INTERNATIONAL SOCIALISM

A quarterly journal

Summer

Contents

Issue 67 of INTERNATIONAL SOCIALISM, quarterly journal of the Socialist Workers Party (Britain)

Published July 1995
Copyright © International Socialism
Distribution/subscriptions: International Socialism,
PO Box 82, London E3.
American distribution: B de Boer, 113 East Center St, Nutley,
New Jersey 07110.
Subscriptions and back copies: PO Box 16085, Chicago
Illinois 60616
Editorial and production: 0171-538 1626/0171-538 0538
Sales and subscriptions: 0171-538 5821
American sales: 312 665 7337

ISBN 189 88 761 0X

Printed by BPCC Wheatons Ltd, Exeter, England
Typeset by East End Offset, London E3

Cover design by Ian Goodyer

For details of back copies see the end pages of this book

Subscription rates for one year (four issues) are:

Britain and overseas (surface):	individual	£14.00 ($30)
	institutional	£25.00
Air speeded supplement:	North America	nil
	Europe/South America	£2.00
	elsewhere	£4.00

Note to contributors

The deadline for articles intended for issue 69 of *International Socialism* is **1 August 1995**

All contributions should be double-spaced with wide margins. Please submit two copies. If you write your contribution using a computer, please also supply a disk, together with details of the computer and programme used.

INTERNATIONAL SOCIALISM ★

A quarterly journal of socialist theory

MILLIONS OF people are turning to Tony Blair's 'New Labour'. Award winning journalist Paul Foot looks at the reasons for Blair's popularity and the prospects for class struggle under a future Labour government. In 'When will the Blair bubble burst?' he examines the limits of Blair's popularity, the economic and political boundaries within which he is imprisoned and outlines an alternative socialist strategy. In 'One Hundred Years of Revisionism', *Socialist Worker* editor Chris Harman looks at previous attempts by leaders of the labour movement to abandon socialist ideas, and shows how Tony Blair is obliged to be more right wing than his predecessors.

THE 50th anniversary of VE day has raised many serious questions about how the ruling classes of Europe were prepared to collaborate with fascists and fought to carve out empires, not to protect democracy. The war ended in a massive eruption of working class radicalisation across Europe. Chris Bambery looks at the rise and fall of those hopes. Even in the darkest hours of the Second World War, workers resisted the Nazis. Alex Callinicos reviews an inspiring account of resistence in the concentrations camps and a study of the German working class under Hilter's Third Reich.

MANY SOCIALISTS and activists accept the idea that the media is responsible for the Tories' election victories and dominates the way workers think about politics. In his article 'Is The Media All Powerful?' Chris Nineham argues that, despite the media empires owned by tycoons like Rupert Murdoch, the media's influence can be challenged.

PETER MORGAN reviews a comprehensive history of the American West which delves into the wars against the Native Americans and the growth of working class organisation and charts the fortunes of the area, from the Gold Rush of the 1840's to the growth of Los Angeles.

CHINA IS one area of the world which seems untouched by the revolutions which swept away the political systems of Eastern Europe. But China has been wracked by revolt, as Charlie Hore's *Bookwatch* shows.

Editor: John Rees, Assistant Editors: Alex Callinicos, Chris Harman, John Molyneux, Lindsey German, Ann Rogers, Colin Sparks, Mike Gonzalez, Peter Morgan, Ruth Brown, Mike Haynes, Judy Cox and Rob Hoveman.

When will the Blair bubble burst?

PAUL FOOT

Paralysis has struck down British Labour. Old commitments to changing the hated Thatcherite society are daily cast aside. One Sunday morning David Blunkett goes on television to reaffirm tentatively Labour's long standing promise to impose VAT on private schools. That same Sunday, in the afternoon, after a call from his Leader, David Blunkett is on again, telling us that Labour has no intention of imposing VAT on private schools. A few days later Derek Fatchett, a Labour front bench spokesman on 'defence', launched a spirited attack on the grotesque waste of public money on homes, servants and cooks for senior officers in the armed forces. The Leader called Fatchett in and told him he must never again attack senior army officers without his permission. Jack Cunningham, the very right wing Labour spokesman on industry, gave a public commitment that privatised coal would be renationalised by Labour—only to read in the newspapers of a speech by a more junior Labour spokesman with the ear of the Leader. The speech told a meeting of coal merchants that there were 'no plans' to nationalise their industry.

Even the health service may not be safe in Labour hands. The rumour as I write is that the party's health spokeswoman Margaret Beckett threatened to resign in order to hang on to Labour's long established pledge to dismantle the NHS trusts and return the health service to some form of more elected control. An 'indissoluble commitment'. to re-nationalise the railways has now been replaced by a 'might do, might not do' compromise written in such gobbledegook that its author must have been John Prescott.

The day by day controversy between Labour and the increasingly absurd Tory government is paralysed too. When the deeply reactionary employment secretary Michael Portillo changed the rules making it more difficult for unemployed people to claim benefit, he was roundly attacked by his 'shadow', Harriet Harman. He lost the argument all down the line until he asked her whether Labour would abolish his new rules. There was a lot of huffing and puffing, but no reply. In the House of Commons the prime minister has taken to replying to questions from Labour leader Tony Blair with a single question: what would you do? Would Labour squeeze the rich? Would they return opted-out schools to the elected authorities? Would they reverse privatisation with public enterprise? Would they repeal the anti-union laws? Exactly what is the minimum wage? No reply, no reply, no reply. Paralysis.

The paralysis flows from the political to the industrial. I recently spoke with Tony Benn at a meeting of nurses called in response to a fantastic offer from the government's 'impartial' review body of a wage increase of 1 percent. The nurses were angry, but the union officials cool. When I remonstrated afterwards with a UNISON official, he replied simply, 'Well, it's Blair, isn't it?' He meant that the new young Labour leader and his glittering successes in the polls had mesmerised union officials who might otherwise have been stung into action.

The same paralysis hit the teaching unions as the government blandly announced new pay cuts for teachers. A campaign against the cuts was launched not by the unions but by the school governors who had been granted new powers over the schools in order to tame the unions. The teachers' union leaders don't want to rock the Blair boat. When, at the annual Easter conference, the National Union of Teachers overturned their leaders' advice and called for a strike ballot, Blair himself led the witch-hunt against the militants. He and his colleagues take every opportunity to make it clear that any industrial action, even the slightest ripple on the social surface, will make it more difficult for Labour to win the next election.

The price of this paralysis is very high: continued exploitation without hindrance. Britain's rulers, hugely enriched by the privatisation, union busting and higher-band tax cuts of recent years, are like burglars who feel that their stealing time is at last running out. They are cramming into their sacks what remains of available booty. The railways, the nuclear industry, even huge savings on slashed disability benefits, are all up for grabs before the election without any meaningful opposition from the Labour or trade union leadership. The most rapacious British ruling class since the war is making hay while its sun still shines. The price, moreover, is not just in pounds and pence: lower wages, longer hours, more sackings and so on. The old defeatist arguments of the mid-1980s, that workers are all frightened or apathetic, are plainly false. There are on all sides signs that more and more of them are ready and willing to fight. Every time they are held back by Labour's paralysis they lose confidence, hope—and a chance to knock the Tories back.

Is it all a bluff?

So headlong and relentless is this stampede that some optimistic Labour Party socialists can be heard to say: 'It is all a bluff. Tony and John are not really as right wing as they pretend. They are just saying they are right wing so that they can win the election. When they get into office they will revert to their true socialist feelings.' This is the exact opposite of the truth. The new leaders' 'true feelings' are that they want to run the country not very much differently than it is run at the moment, with marginal adjustments to make it a little bit fairer. A good guide to Tony Blair's 'true feelings' is his original draft of the alternative Clause Four, which promised to 'work together' with 'trade unions, consumer associations *and employers' organisations.*' (The replacement of the word 'employers' with the word 'other' was the only tangible victory for the trade union negotiators over the new clause.)

Unlike all the other Labour leaders this century, Blair himself has no socialist past. During the whole of his youth and his university education there is not the slightest sign of any ideological commitment to socialism. Unlike every other Labour leader this century, he has never at any time in his life been convinced of the argument for a socialist order of society. It has been argued on his behalf that he joined the Labour Party in the early 1980s when most right wing social democrats were joining the Social Democratic Party. In fact, most of the social democrats who joined the SDP were converts from the Labour Party. They were in many ways the more idealistic and evangelistic of the right wing social democrats. Most political careerists, after glancing at the political and electoral realities, stayed with Labour. A young man intending to make a career of anti-Tory politics in 1981 or 1982 was far more certain of a safe seat in parliament and high office with Labour than with the SDP. Though he gingerly toed the more left wing party line when he fought the Beaconsfield by-election in 1982, Blair's politics were never socialistic. They stemmed from a vague Christian notion of togetherness, encapsulated in his well-worn cliche, 'We achieve more together than we do on our own.' This togetherness has nothing to do with equality or public ownership. It is as achievable, Blair believes, in a corporation like Hanson or Kingfisher as it is in any public enterprise. That's why he throws out the 'baggage' of a constitutional commitment to common ownership, and fixes his sights on a few very simple and easily attainable objectives, none of which have anything to do with socialism.

When does Labour win?

No, the Blair offensive is not a bluff, and most Labour Party members know it isn't. What then is the secret to his enduring appeal among people who suspect his politics? How is it that so many constituency parties have voted to dump Clause Four, to which most of them still feel a strong political attachment?

The main reason is their confidence that Blair will win the next general election. Large numbers of Labour Party members have been convinced by the argument that the election cannot be won unless Labour dumps every vestige of its traditional support for socialism and peace. They are impressed by the awful results of the 1983 general election, in which the breakaway Social Democratic Party with the enthusiastic support of the Liberals got almost as many votes as Labour. They ascribe that defeat to the left wing policies in the Labour manifesto. The argument persists through the two subsequent elections as Labour dropped more and more of its left wing policies. Like desperate adventurers in a punctured hot air balloon, they cry for more and more 'socialist baggage' to be cast overboard. The Blair paralysis is the logical result of that argument.

Political history, however, did not start in 1979. There have been two long periods of Labour government in the last half century. Both these elections, 1945 and 1966, were won with Clause Four in place and far more left wing policies even than in 1983. In 1974 a Tory government was thrown out by the electorate and a Labour government established, even though *Labour's Programme 1973* was far, far to the left of anything written by Labour in the 1980s. The record shows that the results of elections have far more to do with the prevailing popular political mood than with formal policies in manifestos. If Labour does win the next election—and another defeat seems beyond the capacities even of the shadow cabinet—the result will have far more to do with the popular fury with Tory broken promises and sleaze than with the political inclination of the Labour manifesto.

Can Blair deliver?

But what then? What happens after a Blair victory?

Here traditional socialist arguments are inclined to sound irrelevant. Traditionally, socialists in and out of the Labour Party have protested

about the backsliding of previous Labour governments; the broken
promises and unfulfilled aspirations of the past. They dust down the old
manifestos and show how specific promises (for instance, to end the
Polaris nuclear missile programme in October, 1964) have been systematically broken. This argument has lost its force. Indeed it has to some
extent been adopted by Blair and his team as a justification for their
paralysis. 'In the past', they argue, 'Labour tried to do too much. They
promised things they knew they could not achieve. What we offer is
something much more honest. We will say what we can achieve, and we
will achieve it.' This argument is seized on eagerly by all sorts of Labour
Party supporters worn down by years of Tory cruelty and greed. But it
falls to the ground as soon as anyone asks an old and familiar question.

Who runs the country?

However far he moves to the right, there is one crucial characteristic of
past Labour governments which Blair cannot shake off. Like Ramsay
MacDonald, Clement Attlee, Harold Wilson and James Callaghan, Blair
must believe that he, as prime minister, will be in charge of events. I
recall as one of the formative experiences of my youth going down to 10
Downing Street in late October 1964 as an impressionable reporter. The
new young, popular and extremely able prime minister, Harold Wilson,
was holding a press conference. He had just stormed into Downing
Street by overturning a massive Tory majority. The world, it seemed, lay
at his feet. He sat in the cabinet room, puffing on his pipe and beaming
benevolently. He conveyed an impression of child-like amazement at his
new power. He pointed to a series of buttons attached to his telephone. 'I
can sit here', he said, 'and call up the Governor of the Bank of England
or the Chief of the Imperial General Staff.' For anyone interested in politics it was a time of high hope and excitement. The old days of the Tory
dynasty, what Wilson called the 'faded antimacassars of the age of
ancestor-worship', had been removed forever. Here was a new man in
charge, committed to a new order, his power conveyed to him by the
votes of the people.

The disillusionment which followed so swiftly, culminating in the
cuts and wage freeze of July 1966, was not so much about specific policies. It was about political power, or rather political impotence. The man
who pressed the buttons summoning the Governor of the Bank of
England was having his economic policies dictated by that same governor, his foreign policy dictated by that same Chief of the Imperial
General Staff. The thread of democracy which attached the new prime
minister to the electorate was effortlessly cut by wealthy and powerful
people elected by no one. If this seemed true of the first Wilson govern-

ment of 1964-1970, it was doubly true of the second one—which started in 1974 and went on (after Wilson abandoned it in 1976) until 1979. The first real crisis was in the early summer of 1975, when Wilson reversed all his economic commitments and again set in motion a policy of wage controls followed by public spending cuts. He did not do so by choice. He himself described his role in Downing Street as that of an entirely impotent tenant awaiting eviction by bailiffs, whom he specifically defined:

> We were living on borrowed time. But what of the bailiffs, in the shape of the international financial community, from cautious treasurers of multinational corporations, multinationals, to currency operators and monetary speculators? Would they give us time to win the support of the miners and take all necessary corrective action? The answer came on 30th June.[1]

The answer was no. The government and its electoral majority were evicted from its planned and stated policy by 'the bailiffs'. The following year, 1976, which rightly became the bogey for the left for years afterwards, Denis Healey, the Labour chancellor, was similarly stampeded by the International Monetary Fund, which insisted, in exchange for a loan to help Britain out of its balance of payments difficulties, that Labour renege on its promises to increase spending on hospitals, schools and public transport. Was the loan really necessary? Years later, when Healey wrote his memoirs, he thought not. 'The whole affair was unnecessary,' he wrote. 'We could have done without the IMF loan at the time only if we—and the world—had known the real facts at the time'.[2] The Chancellor of the Exchequer, a man of high intelligence, was not informed of the real financial facts! So ill-informed was he about the matters over which he was meant to be in charge that he reversed the entire thrust of his party's policy, and launched his government on a Thatcherite economic policy before Thatcher even came to office. Later in that same *annus horribilis*, 1976, Prime Minister James Callaghan chose the Labour Party conference to make a classical statement of Labour's impotence:

> What is the cause of high unemployment? Quite simply and unequivocally it is caused by paying ourselves more than the value of what we produce. There are no scapegoats. That is as true in a mixed economy under a Labour government as it is under capitalism or communism. It is an absolute fact of life which no government, be it left or right, can alter... We used to think that you could spend your way out of a recession and increase employment by cutting taxes and boosting government spending. But I tell you in all candour that that option no longer exists...

So what option did exist? To coin a phrase, back to basics. Callaghan spelled it out quite clearly. 'We must get back to fundamentals—first, overcoming unemployment now unambiguously depends on our labour costs being at least comparable with those of our major competitors.' The only way workers could ensure unemployment did not rise was to cut their own wages.

Once again, it was not just the breaking of manifesto commitments which disillusioned Labour voters. It was the admission of their government's impotence. Ever since 1945 Labour politicians had been inspired by the economics of John Maynard Keynes. Keynes provided them with an economic theory which enabled them, so they believed, to organise the national economy so that they could 'spend their way out of a recession by cutting taxes and boosting government spending'. Once in office, they believed, they could act on Keynes's theory—and run capitalism fairly without abolishing it. Universal suffrage conferred on them the necessary power to seize the reins without changing the horses. During the 1945-1951 government and, to a lesser extent, the Wilson government of 1964-1970, the Keynesian Labour ministers convinced themselves that they were in charge; and that it was their brilliant management of the economy which for the first time in capitalist history stopped the cycle of booms and slumps. In fact, as the International Socialists (forerunner of the SWP) argued at the time, they were not in charge at all. The economic stability was caused in the main by the huge spending on unused and unsold arms in peacetime. The full extent of the Labour ministers' impotence, and the futility of the Keynesian argument, only became clear to ministers during the Wilson/Callaghan government of 1974-1979. The arch-Keynesian James Callaghan abandoned Keynes and reverted to reactionary free market slogans which Tory ministers of the 1950s and early 1960s would have been ashamed to proclaim. Callaghan's 1976 Declaration of Impotence set the tone for Labour's three remaining years in office. The Labour government, its impotence sealed by an alliance with the Liberal Party, careered away from even its most marginal aspirations, and stumbled to defeat.

Here is the crucial lesson for the Blairites. The point is not, as they argue, that Labour sought to do too much, nor even that they abandoned individual manifesto commitments. It is that Labour's ability to do *anything* for the people who voted Labour was systematically removed. They didn't just abandon individual promises. They lost control altogether.

Why don't Labour governments run the country?

Why were these governments not in control? The history of Labour governments is inexplicable in any other language except that of class. The society we live in is controlled by an unelected class which guards its wealth and power jealously against elected politicians whom it regards as upstarts. If those upstarts try, as *Labour's Programme 1973* suggested they should, to 'shift the balance of wealth and power towards working people and their families,' they come up against the most relentless ruling class opposition. Here then is the Labour dilemma. Because of the history and origins of the party, because the party rests on trade union support, because of the people who vote Labour, because Labour Party members are overwhelmingly workers, all Labour governments must try to do something for the people who vote Labour. Blair might change Clause Four from a commitment to common ownership, but even he must replace it with a statement committing Labour to ensure that 'wealth and power is in the hands of the many, not of the few'.

His supporters today are no longer hoping for socialism. They are not even hoping for any substantial change in the ownership of industries or in the distribution of wealth. They want no more than a few minor reforms to make the society better than it has been under Major or Thatcher. But to do even that Blair will need, above all, to be in control. Indeed, the more he rejects socialist policies, the more his credibility depends on showing that, once elected, he is in control. The more he abandons what Harold Wilson during the 1964 general election called 'the moral crusade' to change the world, the more he relies on his image as an efficient administrator, the more he will depend on being in control. The qualities for which he is renowned—competence, civility, a command of his brief—can only be put to good effect if he can press those buttons in 10 Downing Street much more confidently than even Harold Wilson dared to do.

Is there not, the Blairites argue, at least a chance that with a much more moderate agenda, Blair will usher in more reforms than did Wilson or Callaghan? After all, they argue, even those administrations seem much better than anything we've experienced since 1979. Labour governments in the past *have* introduced reforms. Look at the National Health Service. Look at the high rate of council house building in Wilson's first government, not to mention liberal laws on gays, abortion, capital punishment. Look at the fact that even the 1974-1979 Labour government did, as promised, freeze council rents and take back into public ownership the shipbuilding and aircraft industries.

Yet those reforms were not examples of ministers being in control, still less of their personal determination or administrative abilities. They are, once again, impossible to explain except in terms of class. They depended on three factors: the economic 'leeway' for reform, the strength and confidence of the opposing classes, and, much less important, the extent of Labour's electoral commitment.

i) *The leeway for reform*. All the reforms mentioned above took place against a background in which Britain was in the big economic, industrial and military league, and when there was full employment. After the war Britain was still the second biggest industrial power on Earth. Now it produces 4 percent of world manufacturing output. Even at the height of the Thatcher boom productivity increases in British industry lagged behind those of the US, Germany, Japan and many other countries. Malcolm Rifkind, Britain's defence secretary, tells his supporters that 'Britain is a small island off the north west coast of Europe' and must tailor its defence commitments accordingly. Compare that with the central arguments which wracked the Wilson Labour government less than 30 years ago—whether Britain should keep a substantial military presence 'East of Suez'.

Today even the most enthusiastic Blairites agree that the leeway for reform is tiny. Britain is constantly being overtaken in the league of economic nations. The British economy, even more than its competitors, is plagued by chronic underinvestment. A recent book by a prominent Blairite—*The State We're In* by Will Hutton of the *Guardian*—brilliantly exposes the weakness of the British economy. Hutton ruminates gloomily on the 'globalisation' of modern capitalism. His book has been an outstanding success, but his solutions depend on 'Euro-Keynesianism', that is applying the failed Keynesian policies of past Labour governments on a European scale, where the prospects for the necessary co-operation and joint action are even grimmer than they were on a national scale in the 1960s and 1970s. There is a great gulf fixed between the tasks which Hutton outlines and even the remotest possibility that a timid and cautious Blair government, armed with less conviction and confronted by far more ruthless ruling class opposition, could do anything about them.

ii) *The strength and confidence of the classes*. All the above reforms— the NHS in the 1940s, house building the 1960s, the nationalisation of shipbuilding in the 1970s and others at the same time—took place against the background of strong and growing trade unions, rising confidence in the workplace and (in the case of the 1960s and 1970s) industrial victories for the working class. I will show later that these things constantly change—and are changing—but a glance at the strike figures for 1974 compared to those of 1994 shows that in those 20 years the balance of confidence tipped towards the employers.

iii) *The electoral commitments of Labour.* The democracy of parliamentary elections often clashes with capitalism which is essentially undemocratic and hierarchical. The clashes this century between capital and elected Labour governments were inspired by the ruling class's suspicion and disdain for any government elected by the votes of people it exploits. In these clashes Labour is strengthened at least to some extent by the promises it makes during the election. In 1966, for instance, the Labour Party was committed to abolish health prescription charges and, on taking office, promptly did so. When in 1967 they went to the IMF for a loan, the IMF negotiators insisted *above everything else* on the imposition of prescription charges. Prime Minister Wilson and his colleagues pleaded, begged, and offered more extensive cuts elsewhere—all to no avail. The negotiators for capitalism were determined that the elected government's nose should be rubbed in its most treasured commitment. Yet, at least to some extent, the negotiations depended on the commitments. If there had been no commitment to reform, there would have been nothing to negotiate. Control could be swiped from the elected government without hindrance. This is the folly of Blair's determination to proceed without any commitment to take back any privatised property or redistribute wealth. He will be much weaker without the commitments than with them.

On all three counts a new Blair led Labour administration will be substantially weaker even than its pathetic predecessors. Particularly if he is successful in taming any industrial action or confidence before his election, Blair will find himself at the mercy of an arrogant and contemptuous ruling class, eager at once to humiliate him and subdue him to its purpose. All the signs are that he will be a willing captive. But as his control over events is seen to vanish, as he becomes the servant of events rather than their master, so the very characteristics which now serve him in such good stead will become the instruments of his and Labour's humiliation. His moderation will be ridiculed as weakness, his hostility to dogma as weak minded, his everlasting grin as facetious. A glance at what happened to his hero, Bill Clinton, who won an election after energetically distancing himself from any substantial reforms, reveals just a little of what will happen to Blair in Downing Street. Tossed about like a cork in a whirlpool, he will jettison one commitment after another until, no doubt, he will start to study how his illustrious predecessor Ramsay MacDonald escaped a similar plight and stayed in Downing Street at the head of the Tory party. It won't be long into a Blair government before the Tories and their press start to howl for a government of national unity.

The economic state we're in—and the whole history of Labourism in Britain this century—points to the inevitable collapse of a Blair administration, with horrific social consequences. This will not just be a personal tragedy for Tony Blair. The pit into which Tony Blair will certainly fall beckons all of us. The failure of a government in which so many socialists and trade unions have placed their faith could lead to the widespread cynicism and pessimism.

Why should we vote Labour?

The more this grim prospect looms, the more wretched some Labour supporters become. Some on the left argue for an electoral break with Labour. They announce proudly that they will be abstaining in the polling booths and denouncing Labour on the hustings. This small minority argue that Labour has lost all claim to the allegiance of working class votes, and that there is no longer any substance in the claim that Labour has links and roots in the working class. These people do not seem to have noticed that the most blatant and well-endowed effort to smash British Labour—the SDP—collapsed in ruin. Despite OMOV, John Prescott, John Smith, Tony Blair and all the others, the trade unions are still inexorably entwined with the party. In its basic electoral support and in its links with the unions, Labour is still a party with working class roots. When Labour does well at the polls, its worker supporters feel better, more confident; and when Labour goes down, its supporters go down too.

In the next general election at least, there will be no credible left alternative to Labour. The only effect of alternative candidates or abstentions will be a stronger Tory party in parliament. Those who propose an exclusively electoral answer to the Blair problem are making the same mistake as Blair himself—putting far too much emphasis on what happens in the ballot box. They are also abandoning all those people who cling loyally to Labour for its class roots but are deeply disturbed by the Blair paralysis.

Ironically, indeed, many of the people who voted for Blair as leader in a desperate desire to get rid of the Tories are the most aware of the possible consequences. They know the implications of the history and of the economic background and the utter spinelessness of every statement that comes from the leader's office. They know what to expect, and many of them just hang on, grimly expecting it. At a meeting not long ago in Norwich I was interrupted in mid-flow about the inevitable and dreadful consequences of a Blair Labour government. 'I know, I know,' said a man standing in the aisle holding his head and begging me not to go on. 'I know—but I hate the Tories so much I just want to see them beaten at

the election, and *I don't care what happens afterwards.*' Such people
should not be left to stew in their own hopelessness. Their plaintive
question—is the prospect entirely bleak?—needs an answer.

What happens when the Blair bubble bursts?

No, the prospect is very far from bleak. For a start, there are plenty of
signs that Blair's rightward stampede is resented by large sections of the
people who will vote for him. His relentless march to respectability
seems to have carried the new Labour leader well to the right of most of
his supporters.

In a MORI poll last October, for instance, 68 percent of voters spoke
up for returning privatised utilities to public ownership and 60 percent
were in favour of a wealth tax on people with more than £150,000. An
ICM poll the previous month asked the question: 'Do you think profitable state industries should be run as private companies?' The question
was first asked in 1988 when 30 percent agreed, 53 percent didn't. In
1994 the percentage agreeing had slumped to 16 with 66 percent against.
Even more remarkable, in the same poll 38 percent agreed and 28
percent disagreed with the statement: 'More socialist planning would be
the best way to solve Britain's economic problems'. Six years ago only
29 percent agreed with the statement: 'Trade unions should have more
say in the way the country is run'. Now the figure has risen to 39 percent,
with only 40 percent against—the gap of 25 percent has been cut to 1
percent. In the last poll to ask the question, 60 percent said they would
pay more income tax for more social security—more than half said they
would pay an extra four pence in the pound.

As Blair has moved to the right, his supporters seem to have moved to
the left. Blair refused to support the 1994 signal workers' strike, but more
than 70 percent of Labour voters did so. Perhaps the most fascinating
recent poll was about Clause Four. In February 1995 Gallup asked a cross-
section of voters what they thought of Clause Four. Overwhelmingly the
respondents said they opposed it. Then they were told what it said: 37
percent said they were 'broadly in agreement', 28 percent broadly in dis-
agreement. Among Labour voters 49 percent agreed, 29 didn't.

The people's mood is not cowed or broken. Blair's New Labour
seems like a ray of hope—but certainly not the only possible salvation.
The people who supported Blair's campaign to change Clause Four were
often the same people who were in broad agreement with the clause. The
signal workers dispute showed that 'old fashioned' official strikes can
win as effectively as they ever could, and the sudden unheralded spurts
of militant demonstrations on issues like the export of live animals and
the Criminal Justice Act do not fit into the picture the Tories paint of a

subdued working class. Indeed, ever since the hospital strikes of 1988, political and industrial resistance has grown—through the successful mass uprising against the poll tax in 1990, the Welling anti-Nazi demonstration in 1993 and the big TUC-sponsored demonstrations for the health service and against racism. There have been growing signs on all sides of a rank and file resistance which takes little notice of what the Labour leaders are saying. All this suggests that a Blair government will have to grapple with a strong grass roots working class resistance. In other words, when the Blair bubble bursts, as it must, people are as likely to move to the left as to the right.

If that happens, there will be one crucial difference to last time. Last time the explosion of fury in the working class movement at the right wing policies of the Wilson government after 1974 were held in check by left wing trade union leaders such as Hugh Scanlon of the engineering union and Jack Jones of the Transport and General Workers Union. Their influence was rooted deep in the rank and file. For years the Communist Party had attracted and organised industrial militants, to whom hundreds of thousands of workers responded. During the last Labour government the left wing union leaders and their supporters in the Communist Party had no alternative strategy to that set out by the Labour government. The 'social contract' which, as Callaghan blurted out at the 1976 Labour Party conference, was a device to control wages and salaries, was supported unanimously at the 1975 Trades Union Congress. Labour left and Communist militants encouraged their sceptical supporters to vote for freezing their own wages and cutting their own services.

Today there is no such organisation of Communist militants, no left trade union leaders of anything like the stature of Hugh Scanlon or Jack Jones. This represents, first, the decline of traditional socialist education and propaganda in the British working class. But it also means that the trade union *'gendarmerie'* which controlled the working class movement so effectively in the late 1970s is no longer as influential: that an angry and militant reaction to a Blair government can shoot to the surface with less obstruction.

Last time Labour made some promises and sold most of them out. Next time, even if it doesn't make any promises, Labour will quickly lose its only remaining appeal: its appearance as a fair, rational and efficient administrator, committed, however vaguely, to a better world. Last time the sell out led to a shift to the right. This time the situation is more volatile. If socialists, like that man in Norwich, abandon all their ideas and spirit of resistance to a hopeless and ridiculous faith in Tony Blair, then the vacuum created by the Blair disaster can be filled from the right. If on the other hand there is in place an energetic non-sectarian socialist party which seeks to build from the bottom up, which brings militants together and encourages them with socialist propaganda and a socialist press, which organises at the rank and file level against fascists, Nazis and racialism, and which opposes any further attempt to make workers pay for the capitalist crisis—then there is every chance that socialism can be put right back on the political agenda; and that masses of angry and disillusioned workers will swiftly make up what they have lost in organisation and education by enrolling in the most effective school of all: the school of industrial struggle.

What now?

The conclusions have never been more obvious.

i) Parliamentary democracy, though an enormous improvement on the unelected despotisms which still govern most of the world, is not strong enough to control the increasingly multinational capitalist monopolies which gobble up the world's resources and its labour with the single purpose of boosting their power and their profits.

ii) The only power which can control and overturn those monopolies is the power of the people exploited by them: the working class.

iii) Socialists must come together and organise where that power lies— in the day by day resistance to capitalism. They must build an organisation which provides a focus for fragmented resistance, and a political strategy based on the most implacable opposition to the monopolies, their state and the class which controls them.

iv) In Britain the only party which can do any of this is the Socialist Workers Party.

Notes

1   H Wilson, *Final Term: The Labour Government 1974-1976* (Weidenfeld and Nicolson, 1979), p114.
2   D Healey, *The Time Of My Life* (Michael Joseph, 1989), pp432-433.

From Bernstein to Blair: one hundred years of revisionism

CHRIS HARMAN

Tony Blair's decision to remove 'common ownership' from Labour's constitution met with whole hearted approval from a group of intellectuals and politicians for whom it was the final victory for the 'revisionist' argument begun by Edward Bernstein 99 years ago and Anthony Crosland 49 years ago.

They had sought to 'modernise' socialism by removing from it any notion of a sudden transformation of capitalist society, it was said. But they had been defeated by the forces of conservatism within the socialist ranks. Blair, by contrast, was not afraid to confront these head on and had achieved a long overdue victory for 'common sense'.

Such were the arguments of David Marquand, the Croslandite who left Labour for the SDP in the early 1980s, and of Shirley Williams, the former Labour minister who helped found the SDP. They are echoed by the cheerleaders for Blair in the *Independent* and the *Guardian*—the political columnist Hugo Young, the economic journalist Will Hutton, the former Stalinists Martin Jacques and Dave Aaronovitch, and by the eminent (and virtually unreadable) sociologist Anthony Giddens.

But their arguments are based on a distortion of the history of the century old argument over revisionism that could only arise out of complete ignorance or complete dishonesty.

The distortion is twofold. It is not true that the arguments advanced by Bernstein and Crosland to justify their positions are the same as those advanced by the Blairites today. In fact, their analysis of what was happening to capitalism was the diametrical opposite to that of many influential Blairites today.

Nor is it true that Bernstein and Crosland failed because they 'lost' the argument about the practical direction to be taken by their parties. All reputable histories of the German Social Democratic Party—for instance, Schorske's classic *German Social Democracy*—recognise that, although it rejected the theoretical formulations of Bernstein's book *Evolutionary Socialism* in favour of the allegedly 'orthodox Marxist' views championed by Karl Kautsky, its practical activity was increasingly indistinguishable from that preached by Bernstein. In the same way, the abandonment of the Labour Party leadership's attempt to ditch Clause Four in 1959-1960 certainly did not mean that the party in subsequent years, whether in opposition under Gaitskell or in government under Wilson and Callaghan, followed a policy any more left wing than that preached by Crosland.

The failure of German Social Democracy faced with world war in 1914-1918, with revolution in 1918-1921, with slump in 1929 and with the rise of Hitler in 1931-1933 cannot be ascribed to any rejection of the strategy and tactics promoted by Bernstein in the 1890s, but instead must be laid at their door. Similarly, the failure of the Labour governments of 1964-1970 and 1974-1979 to bring about the improvements in British society which they promised lay not in a rejection of the Croslandite approach, but in its acceptance.

Bernstein's analysis

The analyses of both Bernstein and Crosland were based on one overriding premise. Capitalism, they said, was much less prone to crises, much more amenable to social control and much more able to provide reforms in the interests of workers than previous socialists, especially Marx and Engels, had thought possible.

Bernstein insisted generalised economic crises were no longer an integral part of capitalism. Marx had warned that the ending of one economic crisis 'simply conceals in itself the seeds of a more powerful future crisis'. Engels had asked whether 'we do not find ourselves in the preparatory period of a new world crash of unheard of violence?' Both were wrong, insisted Bernstein. 'Signs of an economic worldwide crash of unheard of violence have not been established.'

This was because Marx and Engels had underestimated factors which countered the tendency of capitalism to enter into crisis. In particular, they had failed to see that the growth of credit made it easier for capitalists to borrow their way out of short term difficulties, while increased government intervention and the making of formal agreements between groups of capitalists ('trusts' and 'cartels') enabled them to prevent generalised crises through the exertion of organised control over the economy:

The enormously increased wealth of the European states in conjunction with the elasticity of the modern credit system and the rise of the industrial Cartels has...limited the reacting force of local disturbances that, at least for some time, general commercial crises similar to the earlier ones are to be regarded as improbable.

Bernstein also argued that, 'The regulation of production...by associations of manufacturers...diminishes the danger of crises.' There could be 'overproduction in single industries', but this did not 'mean general crises'. Nor could speculation any longer play its old destructive role:

The maddest outbursts of commercial speculation come to pass at the dawn of the capitalist era... The older a branch of production is under modern forms the more does the speculative momentum cease to play a decisive role in it... If crises of the money market are not quite banished from the world yet, the tightening of that market by vast commercial undertakings controlled with difficulty is very much reduced.

One further factor making crises less likely was the growth of the world market—what it is fashionable today to call 'globalisation'. 'The enormous extension of the world market has...increased the possibility of adjustment of disturbances...'

But it was not only in their expectation of deeper economic crises that Marx and Engels had been wrong, according to Bernstein. They had also been wrong to see an ever greater polarisation between classes.

On the one hand, there had not been the decline they had expected in the numbers of medium sized capitalists and the petty bourgeoisie:

It is quite wrong to assume that the present development of society shows a relative or indeed absolute diminution of the number of members of the possessing classes. Their number increases... Britain the 'workshop of the world' is far from being in the stage of containing only large industries. In Germany a whole series of branches of industry, small and medium sized undertakings, appear quite capable of existing beside the large industries... In the whole of Western Europe, as also in the Eastern states of the US, the small and medium agricultural holding is increasing everywhere.

On the other hand, the possessing classes were much more prepared to make concessions to the mass of people than Marx and Engels had expected: 'In all advanced countries we see the privileges of the capitalist bourgeoisie yielding step by step to democratic organisations...'

This leads to economic organisation increasingly being subject to democratic control:

> *The economic natural force changes from the ruler of mankind to its servant... Only the antagonism of interests—of private and group elements—hinders the full transition... Yet the common interest gains in power to an increasing extent as opposed to private interest and the elementary sway of economic forces ceases...*

To bring this process to fruition did not require 'dissolution of the modern state system' as argued by Marx in his writings on the Paris Commune. Instead all that was necessary was a further spread of parliamentarianism, with socialists embracing a thoroughgoing 'liberalism'. That did not mean the end of all conflict. Trade unions needed to organise to bargain with employers, and there would be political conflicts between different parliamentary parties. Bernstein insisted he had not 'questioned the necessity for the working classes to gain control of the government...' And 30 years after he first outlined his revisionist ideas, he was still saying that 'the class interests of the workers demands the transfer of economic monopolies into the hands of the society... Social control is to be extended to all fields of production.' But all the conflict would be peaceful conflict, within the confines of the 'modern democratic' state. 'The more the political organisations of modern nations are democratised, the more needs and opportunities of great political catastrophes are diminished', he was writing in 1895, while Germany was still a semi-absolutist monarchy whose emperor had the power to override decisions of the imperial parliament. Once the Weimar Republic was in existence, he went even further. As Peter Gay's political biography of him, *The Dilemma of Democratic Socialism*, says:

> *The task of the social democratic party regarding the realisation of socialism, Bernstein said, lies in the realisation of what Lassalle called 'the idea of the working class'. A glance at the German state was enough to show that the country was approaching that goal. It would be absurd to call the Weimar Republic a 'capitalist republic'... The development of cartels and monopolies had brought about an increase in public control and would lead to their eventual metamorphosis into public corporations.*

The overall picture provided by Bernstein, then, was of a system less and less characterised by catastrophic economic crisis, more under the control of parliamentary institutions, increasingly satisfying the aspirations of workers and increasingly immune to political collapse. There was no need for revolutionary change from capitalism to socialism because capitalism itself was becoming more and more like socialism. Socialists could confidently follow a policy of piecemeal reform within the existing system, without needing to worry about the achievement of their ultimate aims. As he put it, 'the final goal, no matter what it is, is nothing—the movement is everything'.

Crosland's analysis

Crosland, writing nearly a quarter of a century after Bernstein's death, consciously set out to vindicate the original 'revisionist analysis'. He argued that it had remained essentially correct even in the 1930s, when a temporary crisis of the system had caused many people not to notice its continuing overall growth, rising real wages and lessening inequality:

> *The pervasive influence of Marxist analysis in the 1930s was a reflection of an intellectual ferment without parallel in the history of the British labour movement... More and more people came to feel that some thorough going analysis was needed to explain the catastrophe which appeared to be engulfing world capitalism...*
>
> *The belief that the 'inner contradictions' of capitalism would lead to first to a gradual pauperisation of the masses and ultimately to the collapse of the whole system has by now been rather obviously disproved. The British net national income, in real terms, was 3.5 times as high in 1938 as in 1870, and income per head 2.5 times higher, and real wages moved roughly in line with income per head.*
>
> *In addition, over the three or four decades before the Second World War the incidence of poverty fell to...one third of its level at the beginning of the period, and thus there is no evidence, even in the 1930s, of growing pauperisation, nor that the capitalist system was on the point of collapse.*

The picture since 1940 was even clearer, he insisted. The economy had grown massively, the share of the national income going to labour had increased at the expense of that going to capital, and poverty had fallen to an unprecedented degree:

> *And now for a decade since the war, the British economy has singularly improved its performance. Full employment has replaced depression, the instability is vastly less, and the rate of growth appreciably more.*
>
> *From 1948 to 1954 the British national income rose by 20 percent—a figure only slightly below that achieved by the US, conventionally saluted as*

*the world's most productive economy... Production has risen more in Britain
since the war than in any other European country.*

Wages increased their share of the total [National Income] *from 37
percent to 44 percent between 1938 and 1950.*

By 1950 'the poverty line had fallen from 31 percent of the working
class population to under 3 percent, or from 18 percent of the whole population to 1.6 percent' according to Rowntree's surveys of York.

*Thus nine tenths of the poverty that had existed in 1936 had disap-
peared... Moveover there was a general rise in living standards at the lower
end of scale.*

But this was not all. The growth of the economy and the decline in
inequality were a reflection of more fundamental changes:

Today the capitalist business class has lost [its old] *commanding position...
Decisive sources and levers of economic power have been transferred from
private to other hands... The social attitudes and behaviour of the business
class have undergone a significant change, which appears reflected in a pronounced loss of strength and self confidence.*

There was 'a less aggressive pursuit of maximum profit at all costs',
and 'the traditional capitalist ruthlessness has largely disappeared...'
since 'for practical purposes economic decisions in the basic sector have
passed out of the hands of the capitalist class into the hands of a new and
autonomous class of public industrial managers', while 'there has been a
decisive movement of power within industry itself from management to
labour.'
The overall result was a system very different to the one described by
Marx: 'Almost all the basic characteristic features of traditional pre-1914
capitalism have been either greatly modified or completely transformed.'

*The economic power of the capital market and the finance houses, and hence
capitalist financial control over industry, are much weaker. This change
makes it absurd now to speak of a capitalist ruling class.*

*It therefore seems misleading to continue talking about 'capitalism' in
Britain...*

Such changes ensured that the growth without crises that British capitalism had seen for a decade and a half would continue indefinitely,
ruling out recessions or mass unemployment: 'My own view is that the
present rate of growth will continue, and the future is more likely to be
characterised by inflation than by unemployment.'

They also gave governments an unparalleled ability to further improve the conditions of the mass of the population:

> *Acting mainly through the budget, though with the aid of other instruments, the government can exert any influence it likes on income distribution and can also determine within broad limits the division of total output between consumption, investment, exports and social expenditure.*

This did not mean there was no room for improvement. There was a need for socialists to push energetically for reforms, with the goal of 'equality' and not merely of 'equality of opportunity'. And the Labour Party had not always done as much as it could have. This, however, was not a fault of the system but of a lack of will power. The Attlee government's planning failures, Crosland wrote, stemmed not from a lack of economic power but a failure of will. 'If socialists want bolder planning, they must simply choose bolder ministers.'

The judgement of history: Bernstein

Both Bernstein and Crosland wrote at periods when empirical reality seemed to bear out their optimistic picture of workers enjoying ever better lives within a more or less crisis free system. In 1895 there had not been a major crisis of German capitalism for nearly 20 years, real wages had been rising and the government had introduced the first rudiments of a welfare system. In 1956 there had not been a recession for two decades, unemployment was less than 2 percent, employed workers were better off than they had ever been before and a Tory government was content to leave intact the welfare state introduced by the wartime coalition and post-war Labour governments. Yet in both cases the forecasts about the future of the system were proved radically wrong within a relatively few years.

As Rosa Luxemburg pointed out, 'Hardly had Bernstein rejected Marx's theory of crisis than a new profound crisis broke out in 1900, while seven years later a new crisis beginning in the United States hit the world market.' Workers' living standards tended to stop rising in most of the advanced capitalist countries in this decade, laying the ground for a new and unprecedented upsurge of militancy in many countries in 1910-1914. The reliance of capitalism in each country on the growth of cartels and the state led not, as Bernstein expected, to increasingly peaceful development but to growing clashes between the imperial ambitions of rival states—the growing arms race between the German and British navies, the clashes between the great powers over influence in China, then North Africa, and finally the Balkans, leading to the First World War.

Once all the major powers were drawn into this maelstrom, they were all threatened by precisely the 'political catastrophe' Bernstein had insisted would not occur: the four empires that dominated central and eastern Europe (the Russian, the German, the Austro-Hungarian and the Turkish) all collapsed amidst revolutionary ferment, while the British and French empires experienced the first great anti-colonial revolts (in Ireland, India, Indo-China and North Africa) and an insurrectionary mood swept Italy's workers as they occupied the factories. Even a brief spell of economic revival and political stability in the mid-1920s was hardly enough to prove Bernstein right. It had lasted little more than three or four years before the world was experiencing the worst slump it had ever known. A third of the workforce was without jobs in the two largest economies, the US and Germany, where not only the mass of the working class but also wide sections of the middle class faced real impoverishment, creating conditions for the rise of fascism. And the reorganisation of the system through the intervention of rival states that grew out of the crisis, far from leading to renewed peaceful development, resulted in a war even more horrific than that of 20 years before.

Bernstein's attempts to improve society through reform were damned by these developments which his analysis could in no way explain. He was personally devastated by the outbreak of the First World War. His own pacifistic inclinations led him to oppose the war, at first in private and then in public by voting in the *Reichstag* against war credits late in 1915. But the logic of his revisionist analysis was to identify with the national state and its demands for expansion, as Bernstein himself made clear when he defended Germany's 'right' to control parts of China in his *Evolutionary Socialism*.

If he did not draw this conclusion fully during the war, almost all of his revisionist colleagues did. They refused to print his articles in the *Sozialistische Monatshefte* magazine, with which he had been closely associated and then voted to expel him from the Social Democratic parliamentary caucus along with other opponents of the war. The arch-reformist was forced to join the Independent Social Democrats, a growing number of whose members were attracted to out and out revolutionary views. Meanwhile, he found it impossible to influence events himself, as the war precluded reform and his own politics any identification with revolution. He admitted his impotence ten years later when he claimed, according to Gay, 'he wished now that German social democracy and he himself had been able to bring themselves to call for the mass strike in August 1914.'

Yet he could not abandon his analysis, and the moment the war ended he rushed to embrace full blooded reformism again, rejoining the Social Democratic Party in January 1919 because he agreed with them that

'order had to be restored' after the revolution of two months before—
even though the restoration of order meant the Social Democrat leaders
relying on the generals of the imperial army to shoot down workers and
break strikes from one end of Germany to the other. Yet he could neither
be happy nor politically effective in the party, since its alliance with the
generals led to a national chauvinism he detested sweeping through its
ranks. As Gay records:

> *He could write to his good friend Kautsky in 1927 that neither Hilferding's*
> ***Gesellschaft*** *nor Stampfer's **Vorwärts** would accept his articles: he spoke of*
> *his 'political death'... The party was too busy with **Realpolitik** to listen to the*
> *aged Bernstein.*

The man who had been so optimistic about the future of capitalism in
the 1890s and who had been able to see the Weimar Republic as a non-
capitalist state was acutely worried about the future once 1929 brought
renewed slump. He asked in a letter to Kautsky:

> *Will that which we have worked so passionately for all our lives be pre-*
> *served?... The great economic depression has created a general world*
> *crisis...*

His only desperate hope was that somehow the ranks of the Social
Democratic Party would weather the economic and political crisis. But
as Gay notes, he died on 18 December 1932 'six weeks before his last
desperate hope was proved a delusion'.

The judgement of history: Crosland

Bernstein was never himself a member of a government committed to
his vision of social reform. Crosland was a senior minister in two Labour
governments, from 1964 to 1970 and from 1974 until his death in 1977.
By 1974 the experience was already forcing him to reassess some of his
earlier arguments. As his widow recalls in her biography of him:

> *He was over optimistic about economic growth, he admitted... In **The Future***
> *of **Socialism** he had argued that socialism could be pursued within the frame-*
> *work of a mixed economy... A major tool, growth, had proved far more*
> *difficult to achieve than anyone had expected in the 1950s...*
>   *The 1964-1970 Labour government had suffered from a failure on eco-*
> *nomic policy... The performance did not live up to the hopes... Extreme class*
> *inequalities remain, poverty is far from eliminated, the economy is in a state*
> *of semi-permanent crisis and inflation is rampant...*

The reason, he admitted, was that:

British society—slow moving, rigid, class ridden—has proved much harder to change than was supposed... The early revisionist writings were too complacent in tone... More should have been achieved by a Labour government in office and Labour pressure in opposition...

Harsh realities did not lead him, any more than Bernstein, to abandon his revisionist views. 'I see no reason to abandon the revisionist analysis of socialism in favour of a refurbished Marxism...' he wrote, bemoaning the fact that:

The stability of democratic society and the possibility of peaceful reform seem more and more threatened by angry workers, students, squatters, even middle class amenity groups... Even the rule of law is challenged by some Labour councillors and trade unionists...

As environment secretary in the new Labour government he urged the need for a social contract with the unions to hold down wages and told local Labour councils they had to accept harsh cuts on spending because 'the party's over'.

At the same time, however, he was being forced to the conclusion that a Labour Party that was committed in practice to his 1956 analysis was not bringing about the sort of egalitarian society he had hoped for. He wrote:

A move to the left is needed. Not in the traditional sense of a move towards old fashioned Clause Four Marxism, but in the sense of a sharper delineation of fundamental objectives, a greater clarity of egalitarian principles and a stronger determination to achieve them... Public ownership remains one of a number of means (along with taxation, legislation, government controls, trade union actions, and so on) to achieving our socialist ends—and a means which in the light of the improved performance of the public sector, can now be used more freely... We shall require higher taxation of the better off sections of the community...

He could soon see that his egalitarian wishes were not being fulfilled by the 1974 Labour government any more than the previous one. He complained in 1976, 'What the press can't understand is that this is the most right wing Labour government we've had for years.' He was bitter when old right wing Labour colleagues like Denis Healey and Bill Rogers accepted massive welfare cuts in return for an International Monetary Fund loan. In cabinet he toyed for a time with the alternative programme of import controls suggested by Tony Benn and the left. And the man who had insisted, 20 years before, that it made no sense to call Britain 'capitalist' now stunned Foreign Office officials by telling them, 'The IMF is a capitalist body, it's intolerable that a socialist government should have its philosophy imposed on it.'

Crosland's 1950s revisionism had been based on the belief that government intervention could easily ward off slumps and redistribute wealth from the rich to the poor. When he died in 1977 he was a senior minister in a government whose head, James Callaghan, had told the 1976 Labour Party conference that government intervention could not work in that way:

> *We used to think you could just spend your way out of recession by cutting taxes and boosting government borrowing... That option no longer exists and in so far as it ever did exist, it worked by injecting inflation into the economy. And each time that has happened, the average level of unemployment has risen.*

The effect of the policies followed by the government was to push unemployment, which had been about 300,000 when Crosland wrote his book, to over 1.5 million, to bring about the first fall in the living standards of employed workers for about 70 years, to begin a redistribution of income away from labour and towards capital and to start a long term rundown of welfare services.

Capitalism had, in fact, entered a new phase of crisis which rendered Crosland's revisionist belief in improving society for the mass of people as utopian as Bernstein's had been in the First World War and the Weimar Republic. This was shown in the years after Crosland's death when even those of his revisionist co-thinkers like Roy Hattersley who had wanted to resist the IMF cuts in 1976 finally conceded that capitalist governments could no longer control trade and foreign exchange transactions. Paradoxically, by the early 1980s the only people to suggest an 'alternative economic strategy' based on such interventionist, 'Keynesian' policies were the hard left in the Labour Party who had fought so hard against Crosland for most of his life—and most of these had abandoned such views by the mid-1980s.

The new revisionism

The analyses used to justify Blair's policies are, in fact, different in fundamental respects from the old revisionisms of Bernstein and Crosland. For they base themselves not on a belief that capitalism is slowly becoming more controllable and turning into socialism piecemeal, but on the insistence that capitalism today is too powerful and too dynamic to be controlled.

This view was expressed forcibly by Labour's shadow chancellor Gordon Brown at a conference on 'global economic change' organised by the party:

> *Past Labour governments tried to counter the injustice and failure of free market forces by substituting government for the market, and often saw tax, spend and borrow policies as the isolationist quick fix for national decline. The fact is these policies cannot work in the highly integrated world economic environment in which we live.*
>
> *World capital markets have eliminated any notion that economic policy can remain a matter solely for national governments... Countries which attempt to run national go-it-alone macro-economic policies based on tax, spend, borrow policies to boost demand, without looking at the ability of the supply side of the economy, are bound these days to be punished by the markets in the form of stiflingly high interest rates and collapsing currencies.*
>
> *The old Labour language—tax, spend and borrow, nationalisation, state planning, isolationism and full time jobs for life for men...is inappropriate.*

This 'old Labour language' was precisely the language which underlay the revisionism of Bernstein and Crosland. Brown was saying what Marxists had always said, although from the opposite point of view, that it could not work. The *Independent on Sunday*—which goes along with many of Brown's ideas—summed up his speech with the headline, 'Brown ditches Keynes'.

The same pessimism about the ability of reformist governments to control capital is to be found in the writings in the left Labour paper *Tribune* of one of Brown's former advisers, Professor Meghnad Desai of the London School of Economics:

> *It is no longer possible to pursue left Keynesian policies in a single country context... We are now witnessing in the 1990s a return to the sort of world socialists of the 19th century knew, with global movements of capital, and the state incapable of exercising much control over the economy...*

The lack of success of Socialist and Labour Party governments, he insists, do not result from:

> *A failure of will, or the pusillanimity of the leadership. The problem is the resurgence of capitalism... A century after Marx and Engels it continues constantly to reproduce itself.*

Clause Four should be abandoned, according to Desai, not because there is some other way of controlling the economy as Crosland argued, but because 'public ownership of the economy is no guarantee of control of the market...'

But if the market cannot be controlled, what does the uncontrolled market offer? The Labour Party's revised Clause Four talks glibly of 'the enterprise of the market and the rigours of competition'. But one of the most influential economic journalists supporting the Blair-Brown approach, Will Hutton, provides a view of what is happening that is nearly as pessimistic about the future facing the system as the Marxist critics of Bernstein and Crosland were in their time:

There is a mounting and quite proper sense of crisis spreading across all classes about the character and availability of work and its implications for every aspect of society—from the care of our children to the growing dereliction of our cities... Insecurity, low wages and wasted talent are widespread and the problem touches professions and occupations once thought inviolable.

One in four of the country's males of working age is now unemployed or idle... The numbers living in poverty have grown to awesome proportions, and signs of social stress—from family breakdown to the growth of crime— mount almost daily... One in three children grows up in poverty...

The country is increasingly divided against itself, with an arrogant officer class, apparently indifferent to the other ranks it commands. This class is favoured with education, jobs, housing and pensions. At the other end of the scale more and more people discover that they are the new working poor, or live off the state in semi-poverty... In between there are growing numbers of people who are insecure, fearful for their jobs in an age of permanent 'down sizing', 'cost cutting' and 'casualisation' and ever more worried about their ability to maintain a decent standard of living.

Hutton tries to blame what is happening not on the tendencies of capitalism in general, but on the peculiarities of its British form, which he claims is distorted by the role of the financial institutions of the City of London. But he has to admit:

What is happening in Britain is only a more acute version of what is happening elsewhere... There is scarcely a Western country that cannot tell us at least one tale similar to Britain...in Sweden, which used to be portrayed as the finest example of social democratic regulation of capitalism, 'the first attacks on the welfare state since the 1930s' came from a social democrat government 'curbing the rise in government borrowing', while in France the Socialist Party government of the late 1980s embraced 'competitive deflation and economic rigour', leading to 'youth unemployment even higher than in

Britain'. Spanish Socialists and the New Zealand Labour Party have been no less enthusiastic about budget cutting, privatisation and restructuring the welfare state than say the Canadian Conservatives. Everywhere the ideological edge of political competition has been blunted. Different political parties, when in government, offer similar programmes.

And in the US, still the world's biggest single economy:

Job insecurity is endemic, and the wages of the bottom 10 percent of the Labour force are about 25 percent lower than they are for the same group in Britain... Nearly one job in five in the US does not carry sufficient income to rear a family of four.

In fact, one of the most prominent theorists of 'the affluent society' of the 1950s and 1960s was J K Galbraith. His description of the US today is nearly as damning as Hutton's description of Britain: 'In 1988 the top 1 percent of family groupings had annual incomes that averaged $617,000 and controlled 13.5 percent of all income before tax.'

The top 20 percent lived in some comfort with incomes of $50,000 a year (about 700 a week) and above. To them accrued 51.8 percent of all income before taxes.

Their 'comfort and economic well being is being supported and enhanced by the presence in the modern economy of a large, highly useful, even essential class that does not share in the agreeable existence of the favoured community.' This class:

Is integrally a part of a larger economic process and serves the living standard and the comfort of the favoured community. The economically fortunate are heavily dependent on its presence... The poor in our economy are needed to do the work that the more fortunate do not do and would find manifestly distasteful, even distressing.

Gailbraith talks confusingly, of a 'contented majority' of two thirds of people—but he means two thirds of those who bother to vote (half the electorate), not two thirds of the adult population.

In fact, he notes, conditions for the great mass of the American population have been getting worse over the last decade and half, with four fifths of families seeing their incomes fall, the decrease for workers on the median wage being about 5 percent.

He also insists on the 'intrinsic tendency of capitalism to instability, to recession and depression', and on 'the powerful tendency of the economic system to turn damagingly not on consumers, workers or the public at large, but ruthlessly inward on itself...'

He writes of 'recession and depression made worse by long term economic desuetude, the danger implicit in autonomous military power, and growing unrest in the urban slums caused by worsening deprivation and hopelessness...'

And he even makes a comparison between the US today and the USSR in the final years before it fell apart:

Few things could have been further from accepted thought than the possibility that the explosive events in Eastern Europe could have a parallel in the United States or perhaps Britain. Communism had failed. Capitalism was triumphant. Could anyone be so pessimistic as to suggest that lurking in the successful system were grave flaws similarly concealed? Alas there are.

Hutton draws similar conclusions for the system as a whole. Unless those who run 'Western capitalism in general and British capitalism in particular' can be persuaded to reform their ways, he warns, 'they are headed for perdition' with 'a reprise in the early 21st century of the conditions in the early part of this century'—conditions which involved civil war, world war, the rise of Nazi barbarism and working class revolution.

Hutton claims that reform can prevent this prospect. Yet it would be difficult for anyone to claim that the reforms he calls for measure up to the scale of crisis he points to. Thus he calls for British capitalism to abandon its 'short termism' and domination by the financial sector and to adopt a form of capitalism more akin to those which exist in Germany and Japan—but then goes on to admit that German and Japanese capitalism themselves face increasingly intractable problems. Again he calls for a British government that would return to 'Keynesian measures' to deal with recessions—but then admits that the room for manoeuvre by any British government is restricted by its immersion in the world system:

Foreigners own a quarter of British shares, bonds and bank deposits. The capital markets' veto is particularly strong, and any British government will be imprisoned by their demands for fiscal and monetary caution.

He sees the only alternative to such restraints on government action as being 'the construction of a more stable international order' but cannot suggest any way to move towards this apart from 'the European Union and its potential for organising concerted action'.

He claims:

The countries of the EU together have the power to regulate financial markets and control capital flows, and to play a part in compelling the US and Japan to manage their relationship better as part of a world deal. They have the potential to manage demand, boosting and reducing it when necessary, without having their policies blown off course by capital markets... If Europe wants to defend its idea of a welfare state...it will have to do so in a united fashion.

What he does not suggest is how they are going to be forced to behave in this way when all recent experience points to the domination of policy making within each European national state by the influence of nationally based firms and perceived 'national interests'. Hence their complete refusal to aid each other substantially when faced with speculative pressures against currency rates within the European Monetary Union. Hence too their pursuit of opposed foreign policies when faced with the war on the EU's doorstep in former Yugoslavia.

What is more, the internationalisation of the system means that even governments of the largest economies, those of the US and Japan, are increasingly restricted in what they can do by the pressures of worldwide competition.

Finally, and most importantly, the Euro-Keynesians ignore the fact that the long post-war boom was not a result of Keynesian methods. Keynes no more caused the long boom than the cock's crowing causes the sun to rise. Rather he signalled something which was happening anyway, as governments turned to a massive level of military spending and, with it, to massive intervention in the economy. Indeed, his own prescriptions for keeping booms going were rarely used during the 'golden age'. Strangely enough, Hutton, one of the most enthusiastic of the latter day Keynesians, has recognised as much in one of his columns for the *Guardian,* pointing to 'the proof offered by Robin Matthews as long ago as 1968 that the amount of Keynesian pump-priming to manage demand in the...1950s and 1960s...was comparatively small' and could not have been responsible for the long period of economic expansion. Attempts were made to use them in all the advanced countries when this period came to an end in the mid-1970s—and were abandoned everywhere because they did not work. People like Hutton are wishing for the moon when they claim that Keynesianism can work, if used on a European scale, 20 years later.

No doubt it is because they are dimly aware of this that politicians like Blair and Brown—and their equivalents in France, Germany, Italy, Spain and Scandinavia—refuse to promise improvements in welfare benefits, unemployment levels or working conditions. Instead all their emphasis is on 'supply side' economics: on measures that can increase the competitiveness of particular firms or particular national sectors of the world economy. If only, they claim, the country's labour can be more skillful and more competitive, then this will lead to increased exports, increased jobs and eventually higher living standards.

But in putting forward such 'supply sided' arguments, they are retreating completely from the claims about the potential of state intervention accepted by Crosland 40 years ago into the old pre-Keynesian economic orthodoxy as resurrected under Reagan in 1980s America.

'Supply side economics' is about how to fiddle with this or that individual element in the system—how to deal with the 'micro-economy'. It offers no sort of direction over the system as a whole, over the 'macro-economy' which Keynesians and Croslandites used to claim they had mastered. At most it is about how to shift the burden of living in a nasty world on the backs of others, not of how to get rid of the nastiness. And even in terms of its limited goal it is very unlikely to work, since every competing component of the world system is trying to do the same thing and there is no inherent reason why any one should be more successful than any other.

This is not the reformism of hope which Bernstein and Crosland once tried to offer. Nor is it a more 'modern', more effective version of such reformism. Instead it is a reformism which harks back to the versions of pre-Keynesian bourgeois economics that taught there was nothing to be done about the vagaries of the capitalist system apart from the ironing out of 'imperfections' to the free movement of the market. It is the reformism of despair.

The point is to be seen in the writings of Eric Hobsbawm, who in the 1980s earned the praise of former Labour leader Neil Kinnock for preparing the ground intellectually for the new revisionism. Hobsbawm's most recent account of where the system is going is even more pessimistic than those of Desai and Hutton. In his book *The Age of Extremes* he contrasts the period of capitalism since the mid-1970s with the 'golden age' of the post-war boom:

The history of the 20 years after 1973 is that of a world which lost its bearings and slid into instability and crisis. And yet, until the 1980s, it was not clear how irretrievably the foundations of the golden age had crumbled... For many years economic troubles were still 'recessions'. The half century's taboo on the use of the terms 'depression' or 'slump', that reminder of the Age of Catastrophe, was not completely broken... The civilisation that had elevated the world-magic of the advertisers into a basic principle of economy was caught in its own mechanism of delusion. Not until the early 1990s do we find admissions that the economic troubles of the present were actually worse than the those of the 1930s... The problems which had dominated the critique of capitalism before

*the war, and which the golden age had largely eliminated for a generation—
poverty, mass unemployment, squalor, instability'—reappeared after 1973.*

*In the 1980s even many of the richest and most developed countries found
themselves, once again, getting used to the everyday sight of beggars on the
streets, and the even more shocking spectacle of the homeless sheltering in
doorways in cardboard boxes... During the crisis decades inequality unques-
tionably increased in the 'developed market economies', and...the almost
automatic rise in real incomes which the working classes had got used to in
the golden age now came to an end...*

*Between 1990 and 1993 few attempts were made to deny that even the
developed capitalist world was in depression. Nobody seriously claimed to
know what to do about it, other than to hope it would pass... Nobody knew
what to do about the vagaries of the world economy or possessed instruments
to manage them. The main instrument for doing so in the golden age, government policy, nationally or internationally coordinated, no longer worked.*

The economic failure, Hobsbawm insists, is accompanied by growing
political instability:

*The world of the third millennium will almost certainly continue to be one of
violent politics and violent political changes. The only uncertain thing about
them is where they will lead.*

Hobsbawm does not see any alternative to capitalism as an economic
system. But he has no faith in this meaning a better, more equitable or
more secure society:

*No serious observer in the early 1990s could be as sanguine about liberal
democracy as about capitalism... The most obvious thing about the political
situation of the world states was their instability. In most of them the chances
of the survival of the existing regimes over the next 10 to 15 years were, on
the most optimistic calculations, not good.*

Hobsbawm believes it 'probable' that 'the form' of 'universal suffrage' will persist in most advanced countries, but that 'decision making
would increasingly sidestep the electoral process', offering 'no encouraging prospect for the future of parliamentary democracy of the liberal
kind'.

The whole world, in short, is heading for period of immense crises
and unpredictable changes:

*We live in a world captured, uprooted and transformed by the titanic eco-
nomic and techno-scientific process of the development of capitalism which
had dominated the past two or three centuries. We know...that it cannot go on*

ad infinitum. *The future cannot be a continuation of the past, and there are signs...that we have reached a point of historical crisis... Our world risks both explosions and implosions...*

We do not know where we are going. We only know that history has brought us to this point and why. However, one thing is plain. If humanity is to have a recognisable future it cannot be by prolonging the past or the present. If we try to build the third millennium on this basis, we shall fail. And the price of failure, that is the alternative to a changed society, is darkness.

The tone could hardly be more different from that of Bernstein and Crosland, with their insistence that crises and impoverishment were increasingly a thing of the past and that nothing could stop the forward march of liberal democracy, prosperity and security. Hobsbawm's conclusion is, instead, remarkably close to Marx's insistence that every society reaches a point where the alternative is the 'revolutionary reconstruction of society' or 'the mutual destruction of the contending classes'—or, as Rosa Luxemburg put it, 'socialism or barbarism'. Hobsbawm differs from Marx in rejecting the possibility of a socialist road out of this impasse, but not in his assessment that existing society is heading for immense social convulsions. He points to the potential of revolutionary upheaval, even if he rejects it as a preferred option.

Most of the new revisionists are not as apocalyptic as Hobsbawm. But they cannot avoid their arguments leading to similar conclusions. The old revisionists argued that capitalism could not break down, that the class struggle would get more gentle and that capitalism was slowly turning into a peaceful, prosperous, 'affluent' system. The new revisionist argument is the opposite—that breakdown is likely, that reform probably won't work but that it has to be tried as the only alternative to breakdown.

The analyses of Bernstein and Crosland presented Marxists of the time with a serious task of counter-analysis. It required much intellectual effort and argument to show, in decades in which crises were less severe and real wages were rising, that the fundamental contradictions of the system were intensifying. That is why Rosa Luxemburg's polemic against Bernstein, *Reform or Revolution,* was so important at the turn of the century. It also explains the importance of the analyses of the permanent arms economy produced in the 1950s by T N Vance, Tony Cliff, Mike Kidron and others. The analyses of the new revisionists do not confront us with any such problems. We can fault them for not understanding why the capitalist system spun out of control in the 1970s. And we can put forward our own explanations, as I have attempted to in my book *Explaining the Crisis* and my recent articles in this journal, 'The State and Capitalism Today' and 'Where is Capitalism Going'. But we do not need to prove that it is out of control. Their own accounts show the system to be in a period of insoluble crises, with class antago-nisms that are getting more bitter and barbarism a likely prospect. And, if that is so, it is difficult so see what credence anyone should give to a politics which refuses to talk about any fundamental challenge to the system at all.

There is a serious argument to be had with such people about the working class being a potential agent for revolutionary change. There is another argument about the possibility of establishing a democratically planned economy. But there should be no argument about the convul-sive, revolutionary character of the present epoch and the complete impossibility of Blairism coping with this.

References

E Bernstein, *Evolutionary Socialism* (London, 1909).
S Crosland, *Anthony Crosland* (London, 1982).
C A R Crosland, *Socialism Now* (London, 1974).
C A R Crosland, *The Future of Socialism* (London, 1956).
J K Galbraith, *The Culture of Contentment* (London, 1921).
P Gay, *The Dilemma of Democratic Socialism* (New York, 1952).
E Hobsbawm, *Age of Extremes* (London, 1994).
W Hutton, *The State We're In* (London, 1995).
R Luxemburg, *Reform or Revolution* (Colombo, 1966).
C E Schorske, *German Social Democracy 1905-1917* (London, 1955).

Was the Second World War a war for democracy?

CHRIS BAMBERY

For the overwhelming majority of those who fought in the Second World War, it was a war for democracy. Whatever their own experiences, the newsreel footage they saw in 1945 as the concentration camps were liberated meant that until the end of their lives they believed that Britain's war with Nazi Germany was a 'just war'. That contrasted with the experiences of those who had taken part in the First World War. Few, at least by the war's end, would have argued that that war was 'just'.

Fifty years after the end of the Second World War most people still see this war as different. So in his recent history of this century Eric Hobsbawm argues that the Second World War in the West can be:

> ...best understood, not through the contest of states, but as an international ideological civil war... And, as it turned out, the crucial lines in this civil war were not drawn between capitalism and communist social revolution, but between ideological families...between what the 19th century would have called 'progress' and 'reaction'—only that these terms were no longer quite apposite.[1]

This was the theme taken up by the London *Evening Standard* in that memorable summer of 1940 as Britain faced threatened invasion. This paper was owned by Lord Beaverbrook and it was, as it still is, pro-Tory. In 1940 it stood behind Churchill against that section of the British ruling class who wanted to deal with Hitler. In order to mobilise popular support for Churchill it moved leftwards. On 15 June 1940 the paper responded to Italy's attack on France by declaring, 'It is a war not of nations at all. It is a mammoth civil war. Goethe and Garibaldi, a great German and a great Italian, are on our side.' Three days later it reacted to Marshal Pétain's surrender of France by proclaiming, 'Every rebel is our ally. We do not only fight a war. We must conduct a Continental revolution'.[2]

What separates the Second World War from the First World War is the ideological factor.[3] This is something the ruling class had to take into account. And despite the flood of films in the 1950s and the tone of the official celebrations of the anniversary of D Day in 1984 and 1994 and now of the 50th anniversary of the war's end, this is something that cannot quite be concealed.[4]

From the start it was clear to millions of people that this was not simply a war against Nazism but a war in which their own ruling class was divided. Nowhere was this more true than in France. The election of a Popular Front government under the Socialist Leon Blum with Communist support in May 1936 and the subsequent strike wave with its factory occupations terrified the French bourgeoisie. Increasingly they approached the war with an attitude of 'revolutionary defeatism'. The fall of France in May and June 1940 can only be understood against this background:

> *'It would be difficult to exaggerate'*, stressed the French historian, Marc Bloch, *'the sense of shock felt by the comfortable classes, even by men who had a reputation for liberal-mindedness, at the coming of the Popular Front in 1936'... Dangerously, the French conservatives, in their alarm, persisted in regarding the enemy within as infinitely more menacing than the menace without. 'Rather Hitler than Blum' became their motto.*[5]

Julian Jackson argues, 'The Vichy regime was largely a reaction against the revolution that the Popular Front had represented in the eyes of much of the French bourgeoisie'.[6]

In contrast to 1914 the French ruling class was deeply divided.[7] A former right wing foreign minister, Yvan Delbos, reacted to a suggestion by Blum for a government of national union following the *Anschluss* (Hitler's takeover of Austria) by telling deputies, 'The Communists, frightened by their defeat in Spain, and the Jews, hunted down everywhere, are searching for salvation in a world war'.[8]

The French officer corps were highly politicised. Leon Blum believed that '...important military leaders—including Marshal Petain and General Weygand—were more than doubtful... a great number of officers were suspect'.[9] Two secret right wing organisations existed in the French army in the late 1930s, the *Corvignolles* cells and the *Cagoule*, which had widespread support even from senior army officers.[10] Marc

Bloch recalled that so reactionary were the newspapers around his own officers' mess in 1939 that the highly conservative *Le Temps* might have been taken to represent the political views of the extreme left.[11]

These ruling class fears contributed to the Munich Agreement of September 1938. German attempts to seize the Sudetenland threatened war, while fighting in Spain still continued. Whatever the interests of France and Britain, this would have been a highly politicised conflict which they were anxious to avoid. One French diplomat remarked in March 1937, 'Who knows if around Brno, a new Catalonia will not spring up?' referring to the revolutionary centre of the Spanish Civil War.[12]

The British ruling class had not suffered such a scare as its French counterpart but it too entered the war divided. One of the most successful pamphlets in British history was called *Guilty Men*. It was a polemic against the appeasers who would have preferred not to fight Hitler. Though full of praise for Churchill, this pamphlet was boycotted by many booksellers and sold in bundles on the streets—'like a porno-graphic classic', one of its authors, Michael Foot, modestly observed.[13] As Angus Calder wrote:

> *A Gallup poll at this time suggested that three quarters of the public now wanted Chamberlain removed from office. There were strong feelings against the lesser 'Guilty Men', Halifax, Wood and Margesson. Churchill could not remove them; partly because they were able ('If one were dependent on people who had been right in the last few years,' he remarked at the time, 'what a tiny handful one would have to depend on'), and still more because the Tory benches might turn on him.*[14]

Within the normally closed political lives of the British ruling class the pamphlet represented an unprecedented *glasnost* in which a minority section of the Tory Party round Churchill relied on their media friends and the Labour Party to oust their opponents.[15] Angus Calder writes, 'The "old gang", the old system, the "Old World" (as men came to call it) had failed... Hatred focused on Chamberlain, Hoare, Simon, and beyond them the Conservative Party, and beyond them the businessmen whom they represented in parliament'.[16]

The vicious nature of that split is caught in these words of Lord Dunglass (later the Tory prime minister Sir Alex Douglas Home) recorded by a dinner guest on the day of Churchill's 'Finest Hour' speech in June 1940:

> *Alec said in the last fortnight, and indeed since W [Winston Churchill] came in, the H of C [House of Commons] had stunk in the nostrils of decent people. The kind of people surrounding W are the scum...*[17]

The Labour Minister for Economic Warfare, Hugh Dalton, noted that after Churchill's speech:

> It is noticeable how he is much more loudly cheered by the Labour Party than by the general body of Tory supporters. The relative silence of these latter is regarded by some as 'sinister'.[18]

This opposition to Churchill continued into 1941. Andrew Roberts writes of the Chamberlain wing as 'the Respectable Tendency' who 'spent 14 months putting party before country, and love of intrigue before both'.[19]

Their figurehead was Chamberlain's foreign secretary, Lord Halifax. Halifax was of course equally as responsible as Chamberlain for the surrender to Hitler at Munich. In July 1939 Hitler's adjutant reported Halifax as saying that he 'would like to see as the culmination of his work the Führer entering London at the side of the English King amid the acclamation of the English people'.[20] Halifax did not deny this statement when it was made public after the war.

In early February 1940 Lord Halifax passed a peace proposal to Hitler's deputy Goering through a Danish contact of the pro-Nazi historian Sir Arthur Bryant.[21] One of Halifax's closest friends was Lord Londonderry, a former leader of the Northern Ireland Senate and aircraft minister in the MacDonald coalition government. After being sacked from that job, Londonderry toured Germany in early 1936 striking up a friendship with Goering. Back home the Nazi ambassador, Ribbentrop (who would become Hitler's foreign minister), was a regular house guest. In 1938 Londonderry published *Ourselves and Germany*, a defence of appeasement and the Nazi regime, and in January of that year he signed a message of support published in the *Berliner Tageblatt* on the anniversary of the Nazi 'revolution'.[22]

Opposition to Churchill's appointment extended to the royal family. George VI told Chamberlain when he accepted his resignation:

> How grossly unfair I thought he had been treated and that I was terribly sorry that all this controversy had happened. We then had an informal talk over his successor. I, of course, suggested Halifax.[23]

The permanent secretary at the Foreign Office recorded in his diary for September 1939: 'Buck House to see King, called in about 6.10 and stayed till 6.50. He was depressed—and a little *defeatiste*...' As Andrew Roberts comments, 'Putting the word into French makes it no less extraordinary that within a week of the outbreak of war, the senior official at the Foreign Office could find the King-Emperor to be defeatist about Britain's war prospects'.[24]

The present Queen Mother wrote to Chamberlain just as the Germans were invading the Low Countries, concluding, 'You did all in your power to stave off such agony and you were right. With again my heart-felt thanks for all you have done for this dear country of ours, I am, yours very sincerely, Elizabeth R'.[25]

The Duke of Windsor and his wife were openly pro-Nazi. Robert Bruce Lockhart, a journalist and spy, described a conversation he had with the Duke in 1933, when the Duke was still the Prince of Wales. The Duke,who 'was quite pro-Hitler, said it was no business of ours to interfere in Germany's internal affairs, either re Jews or re anything else, and added that Dictators were very popular these days and we might want one in England before long'.[26] After his abdication he toured Germany giving Nazi salutes. After Paris fell to the German army in 1940 he quit his home there, at first for the Riviera and then for Franco's Spain. There a plot was hatched by his old friend the German foreign minister, Ribbentrop, with Hitler and Franco's knowledge, to lure him to Berlin. It took much manoeuvring to get the Windsors back to Britain from where they were carefully sent by Churchill to preside over the Bahamas.[27]

The general attitude to Churchill was that 'he was seen as essentially a war leader, and his rejection by the electorate in 1945 was the result of this long standing image of him, not any sudden access of ingratitude'.[28] Yet in many working class households Churchill was seen as a 'bastard', who had sent troops to shoot the miners of Tonypandy in 1911. But he was seen as a bastard necessary to oversee victory.

Yet, despite Churchill being a blue blooded High Tory, the rhetoric of *Guilty Men* and the propaganda the BBC and the newsreels helped spur a growing radicalisation. The author J B Priestley gave a series of radio broadcasts in the summer of 1940 which won a mass audience and worried Churchill with their radical tone. In one in July 1940 Priestley attacked the idea of property as being 'old fashioned' and suggested it should be replaced by 'community'. Pointing to a house with a large garden near his own home, which lay empty after the owner had fled from the blitz to America, he said:

> *Now, according to the property view, this is all right, and we, who haven't gone to America, must fight to protect this absentee owner's property. But on the community view, this is all wrong. There are hundreds of working men not far from here who urgently need more ground for allotments so that they can produce a bit more food. Also, we may soon need more houses for billeting. Therefore, I say, that house and garden ought to be used whether the owner, who's gone to America, likes it or not.*[29]

Tom Wintringham, an ex-Communist and commander of the British contingent of the International Brigades, coined the term 'a People's War' that summer. The socialist novelist George Orwell took things further:

> The defeat in Flanders will turn out to have been one of the great turning points in English [sic] history. In that spectacular disaster the working class, the middle class and even a section of the business community could see the utter rottenness of private capitalism.[30]

Mass Observation, which closely surveyed British public opinion, reported in November 1940: 'In the last few months it has been hard to find, even among women [!], many who do not unconsciously regard this war as in some way revolutionary or radical'.[31]

A war against fascism and for democracy?

The dominant message around the 50th anniversary of the war's end—a message propagated by historians and politicians on the right and left—is that this was a war against fascism and for democracy. But fighting fascism was never the main concern of Allied rulers. Britain's wartime leader, Winston Churchill, was opposed to Germany from the mid-1930s onwards because he recognised it threatened Britain's position in Europe and the world. He had no problem with the Italian fascist dictator, Mussolini. In 1927, following a visit to Il Duce in Rome, Churchill told the fascist press, 'If I had been an Italian, I am sure I should have been wholeheartedly with you from the start to finish in your triumphant struggle against the bestial appetites and passions of Leninism'.[32]

Churchill's Secretary of State for India, Leo Amery, said in August 1941, after the Atlantic Charter signed by Roosevelt and Churchill promised that each nation could decide its own form of government, that, 'If Italy prefers, after we have got rid of Mussolini, to retain their corporative and functional basis of government, there is no reason why she should not do so, and Point Three [of the Charter] has already given comfort to Salazar in Portugal and friendly dictators elsewhere'.[33] Commenting on the fall of Mussolini, Churchill wrote:

> He was, as I had addressed him at the time of the fall of France, 'the Italian lawgiver'. The alternative to his rule might well have been a Communist Italy, which would have brought perils and misfortunes of a different character both upon the Italian people and Europe... Even when the issue of the war became certain, Mussolini would have been welcomed by the Allies.[34]

When Mussolini fell, the government which the allies recognised was headed by the fascist Marshal Badoglio and King Victor Emmanuel who had appointed Mussolini as Italy's prime minister. They brutally suppressed the massive demonstrations which followed the fall of Mussolini:

> *In Bari 23 people were killed and 70 injured when the army opened fire on the crowd in Piazza Roma. Outside the Alpha Romeo factory in Milan machine guns were trained on the exits to prevent workers leaving the factory to join their colleagues on the streets. In mid-August...the authorities agreed to release political prisoners but also responded with more bloodshed and a massive wave of arrests.*[35]

After the Allied advance the old order still remained: '...in countless communes the ex-Fascists or their collaborators stayed in office... In essence those that had loyally served Fascism for decades, including many who had joined the Party, still dominated the post-Mussolini civil, military, and police systems'.[36] Of Churchill's attitude to this it has been written, 'He was not interested in eradicating Fascism from the Italian state apparatus, and was content, as Pavone has written, "to offer immunity in return for obedience".'[37]

The end of the war brought the chance of popular vengeance against the Fascists, but the Communists played a key role in enforcing restraint. This missed opportunity meant that in Portugal and Spain fascist dictatorships would survive until 1974 and 1975. In 1942, at the time of the Allied landings in North Africa, President Roosevelt wrote to the Spanish dictator, Franco, describing himself as 'your sincere friend' and 'assured him that he had nothing to fear from the United States'.[38] On 24 May 1944 Churchill told the Commons that 'the internal affairs of Spain were a matter for Spaniards alone'.[39] The former leader of the Spanish Communist Party, Fernando Claudin, points out that this position was accepted by Stalin: 'The maintenance in power of the Fascist dictatorship in Spain after the Second World War is one of the clearest results of Stalin's policy of sharing out "areas of influence".'[40]

In December 1940 Sir Alexander Cadogan, permanent under secretary of state at the British Foreign Office, had warned Lord Halifax of the need to be cautious about war aims:

> *The difficulty that I see is that to proclaim 'democracy' and 'liberty' enables the enemy to say that we stand for the 'Front Populaire' and the 'Red' government in Spain. And millions of people in Europe (I would not exclude myself) think that these things are awful.*[41]

Even in Germany the British argued in the first weeks of their occupation for a 'soft peace' which meant maintaining the old apparatus: 'The first few weeks of the occupation of defeated Germany reflected this British conception in the bluntest fashion possible: the deliberate continuation of the Nazi government under Doenitz and his aides at Flensberg, a government Hitler himself designated'.[42]

In France the *epuration*, the purge of Vichyite collaborators, saw 10,000 people killed by local resistance fighters. In contrast: 'Nearly 7,000 people were legally sentenced to death, but only 770 were actually executed, and over 38,000 of the roughly four times that number who were tried for collaboration were sent to prison or forced labour for some term'.[43]

The Communist Parties offered no alternative. Stalin of course had been perfectly prepared to sign a pact with Nazi Germany in 1939 and as a demonstration of goodwill had handed over some German Communists to the tender mercies of the Gestapo. On his return to France the Communist Party leader, Maurice Thorez, backed De Gaulle in demanding an end to the *épuration* and demanded the dissolution of all extra-parliamentary institutions.

De Gaulle himself was far from being a pure democrat. Prior to the war, in 1934, he had advocated the formation of a shock army of six mechanised divisions. The priority of this proposed force was to prevent 'a situation of anarchy, perhaps of civil war'. Attacking the police's ability to cope in this situation he also said the army could not cope because 'its units are now all formed of voters or natives'.[44] After the war his *Rassemblement du Peuple Français* employed 'shock troops' against the Communists in a series of bitter street clashes.[45]

In Britain Jewish refugees had found it hard to enter the country before the outbreak of the war. After Dunkirk, refugees from Germany and Austria were interned and shipped off to Canada and Australia. One Jewish refugee from Germany recalled, 'Churchill had the right kind of instincts "we've got to do something" and, like in Germany, you immediately turn on the Jews'.[46] In June 1940 his father (who had been held in Buchenwald), his brother and he were taken by detectives from their home in London to a detention camp in a Liverpool stadium. He and his brothers were shipped off to Australia—despite the fact the Australian government had refused to accept such refugees!

The leader of the British Union of Fascists, Sir Oswald Mosley, was released from (very free and easy[47]) detention in November 1943 after his relations lobbied establishment figures. By the following year Nazi groups had began to operate again as Mosley prepared to relaunch the BUF in the form of the Union Movement. There was no official attempt to block any of this. One anti-fascist Jew wrote of 'going from a cinema showing newsreels of piles of Jewish men, women and children being bulldozed into limepits in the concentration camps, and then passing an outdoor fascist meeting or seeing swastikas whitewashed on Jewish homes and synagogues...'[48]

So the Second World War was not, in the minds of those who ruled the Allied powers, a war against fascism. Neither was it a war for democracy. After all, Britain and France refused to fight in defence of a democratically elected government in Czechoslovakia but did go to war in defence of Poland, a country ruled by a military clique with pronounced anti-semitic policies. One of Britain's allies was Greek dictator Metaxas whose regime had many fascist traits. Britain's major concern when its forces entered Greece (after the Germans had withdrawn) was not to enforce democracy but to crush the Communist led resistance army, ELAS, and its civilian wing, EAM, in order to restore the old order:

In October 1944, when the Germans were evacuating Greece, the Papandreou government entered Athens with a British naval and military force. Churchill had instructed the British commander, General Scobie, that 'the clear objective is the defeat of the EAM'.[49]

When Scobie called on ELAS to disarm in December 1944 these security forces opened fire on a mass peaceful demonstration in Athens' Constitution Square, killing 28. Fighting flared across the city and the British were on the point of defeat when the Russian military delegation insisted ELAS/EAM accepted Royalist rule in line with accords reached between Stalin and Churchill. The new regime began rounding up ELAS members. Those who had carried firearms during the German occupation were now guilty of a punishable offence.[50]

In terms of the colonial world, talk of a war for democracy must have seemed like a joke. When Chamberlain declared war on Germany he also committed India to the conflict without any Indian having the slightest say in the matter. Two million Indians would fight for the 'King-Emperor'.[51] The nationalist Congress Party had swept into control of most of India's provinces in the elections of 1937 (central control remained in British hands). After the Viceroy, Lord Linlithgow, had declared India to be at war, bargaining began because the Congress demanded independence but Britain needed the Congress to rule India.[52]

Churchill, a violent opponent of Indian independence, was forced to reopen negotiations, pressured from Washington. As the Japanese pushed to India's borders, the Leader of the House of Commons, Labour's Sir Stafford Cripps, was sent to India to reopen negotiations. Churchill and Linlithgow, vetoed the agreement which Cripps brokered. The effect in India was dramatic. One Congress leader recruited tens of thousands of captured Indian soldiers into the Indian National Army which would assist the Japanese in the forthcoming conquest of India.

Gandhi and Nehru launched the Quit India movement. Gandhi told his followers to 'Do or Die'. The day the movement was launched the Viceroy had him and other Congress leaders jailed. The Quit India movement,

> *...amounted to the biggest threat to British control of India since the mutiny. The railway line between Delhi and Calcutta—the main artery of government—was blown up in Bihar, where, for more than two weeks, the British completely lost control and so could not organise repair teams. Supplies could not be sent to the Burmese front, where a Japanese invasion was feared. In many parts of the country police stations were burnt, policemen killed, British people on the roads were stopped by gangs and beaten up, telegraph wires cut... The Government did all it could to suppress news of what was happening in order to preserve morale in both India and Britain. For a week or more it was unclear whether the British would be able to reassert control.*[53]

Control was reasserted by using a carrot and stick methods combined with traditional British policy of divide and rule. In order to suppress popular unrest huge numbers of troops were used and the RAF bombed villages. Congress was banned. In order to appease the upper classes 11 Indians were brought onto the Viceroy's 14 strong Executive Council. It was at this point that Britain promoted Mohammed Ali Jinnah's Muslim League which was invited to form regional governments in Sind, Assam, Bengal and the North West Frontier Province. The stage was set for the tragedy of partition.

The situation in British-run Egypt was critical as German troops neared Alexandria in 1941. King Farouk appointed a prime minister who sympathised with the large pro-German element in Cairo.[54] The British demanded Farouk appoint the pro-British Nahas Pasha as prime minister. Farouk refused. The British then issued him with an ultimatum, to appoint Nahas Pasha prime minister by 6pm or face the consequences:

> *At 6.15 the King delivered his reply. The ultimatum was an infringement of the Anglo-Egyptian treaty and of the rights of Egypt: the King could not assent to it. Lampson [the British ambassador] sent a message to say that he would be calling on the King at 9pm. By the time he did so, British tanks and armoured vehicles had surrounded the Abdin palace. The King prudently ordered his royal guard not to resist.*[55]

Farouk gave way after being threatened with forced abdication. A young Egyptian officer serving in the Sudan wrote of these events of 4 February 1942, 'What is to be done now that this has happened and we accepted it with surrender and servility? ...I believe that colonialism, if it felt that some Egyptians intended to sacrifice their lives and face force with force, would retreat like a prostitute'.[56] Lieutenant Gamal Abdul Nasser spoke for a generation of young Egyptians.

The British ruling class's real agenda was summed up by Leo Amery at the India Office, who stated in December 1942, 'After all, smashing Hitler is only a means to the essential end of preserving the British Empire and all it stands for in the world'.[57]

The United States was prepared to openly attack British colonialism (though hiding its own version of colonialism in places like the Philippines) in order to supplant its allied rival. But democracy was also absent from one area of America itself. In the US the Southern states operated a Jim Crow policy of racial segregation. In one incident, 'A German prisoner of war on the run from a POW camp in the Southern states gave himself away by his behaviour on a long distance bus; not only did he seat himself in the "Coloured People Only" section at the back, but he then gave up his place to an elderly black who was having to stand'.[58] To the north in Detroit 34 people died in February 1943 in a race riot which swept the city. Racial segregation was even enforced in the US armed forces.

New forces had been unleashed by the war, however. On VE Day in Setif in Algeria 8,000 Algerians demonstrated under the slogan, 'For the Liberation of the People, Long Live Free and Independent Algeria'. 'They were also flourishing, for the first time, the green and white flag that had once been the standard of that legendary hero of resistance against the French, Abdel-el-Kader, and was later to become that of the FLN liberation movement'.[59] The French sub-prefect of Satif, Butterlin, ordered his chief of police, Valere,

> to intervene and seize the banners. Valere warned that that might mean a fight *(une bagarre)*. *'All right'*, replied Butterlin, *'then there'll be a fight'.*[60]

The police opened fire but were overcome by the crowds. Arms were seized and demonstrators fanned out across the area attacking colonists, killing 103 of them. The French repression that followed was fierce: 'The casualties inflicted by the armed forces were set officially (by the Tubert Commission) at 500 to 600, but the numbers of Muslim villagers killed by the more indiscriminate naval and aerial bombardments may have amounted to more'.[61]

The Algerian Communist Party, loyal to Moscow's line that it should maintain unity with the Paris government, denounced the uprising as 'Hitlerian'. The party's journal *Liberté* proclaimed that, 'The organisers of these troubles must be swiftly and pitilessly punished, the instigators of the revolt put in front of the firing squad'.[62]

What had changed in Algeria? Alistair Horne explains, albeit in rather patronising terms: 'The Second World War came and with it France's crushing defeat in 1940. To Muslim minds, particularly sensitive to prestige and *baraka* [good fortune], the humiliation made a deep impression'.[63] Events at Setif helped spark the eight year liberation war which would drive France out of Algeria.

The world had been turned upside down. The defeats inflicted on Britain in Singapore and elsewhere had sent out the same message. Yet on VE Day in 1995 who will remember those killed in Setif and in its aftermath?

Rival imperialisms in the age of dictators

No one can deny the horrors of Nazism. But the Nazis were not some parasitical growth on capitalism. They were brought to power in the world's second industrial state by the German ruling class. However much that ruling class might dislike political power being exercised by a former house painter, they shared with Hitler common war aims. German capitalism stood by the Führer until his suicide in the burning ruins of Berlin.[64]

The Second World War was a war dictated by the logic of imperialism. This conflict was fuelled by the 1929-1932 crisis, the gravest the world capitalist system had yet experienced. In order to escape from this crisis Germany, the US, Japan and Britain, together with the lesser powers, France and Italy, adopted a similar strategy. To various degrees they looked towards creating their own protected trade areas together with state direction of the economy.

Just two days after the outbreak of war the exiled Russian revolutionary Trotsky argued, 'The struggle is going on between the imperialist slaveholders of different camps for a new division of the world...the present war is a direct prolongation of the previous war...'[65] He summed up the situation thus:

> The initiative for the new redivision of the world this time, as in 1914, belonged naturally to German imperialism. Caught off guard, the British government first attempted to buy its way out by concessions at the expense of others (Austria, Czechoslovakia). But this policy was short lived.[66]

The British historian A J P Taylor has argued against the idea that Hitler was responsible for the Second World War, claiming that he was simply an opportunist who was trying to redress the injustices of the Treaty of Versailles in 1919.[67] In this sense Hitler,

> ...was the creation of German history and of the German present. He would have counted for nothing without the support and co-operation of the German people... Hitler was a sounding board for the German people. Thousands, many hundred thousands, of Germans carried out his evil orders without qualm or question... In international affairs there was nothing wrong with Hitler except that he was a German.[68]

Taylor argued that Hitler's foreign policy was that of his predecessors 'and indeed virtually all Germans'.[69] He also argued that in 1940 Hitler could have contained the war within Europe. Hitler's mistake was to invade Russia and to globalise the conflict. Taylor claims Hitler was acting 'without design'.[70] In terms of long term plans it was 'doubtful whether he had any'.[71]

In reality Hitler's New Order could not have been created without war with Britain, France and, inevitably, Russia. The creation of a single European power also posed a threat to the United States. And if Germany had succeeded in its long term aims it would also have posed a threat to Japan.

Hitler was clear about this:

> The struggle for hegemony in the world will be decided for Europe by posses-sion of the Russian space. Any idea of world politics is ridiculous (for Germany) as long as it does not dominate the continent... If we are masters of Europe, then we shall have the dominant position in the world.[72]

In the winter of 1940 Hitler explained to his generals:

> Britain's hopes lie in Russia and the United States. If Russia drops out of the picture, America, too, is lost for Britain, because the elimination of Russia would greatly increase Japan's power in the Far East. Decision: Russia's destruction must be made a part of this struggle—the sooner Russia is crushed the better.[73]

But Taylor is right to argue that in this regard German imperialism was no different from its rivals. This is not to ignore the horrific nature of the Nazi regime, merely to point out that at the core of Hitler's war drive were the same factors which drove on his enemies and allies.

The background to all this was the Wall Street Crash. By January 1933, when Hitler took power, there were 6 million unemployed in Germany. Hitler's initial economic programme was similar to Roosevelt's New Deal package in America. Public spending on the *autobahns* and railways (both of military importance) increased, subsidies were given to housing, firms were forced into cartels, industry was offered cheap loans and tax exemption while wages were pegged at the level they were at the bottom of the slump. Industrial production rose from 53.8 percent of the 1929 figure to 79.8 percent in 1934.[74] Yet unemployment remained at three times the 1929 figure and inflation began to mount. The Nazis increased their state capitalist measures. From 1935:

> The major capitalist groups remained intact. But from now on they were subordinated—as in 1914-1918—to the needs of an arms drive which they themselves wholeheartedly supported. The mild reflationary measures of 1933 gave way to the 'preparedness economy'—the arms economy—of 1935 onwards.[75]

By 1936 Germany's economic output equalled the 1929 figure. Three years later it had grown by a further 30 percent. Such expansion was at the expense of Germany's middle and working classes.[76] And in 1938-1939 the German economy fell into a grave economic crisis. A huge budgetary deficit existed—public expenditure was 55 million Reichmarks in 1938-1939 but tax and custom receipts were only 18 million Reichmarks.[77]

Much of Germany's economic policy was based on 'autarky'—economic self sufficiency. Export possibilities were limited in a recession wracked world and in order to curb earlier trade deficits the Nazis limited exports.

But there was a limit as to how far they could go down that road. Rearmament fuelled the need to import raw materials. But the only way Germany could find the necessary raw materials in a world dominated by protectionism was to physically expand the borders of the Third Reich: 'The only "solution" open to this regime of structural tensions and crises produced by dictatorship and rearmament was more dictatorship and more rearmament, then expansion, then war and terror, then plunder and enslavement'.[78]

Similar pressures were affecting Britain, the United States and Japan. All were locked into a system of trade protection where the only solution to their economic problems was a repartition of the world. Russia was a partial exception given its vast territory and raw materials. But even Stalin could not separate the autarkic Russian economy from the competition between states.

The Second World War was a conflict between rival imperialisms. A conflict as much between the victorious Allies as between them and the Axis. Trotsky understood this when in 1934 he wrote:

US capitalism is up against the same problems that pushed Germany in 1914 on the path of war. The world is divided? It must be redivided. For Germany it was a question of 'organising Europe'. The United States must 'organise' the world. History is bringing humanity face to face with the volcanic eruption of American imperialism.[79]

The conflict would see America finally eclipse Britain as the major imperialism and it would lay the basis for the economic and political arrangements which dominated the following half century. Cordell Hull, Roosevelt's Secretary of State, explained in a public address in July 1942 that:

Leadership toward a new system of international relationships in trade and other economic affairs will devolve very largely upon the United States because of our great economic strength. We should assume this leadership, and the responsibility that goes with it, primarily for reasons of pure national self interest.[80]

Warring allies

At 2.41am on 7 May 1945 Generals Friedeberg and Jodl signed the surrender of Germany on behalf of Adolf Hitler's designated successor, Admiral Doenitz, at General Eisenhower's headquarters at Reims in Northern France. No senior British officer or minister was present. Field Marshal Montgomery had to stage his own separate surrender ceremony for the cameras. A relatively junior Russian officer was flown into Reims at the last minute. The Americans drew up the surrender document with no reference to either of their allies. Meanwhile far to the east the Russians were in control of the German capital, Berlin.

Three months later on 14 August in Tokyo Bay both the British and the Russians were excluded when General Douglas MacArthur accepted the surrender of the Japanese. Both countries were also excluded from any say in the American occupation of the country. In the Pacific there was little pretence that the Allies were on an equal footing: 'For such heroes of America's Pacific struggle as Admiral Nimitz and (especially) General Douglas MacArthur, the Grand Alliance was, in the main, a ritual rather than a practical bond'.[81] This was the American policy on which the army and navy were unanimous.

Already by the time Churchill and Roosevelt, travelled to meet Stalin at Yalta in the Crimea in February 1945 the Anglo-American alliance was little more than a facade: 'By Yalta the vital unity between the two nations depended largely on their mutual enemies and the common Anglo-American fear of Russia and the threat of the left'.[82]

The Yalta summit saw a cynical division of Europe between the three victorious powers. Britain was excluded from discussions over Japan. Stalin was able to gain his essential goal—the creation of a buffer zone to the west of Russia's European frontier. He could do so because in the words of the British foreign secretary, Anthony Eden, 'at Yalta the military situation was still conspicuously in his favour'.[83] This was because Russia was carrying the bulk of the war against Germany.[84]

In December 1944 the Germans had launched their assault in the Ardennes aimed at driving a wedge between the Allied forces in northern France and Belgium. In near panic Roosevelt and Churchill had pleaded with the Russians to bring forward a planned offensive to relieve the pressure on the Western Front.[85] By the time of Yalta that offensive had brought the Russians to within 100 miles of Berlin. Similarly in the Far East the Americans, unsure of the effectiveness of the atomic bomb, were relying on a Russian attack on Manchuria to drive the Japanese out of China.

Hitler did order the removal of troops from the Western Front to face the Russian assault on Germany but the Anglo-American forces had no intention of launching an assault on Berlin—despite much post-war bombast from figures like Britain's Field Marshal Montgomery.

Firstly, all three Allies had already agreed on the division of Germany into zones, including Berlin, so as Eisenhower explained: 'It was futile... to expend military resources in striving to capture and hold a region which we were obligated, by prior decision of a higher authority, to evacuate once the fighting was over'.[86] The 'military resources' that the Russians expended on the German capital were 305,000 men killed, wounded or missing.

Secondly, Eisenhower was concerned that the Russian advance might extend to the Atlantic coast. Therefore, he ordered Montgomery to advance to the Baltic port of Lubeck at the eastern foot of the Danish peninsula. 'Head off our Soviet friends', was Churchill's instruction.[87] The British reached the town just six hours ahead of the Russians. Meanwhile the Americans advanced into Austria to prevent the Russians similarly extending their advance.

The need for Russian aid in the war against Japan still influenced American strategy at the Potsdam summit in July 1945. On 23 July Truman met with Churchill and the Combined Chiefs of Staff 'and reiterated the policy to, "Encourage Russian entry into the war against Japan".'[88]

It is this which explains America's decision to use its newly developed atomic weapons on Japan. Truman still needed Russian help in Manchuria but the successful detonation of the atomic bomb was intended as a marker laying down America's post-war position in the world.

Truman's decision to bomb first Hiroshima in August 1945 and then Nagasaki concluded a long series of negotiations with the Russians over the final conquest of Japan. Kolko writes that in May 1945:

> ...the Allies had effectively defeated Japan and reduced its industrial capacity and manpower to nearly a last-stand posture... The Americans now tried to weigh the atomic bomb both from the viewpoint of its use against Japan and its implications to future relations with the Soviet Union... One must remember that at no time did the Americans see the bomb as a weapon for defeating the formidable Japanese army in China, and at no time did they consider it desirable that the Soviets invade the Japanese mainland. The bomb did not reduce the importance of Soviet entry into Manchuria and north China.[89]

The desperate Japanese resistance and the resulting American casualties in the fighting at Okinawa, as the Americans neared the Japanese island chain, determined Truman's position at the Potsdam summit in July 1945. Truman wrote, 'There were many reasons for my going to Potsdam, but the most urgent to my mind, was to get from Stalin a personal reaffirmation of Russia's entry into the war against Japan, a matter which our military chiefs were most anxious to clinch'.[90]

On 9 August the Russians attacked the Japanese positions in Manchuria and liberated much of northern China. The Americans now pressed for a quick Japanese surrender, accepting the continuance of the emperor as part of the price. It was within this context that both Russia and Britain were excluded from the surrender ceremony in Tokyo harbour and from any role in the occupation of Japan.

Britain—the lion in winter

To understand the war it is necessary to look at each of the four major players. The starting point is Britain, simply because Britain had the most to lose and the least to gain in any new world war. In April 1939 the British Treasury warned: 'If we were under the impression that we were as well able as in 1914 to conduct a long war we were burying our heads in the sands.' By February 1940 they believed Britain's resources might just last for two or three years with care.[91]

Britain was being squeezed out of its position as the number one world power by its rival across the Atlantic. Since the 1890s Whitehall had ruled out war with the US because of its economic strength and the vulnerability of Britain's imperial possessions in the western hemisphere. In 1918 the British cabinet had to accept that America had overtaken the Royal Navy and that the days when Britannia ruled the waves were over.

Britain could no longer plan on fighting a war both in Europe and the Far East nor in these circumstances could it guarantee to protect its imperial colonies and dominions in the Far East. In 1925 Winston Churchill assured the Cabinet, 'I do not believe Japan has any idea of attacking the British Empire, or that there is any danger of her doing so for at least a generation to come'.[92] But six years later Japan seized Manchuria and began its expansion into China.

In 1942 after the fall of Singapore and with the Japanese at the gates of India Churchill told the House of Commons, 'There has never been a moment, there never could have been a moment, when Great Britain or the British Empire, singlehanded, could fight Germany and Italy, could wage the Battle of Britain, the Battle of the Atlantic and the Battle of the Middle East—and at the same time stand thoroughly prepared in Burma, the Malay Peninsula, and generally in the Far East.'[93]

Yet at no point had Whitehall told Australia and New Zealand this. Labouring under the belief that the Royal Navy would defend them Anzac troops were sent to the Middle East in 1940.

One thing which united both the Chamberlain and Churchill wings of the Tory party by 1939 was a consensus that the crucial issue was the maintenance of Britain's position in the Mediterranean and the Middle East. This position remained unchanged throughout the war. After the fall of France Britain's priorities were seizing French territory in the Middle East, liquidating Italy's African colonies and taking control of the Iranian oilfields. After America entered the war Churchill desperately tried to avoid a land invasion of northern Europe until shortly before D Day in favour of further operations in Italy, the Balkans and even the Greek islands.

By the 1930s Britain's share of world manufacturing was well below Germany's and a third of America's. Britain was attempting to control a quarter of the world with just 10 percent of global manufacturing. During the First World War it was only Britain's ability to import steel and shell from the United States which staved off disaster. By the late 1930s British steel production was half that of Germany's and Britain was increasingly dependent on American imports. Rearmament from

1935 onwards saw imports rise by 400 percent. Britain had already defaulted on loan repayments to America dating from the First World War. This meant it had to pay up front for its American orders. Its financial reserves simply could not meet the costs of a lengthy war. In July 1939 the Treasury argued, 'Unless, when the time comes, the United States are prepared to either to lend or to give us money as required, the prospects for a long war are exceedingly grim'.[94]

Yet such American largesse was not forthcoming. The United States objected strongly to the creation by Britain of a sterling bloc and imperial trade preference scheme. Britain used the political legacy of empire to create a trading zone from which its rivals were excluded. This contained British colonies and dominions, much of the Middle East and countries like Argentina. Prior to the war the Sterling Area and North America accounted for half of total world trade. Any settlement between the US and Britain would shape the new world order following the war.

The destruction of this set up was America's key aim in its dealings with Britain throughout the war, as the British ruling class were well aware. They were trapped between the devil and the deep blue sea—in the shape of Hitler and Roosevelt. Rab Butler, junior foreign minister, a pillar of the Tory party and a leading appeaser, wrote a month before war broke out, 'In my political life I have always been convinced that we can no more count on America than Brazil'.[95]

This awareness goes some way to explaining the depths of appeasement towards Hitler in the Tory party of the late 1930s. Neville Chamberlain noted of his predecessor as prime minister, Stanley Baldwin, that, 'SB says he loathes the Americans so much he hates meeting them'.[96] Chamberlain nursed a deep dislike of the US and of President Roosevelt in particular.

So Britain entered the war in a dire position. It could not defend its territories which stretched across the globe. It faced two powers but only had the economic and industrial resources to confront one of them. Rearmament had strained its economy to the limits but Britain's military readiness was no deterrent to Germany or Japan.

The Baldwin and Chamberlain governments knew all this. If war broke out victory was only possible if America and possibly the USSR entered the war. The price of this would be to further reduce Britain's position as a world power. The British ruling class chose a twin track approach of offering concessions to Germany, Italy and Japan while trying to create an effective military deterrent.

Hitler's demand for the Sudetenland, part of Czechoslovakia, in the autumn of 1938, brought matters to a head. Chamberlain accepted Hitler's claim that this was simply reuniting ethnic Germans in the region with their homeland, telling journalists invited to meet him at

Lady Astor's home, 'Hitler wants all the Germans he can lay his hands on, but positively no foreigners'.[97]

More crucially it was hoped German expansionism could be directed eastwards towards Russia. A German diplomat reported that he had been told by Chamberlain's close adviser, Sir Horace Wilson:

> *Britain and Germany were in fact the two countries in which the greatest order reigned and which were the best governed... It would be the height of folly if these two leading white races were to exterminate each other in war. Bolshevism would be the only gainer... A constructive solution of the Czech problem by peaceful means would pave the way for Germany to exercise large scale policy in the South East.*[98]

But in the aftermath of the Munich agreement of September 1938, which surrendered Czechoslovakia to Hitler, any further concessions would seriously erode Britain's position as a great power. Chamberlain reacted to Hitler's gobbling up of the remainder of Czechoslovakia by issuing guarantees of protection to both Poland and Romania.[99]

Even so, when Chamberlain entered the Commons two days after the invasion of Poland he intended not to deliver an ultimatum to Germany but to float the possibility of Britain being 'associated' with possible talks to end the 'present hostilities'.[100] Just days before, on 29 August, a friend of Lord Halifax, the foreign secretary, noted in her diary, 'Edward thinks if we can keep Hitler talking for two more days the corner will be turned'.[101]

What precluded this was the emergence of an alliance between the Labour Party and a growing section of the Tory party who realised that any retreat would mark the end of Britain as a great power.

This meant that the British ruling class were deeply divided. After the announcement of war Lord Halifax, the foreign secretary, asked his permanent secretary what Britain's war aims were:

> *I told him I saw awful difficulties. We can no longer say 'evacuate' Poland without going to war with Russia, which we don't want to do! I suppose the cry is 'abolish Hitlerism'. What if Hitler hands over to Goering! Meanwhile what of the course of operations? What if Germany now sits tight? What do we do? Build up our armaments feverishly? What for?... Must try to think this out.*[102]

Field Marshal Montgomery wrote in his memoirs that in September 1939 he believed the British army 'was totally unfit to fight a first class war on the continent'. Britain's leaders believed any loss of life on the scale of the previous war would be unacceptable domestically.

Accordingly Britain placed a heavy emphasis on sea power and, in particular, heavy air bombing. Rearmament was weighted towards the Royal Navy and the RAF.

Under Chamberlain Britain's war 'strategy' was to hope that while the French army kept the *Wehrmacht* in check, a naval blockade of Germany would lead to its economic collapse and the war would fizzle out. This illusion was blown apart with the fall of France in the spring of 1940.

Churchill was not the choice of the Tory party, Chamberlain or even King George VI. He was a ruling class maverick. Chamberlain wanted to pass the mantle of office to Lord Halifax, but Halifax turned it down. This was appreciated in Germany:

> *'Churchill', Dr Goebbels noted in his diary after a discussion with Hitler early in 1942, 'has never been a friend of the Tories, He was always an outsider, and before the war was regarded as half crazy. Nobody took him seriously. The Führer recalled that all Englishmen whom he received before the outbreak of the war were in agreement that Churchill was a fool. Even Chamberlain said so to the Führer.*[103]

Churchill's determination to fight on after Hitler conquered France, Belgium and Holland was not matched by the reality of the situation. In its evacuation from Dunkirk the British army lost nearly all of its equipment. As the military chiefs told the cabinet in May 1940, 'Should the enemy succeed in establishing a force, with its vehicles firmly ashore, the army in the United Kingdom, which is very short of equipment, has not got the offensive power to drive it out'.[104]

A section of Churchill's government entered into peace negotiations in that summer of 1940. Rab Butler called the Swedish ambassador to the foreign office to ask the neutral Swedes to open negotiations with Hitler. During the conversation Butler complained of 'diehards' in the cabinet who should not be 'allowed to stand in the way'. Butler described the prime minister as 'a half breed American' and his war speeches as 'beyond words vulgar'.[105]

Tory ministers in favour of peace with the Nazis included the foreign secretary, Lord Halifax, and 'Chips' Channon (father of one of Margaret Thatcher's ministers). The former prime minister in the First World War, Lloyd George, talked of 'this damn crazy war'. A Churchill supporter, Harold Nicolson, noted on 22 July that 'Lothian [Lord Lothian, British Ambassador in Washington] claims that he knows the German peace terms and that they are most satisfactory'.[106]

Churchill vetoed the peace deal but, as Field Marshal Lord Alanbrooke admitted, up until December 1941 Britain had no strategy for victory independent of the Americans. Churchill summed this up in June 1940 when he wrote, 'I think I can see my way through it... I shall drag in the United States'.[107]

He was lucky in that until the spring of 1941 the British were not fighting any part of the German army, just the far weaker Italians. Even then until the end of 1942 the British army never fought at one time more than four German divisions out of a total of more than 200. As Churchill admitted to Roosevelt at the close of 1940, Britain was unable to match 'the immense armies of Germany in any theatre where their main powers can be brought to bear'.[108]

Another problem was the weakness of Britain's generals and its officer corps. Matters came to a head in 1942 with the loss of Tobruk, Burma and Singapore. The head of the Foreign Office, Sir Alexander Cadogan, wrote in his diary, 'Our generals are no use. Our army is the mockery of the world'. Field Marshal Rommel wrote of the British army's 'immobility and rigidity', of 'the ultra-conservative structure of their army' and of 'the machinery of command—a terribly cumbersome structure in Britain'.[109]

In this respect Britain remained trapped in the legacy of the First World War with a senior officer corps who were still upper class, had little military knowledge and were remote from their men. Britain's most successful general, Montgomery, always relied on building up massive technical and numerical superiority before any offensive, but failed to capitalise on his success.[110]

Britain's industry was hopelessly ill equipped to deal with the demands of modern warfare. It relied on America for steel. By late 1942 production of ammunition was falling. By mid-1943 so was production of military vehicles and by the year's end production of artillery and small arms was also declining. By D Day two thirds of the British Army's tanks and trucks were American.

Great claims were made for the bombing offensive against Germany but very early on officials were noting the realities of the air assault. An official British history of the air offensive concluded, 'Area attacks against German cities could not have been responsible for more than a very small part of the fall which had occurred in German production by the spring of 1945, and...in terms of bombing effort, they were also a very costly way of achieving the results they did achieve'.[111]

Britain constantly manoeuvred to oppose a landing in France, putting forward all sorts of alternative schemes—including an invasion of neutral Portugal. Even after the US insisted on the Overlord operation, the invasion of Normandy, going ahead—Churchill could ask in February 1944, 'Why are we trying to do this?'[112] On D Day the British provided half the troops (including Canadians and Poles). This was the maximum force it could mobilise. From then until the end of the war British troop levels declined while America's mushroomed until they had five times as many troops fighting the Germans.

Churchill described the United States and the United Kingdom as 'a noble brotherhood of arms'. The truth was somewhat different. After America's entry into the war Churchill knew Britain could not hope to dominate a land war in northern Europe. Gabriel Kolko writes, 'The British objective was to employ their very limited resources carefully in a global struggle at precisely those points where they might have the maximum political effect'.[113] All Britain could hope to do was to reclaim its dominance in the Mediterranean.

As early as 1926 a Foreign Office memorandum had stated, 'We have no territorial ambitions nor desires for aggrandisement. We have got all that we want—perhaps more'.[114] That summed up Britain's whole approach—simply hanging on to as much as it possessed.

Matters came to a head over Middle Eastern oil with the Americans determined to exclude the British from the Saudi Arabian oilfields. The outcome was: 'The United States had defeated British imperialism in the Near East'.[115] As the wrangle continued Churchill wrote to Roosevelt:

> *Thank you very much for your assurances about no sheep eyes at our oilfields in Iran and Iraq. Let me reciprocate by giving you fullest assurances that we have no thought of trying to horn in upon your interests or property in Saudi Arabia. My position in this as in all things is that Great Britain seeks no advantage, territorial or otherwise, as a result of the war. On the other hand she will not be deprived of anything which rightly belongs to her...*[116]

But deprived Britain was—and in the main by its brother in arms, the United States.

Hitler's war

Until the autumn of 1941 Hitler planned 'short wars with long stretches of quiet in between', as his war production minister, Albert Speer recorded. Hitler hoped to be allowed to get away with a policy of foreign expansion (as had happened in the Saar, the Rhineland, Austria and Czechoslovakia) whilst avoiding the economic and political strains which had brought revolution to Germany in 1918.[117] In Speer's words, 'He always wanted everything at once'. Speer pointed out that Hitler was concerned,

> *To keep the morale of the people in the best possible state by concessions. Hitler and the majority of his political followers belonged to the generation*

who as soldiers had witnessed the Revolution of November 1918 and had never forgotten it. In private Hitler indicated that after the experience of 1918 one could not be cautious enough.[118]

When he unfolded the plans for the invasion of France, Hitler told his generals, 'I shall stand or fall in this struggle. I shall not survive the defeat of my people. No surrender abroad! No revolution at home!'[119] Hitler did not trust the German masses. The working class had never transferred their support to him even in the elections following his taking of power in 1933. Accordingly he determined they should be spared the deprivations visited on them in 1916-1918. Nazi labour policy was dominated by this political consideration.

Doubts about popular support for war were crucial in delaying the switching of the economy to a total war footing until after the tide turned in 1942:

> ... *the ambivalent attitude of National Socialism towards the workers (terror directed against all expressions of political opposition; and attempts at social integration, even at the expense of rearmament) was determined first and foremost by its ideological assimilation of the lessons of the revolution of November 1918. The future struggle for hegemony in Europe was not to be hampered by disorder on the home front and the threat of revolutionary upheaval. Nazi labour policy, therefore, can be seen as the precautionary pacification of the home front. And for this, carrots were needed as well as sticks.*[120]

The hesitation produced by such fears more than anything else, and far more than the Allied bombing offensive, hampered Germany's war effort.

By 1938-1939 Hitler's regime was caught between the economic consequences of rearmament and their fear of political unrest. Hitler was committed to both a war of expansion and creating a cohesive Germany, immune to a repeat of 1918-1919.

British Marxist Tim Mason has produced strong arguments explaining why Hitler committed himself to war in the summer of 1939. In January the head of the *Reichsbank*, Schact, resigned. The cost of rearmament had meant that the national debt had tripled since the Nazis had come to power, public spending took up some 50 percent of national income and in a hot-house economy inflation was mounting. Yet because of fears of internal unrest Hitler refused to sanction tax increases or other unpopular measures. Despite a policy of economic autarky the German economy was not immune from outside pressures. Mason points out:

It was only a significant and completely unexpected improvement in world trade in 1937, which increased German imports by 30 percent and exports by 25 percent, that created the basis for accelerated rearmament foreseen by the Four Year Plan. This respite came to an abrupt end with the American recession late in 1937...[121]

The seizure of Austria and Czechoslovakia could meet at most a third of Germany's import requirements. Mason also points out that in 1938 the clothing needs of the German population accounted for a third of industrial imports while 'quasi-luxuries' like tobacco, coffee and cocoa were above the 1929 figure which contrasted sharply with acute shortages in the raw materials needed for rearmament. These shortages provided justification for 'a war of plunder'.[122]

Such a war could also solve the labour shortages plaguing the German economy. For, as the military prepared to attack Poland, the regime was planning to conscript German school children to bring in the harvest. This was avoided by using Polish prisoners of war and several army divisions freed from the front by the speed of the campaign.

Mason details massive labour shortages, such as a shortfall of 30,000 miners in the Ruhr which halted coal exports.[123] The regime was not prepared to encourage women to work both for ideological reasons—their stress on women's role in the family—and because to maintain morale in the army the government paid higher separation allowances, 85 percent of the husband's previous earnings, than any other country in the Second World War.

The irrationality of the Holocaust—in 1942 among the first victims of the death camps were skilled Polish Jewish armaments workers—flowed not just from the regime's ideology (though this was crucial) but from Hitler's refusal to rationalise the German economy. He ruled out such measures on the grounds of time but also because such rationalisation would have upset the alliances on which the Third Reich was based and would have required unpopular measures aimed at the working class. Such fears were real. Mason writes:

As we can deduce from Hitler's ever rarer public appearances, the regime was beginning to admit to itself that its hopes of maintaining mass enthusiasm for its project of racial imperialism had not been entirely fulfilled. After the summer of 1938 it was more a case of holding the population down and stemming the rising wave of discontent, opposition and demoralisation. State backed police terror, so effective against political opposition, proved quite inadequate to the changed circumstances. Exemplary punishment of randomly selected 'layabouts', contract breakers or 'saboteurs' had little success.[124]

Mason's conclusion is that Germany was propelled into war by internal crisis and the need for resources to fuel rearmament. The defeat of France in May-June 1940 was achieved, despite the French and British having numerical superiority, by German audacity and the incompetence of her opponents.

The attack on France was not preceded by any noticeable shift in the German economy towards a war footing. The economics minister, Funk, had to explain this to the generals saying, 'To live through this mess one has to be either mad or drunk: I prefer the latter'.[125] In 1940 German consumer expenditure was actually greater than its military spending. The German standard of living remained higher than Britain's until 1944. Military output was actually reduced after the fall of France so that tank production stood at just 40 a month (compared to 2,000 a month reached in 1944).

The result was a remarkably ramshackle and ill equipped force which attacked Russia in June 1941. Only 46 out of 150 divisions were fully equipped with German arms. The rest depended on captured Czech and French material. Far from Germany facing economic collapse, as Britain had hoped, its economy was working under capacity for the bulk of the war.

But neither Hitler nor his generals believed that a lengthy European war was on the agenda. Hitler's calculation in 1939 was that once Britain and France had entered the war following the attack on Poland he had to deliver a knockout blow before both countries' rearmament programme would decisively shift the balance. Hitler believed Britain would either surrender after the fall of France or concede to German demands. One of Hitler's generals, Halder, recorded in his diary after a discussion in July 1940 that the German dictator was reluctant to defeat Britain and dismantle the empire:

> *Reason: if we smash England militarily, the British Empire will collapse. Germany will not benefit from this. With German blood we would obtain something whose beneficiaries would only be Japan, America and others.*[126]

In late 1940 Hitler decided he could conquer the USSR by the end of 1941(the timescale for operation Barbarossa was five months), integrate its economy with that of the *Reich* and return to the attempt to defeat Britain. The primary objective was to win the vast territory and resources of the east, but it would also remove any immediate source of help to Britain and force it to the peace table. Such calculations were mistaken and left Germany fighting a war on two fronts, the long term dread of its rulers. The crucible of the Second World War was the eastern front.

Hitler sent 3 million men into Russia equipped for one decisive offensive. He planned for the war to be over by winter and to leave a garrison of not more than 275,000. German armour reached Leningrad but then had to wait for its infantry to catch up. Then German armoured vehicles halted because spare parts could not be supplied in time to sustain the advance. Half the *Ostheer (the Eastern army)* relied on horse drawn supplies from railheads. The German army took into service more horses in the Second World War than it did in the First—2.75 million to 1.4 million (the Russians mobilised 3.5 million horses).[127] The technical ability of the supposedly racially inferior Russians to replace their tremendous losses came as a shock to the Germans. One soldier wrote:

*Today three months ago the campaign against Russia began. Everybody supposed at the time that the Bolsheviks would be ripe for capitulation within no more than eight to ten weeks... That assumption, however, was based on a widespread ignorance of the Russian war material... We are spoilt by the preceding **Blitzkrieg**.*

Omar Bartov argues that:

*...between 1941 and 1942 the Wehrmacht's combat units underwent a radical process of de-modernisation... Although the **Reich** actually produced a growing number of war machines, the vast majority of German troops lived and fought in conditions of the utmost primitiveness.*[128]

When in early 1942 Albert Speer was given limited authority over the war economy he discovered only 37.5 percent of Germany's crude steel production was going into the war effort—9 percent less than during the First World War. Food consumption never collapsed as in the First World War. Even in 1944 adult male rations were 83 percent of normal and in European terms were only comparable to Britain's.[129] This was achieved at terrible cost to occupied Europe (360,000 Greeks, for instance, died of starvation). It is estimated that the conquered territories paid for 40 percent of Germany's war effort in 1942-1943 while by September 1944 foreign workers made up 21 percent of the German labour force (of 5.5 million foreign workers, 1.8 million were prisoners of war).[130] German industry became dependent on such labour: 'All told, foreign workers made up about one third of the workforce of the armaments industries, and in some instances, such as Krupp's tank manufacturing plant in Essen, about 50 percent...'[131]

But as A D Harvey points out, the productivity of foreign workers was low: 'Various figures have been given; one set for 1944 gives the Italians as having only 70 percent of the productivity of German workers and the Danes and Dutch even less'.[132] Reliance on forced labour meant that in 1944 the average working week for German workers was still three hours less than in Britain. Yet this cushioning of the impact of the war on Germany's population was accompanied by harsh repression aimed at any dissent on the shopfloor. By July 1944 at least 87,000 workers had been imprisoned for violating work norms. Anyone uttering anything smacking of defeatism could be punished, including by execution, and many were, especially after 1943. Executions increased sixfold between 1940 and 1943, reaching 5,336. This repression was aimed at the German working class.[133]

In the year November 1942 to October 1943 the Eastern army had lost 1,686,000 men who were either dead, wounded or missing and had received only 1,260,000 replacements. Between January and December 1943 Germany's stock of tanks declined absolutely from 5,700 to 5,200. Stalingrad was a terrible blow. Hitler complained in the spring of 1944 to an army doctor that his nights were filled with nightmares: 'I can sketch exactly where every division was at Stalingrad. Hour after hour it goes on'.[134]

But terrible as Germany's defeat at Stalingrad was, it cost Hitler 20 divisions (two armoured), just a tenth of the *Ostheer*'s strength and a fifteenth of the *Wehrmacht*'s whole strength. This was dwarfed by the losses inflicted in June 1944 in Byelorussia. This little known battle resulted in German losses of 300,000 with 28 divisions simply written off. This is the greatest defeat ever inflicted in warfare. It dwarfed the battle for Normandy which followed D Day. Yet despite this the *Wehrmacht* kept fighting until the bitter end. Why?

One answer which has gained widespread acceptance centres on the discipline and camaraderie of the German army.[135] There is no doubt that German soldiers received longer basic training than their British or American counterparts right up to the end of the war. Also German officers mixed with their men far more than their Allied counterparts while even the most junior NCO was expected to take command in an emergency. In addition units were recruited from the same area. Yet these 'primary groups' of officers and men were largely destroyed in the first two years of the war in the east.

Omar Bartov argues that the prime motivation in the *Wehrmacht's* continued resistance was 'ideological'. Yet this overlooks, as Gabriel Kolko points out, 'that many men still came from the working class and the peasantry, where socialism, religion, and a very great deal else were still highly regarded' and further that, 'to argue ideology could have overcome constant experience is to claim that Germans were more stupid than soldiers have ever been anywhere'.[136]

Bartov centres his argument on the brutality of Germany's racial war in the east. During the Russian campaign 5.7 million Russian soldiers were captured and 3.3 million died (57 percent). By early 1942, 2 million were already dead. The German commander in Byelorussia claimed to have shot 10,431 out of 10,940 prisoners in October 1941 alone.[137]

Bartov demonstrates that the *Wehrmacht* was involved in the Nazi racial extermination programme at every level. He goes on to argue that this murderous brutality was mirrored inevitably in the army's own organisation. During the First World War the *Kaiserheer* executed just 48 of its own soldiers (less than the French or British). In the Second World War Bartov estimates the *Wehrmacht* killed 13,000 to 15,000 of its own soldiers and that between January 1940 and March 1942 (when Germany seemed sure of victory): 'four fifths of the death sentences were based on ideological-political grounds.'[138]

The mass murder committed by the *Wehrmacht* in Poland, Yugoslavia and above all Russia had a brutalising effect. It also meant that most German soldiers believed that the Russians would exact revenge from the Reich. The Nazi propaganda chief, Goebbels, wrote in his diary in November 1943 that Germany's war effort was sustained 'partly owing to our good propaganda, but partly also to the severe measures which we have taken against defeatists'.[139] This was accompanied by strenuous efforts to maintain civilian morale by maintaining living standards at the highest level possible.

But there was another crucial factor. Neither the Americans, British or Russians wanted to inherit a Germany wracked by the same political chaos as that following the First World War. All were determined to maintain as much as possible of the existing social structure. This meant there was to be no attempt by the Allies to develop internal unrest. All three powers agreed on a simple militaristic solution which would impose an unconditional surrender on Germany. The mass firebombing of German cities had the effect of rallying civilians behind the regime, as did the violence inflicted on the population by the rear echelons of the Red Army.

In March 1943 Britain's Anthony Eden arrived in Washington for talks with Roosevelt's close adviser, Harry Hopkins. Hopkins stated,

It will, obviously, be a much simpler matter if the British and American armies are heavily in France or Germany at the time of the collapse or one of two things would happen...either Germany would go Communist or an out and out anarchic state would set in.[140]

Stalin shared the same concerns as Eden reported to Churchill in March 1943, 'If Germany collapsed, he [Stalin] had no desire to take full responsibility for what would happen in Germany or the rest of Europe, and he believed it was a fixed matter of Russian foreign policy to have both British and United States troops heavily in Europe when the collapse came'.[141]

Why did the German ruling class remain wedded to the Third Reich—including its unleashing of the Holocaust—until the bitter end? Tim Mason has described the Third Reich as being characterised by 'the primacy of politics'.[142] Mason argues:

> ...it was apparently the case that both the domestic and the foreign policy of the National Socialist government became, from 1936 onwards, increasingly independent of the influence of the economic ruling class, and even in some essential aspects ran contrary to their interests. This relationship is, however, unique in the history of modern bourgeois society and its governments; it is precisely this that must be explained.[143]

The weakness of the German ruling class meant that in the Depression of the 1920s they were 'incapable of solving the great problems of domestic, economic and foreign policy and of thereby giving bourgeois society a new structure and a new direction in which to develop'.[144] The National Socialists appeared to be an organisation which could solve the ruling class's problems.[145] Big business might not like giving power to Hitler, it might believe it could ease him out, but the fears that brought it to support Hitler were never removed.

The new regime, the military and big business all accepted that rearmament was their goal. Individual capitalists were prepared to sacrifice their immediate interests to further that goal. The most obvious example was the expropriation of one of the heads of Germany's key concerns, Thyssen, despite his crucial support in raising Hitler to power. This was a policy of state capitalism. This created a German replica of the situation in Washington where managers seconded from big business ran the war economy in tandem with the military.[146] This did not mean a lessening of cut throat competition between the rival capitals bound together in a war economy:

> To increase his profits every contractor tried to obtain these orders and to fulfil them as punctually as possible, so that he would be taken into consideration when contracts were next distributed. This, in conjunction with the shortage of labour and raw materials brought about by the rearmament drive, led to ruthless competition between firms, not for markets, which were well-nigh unlimited for the industries concerned, but for the basic factors of production.[147]

Where the 'pure politics' came to play a crucial role was in the prosecution of the war in the east and the pursuit of the Holocaust which followed Hitler's conquests there. Capitalists and the military could accept the use of vital rail links being used to transport Jews to their murder instead of being used to provision German forces, or the refusal to consider the Slavic populations as being any more than slaves, because this represented the culmination of methods employed by capitalism elsewhere in carving out its vast economic empires. Hence the involvement of German capital in the death camps and in the murderous exploitation of forced labour. Yet as the French socialist, Daniel Guerin, argued in 1945 in his *Fascism And Big Business*: 'The bourgeoisie remained an autonomous force, pursuing its own ends in the totalitarian state'.[148]

The US—making the world safe for democracy?

Immediately after Pearl Harbour and America's entry into the war Alfred C Wedermeyer of the War Plans Department formulated a plan which would largely determine how and where America's army would fight the Second World War. It was presented to President Roosevelt in December 1941 and it was entitled 'Victory Programme'. This policy became known as 'Europe First'.

The policy was based on seizing a foothold in Western Europe by landing a vastly superior force on the shoreline of Western Europe at the earliest possible date after the Atlantic was cleared of German U boats. Wedermeyer calculated US troops would have to outnumber the *Wehrmacht* by three to one. His conclusions were at odds with Britain's plans:

> *We must prepare to fight Germany by actually coming to grips with and defeating her ground forces and definitely breaking her will to combat... Air and sea forces will make important contributions, but effective and adequate ground forces must be available to close with and destroy the enemy inside his citadel.*[149]

America, although having twice the population of Germany, could not build the necessary military force (reckoned to be 8.8 million strong) and fight a major war against the Japanese. Japan had to be engaged but it was 'Europe First'. The man put in charge of this 'Victory Programme' was Eisenhower. He was one of the few senior officers in any of the armies who was experienced in industrial mobilisation.

There was widespread isolationist feeling in the US between the wars but this had largely been overcome by the realities of the US's economy at the close of the 1930s. In 1932 Roosevelt won the presidency, promising a 'New Deal', but his timid state capitalist measures could not prevent the economy re-entering recession. Unemployment rose to 18 million. As Gabriel and Joyce Kolko point out, a turn to the world market became vital. The war in Europe would begin a massive American export drive which together with rearmament pulled the economy right out of recession: 'From the 1932 low of $1.6 billion, US exports rose to $12.8 billion in 1943 and $14 billion in 1944. The figure of $14 billion in post-war exports—well over four times the 1939 level—therefore became the target of most wartime planners, and their calculated precondition of continued American prosperity'.[150]

The American ruling class determined that the world economy would be reorganised to secure that goal. Isolationism was dead as a realistic option by the 1940 presidential election. Roosevelt was convinced that, 'If Britain fell, a disastrous war for the United States would be inevitable, Germany would attack the western hemisphere, probably at first in Latin America, as soon as she assembled a sufficient naval force and transport and cargo fleet (not too long a process with all the ship-building facilities of Europe at Germany's disposal) and Japan would go on the rampage in the Pacific'.[151]

South of the US's border with Mexico, Trotsky echoed that argument in May 1940 as the battle for France raged:

> The potential victory of Germany over the Allies hangs like a nightmare over Washington. With the European continent and the resources of its colonies as her base, with all the European munition factories and shipyards at her disposal, Germany—especially in combination with Japan in the Orient—would constitute a mortal danger for American imperialism.[152]

Across the Atlantic Hitler's Directive Number 18 of November 1940 mentions the need to capture the Canary and Cape Verde Islands, the Azores and West Africa because of their strategic importance in relation to the US.[153] These exact positions plus Iceland were seen as the US's front line of defence and the first step to the invasion of Europe.

American aid to Britain was always based on self interest. Prior to 1941 aid was given to Britain and France so that German ambitions were limited to Europe. This also won the US time to rearm.

In the summer of 1940 when Britain faced Germany alone, Roosevelt demanded assurances that if Britain sought peace the Royal Navy would be sent to Canada to avoid it falling into German hands and threatening American control of the Atlantic. Churchill refused, arguing, as Vichy France had argued to him weeks earlier, that the navy would be a crucial pawn in any peace negotiations.

Yet American aid was only granted in return for the surrender of British bases in the western hemisphere, on the sale, at reduced prices, of British owned companies and investments in the US, Canada and Latin America, the virtual seizure of South Africa's gold production by American warships, restrictions on British exports and finally the removal of the UK's currency and trade controls which could have been used to rebuild its pre-war international trade zone.

Britain was saved from having to sue for peace with Hitler by American intervention. This was given because it was in America's national interest. The longer Britain fought on, the longer the US had to make its own preparations. British war orders in 1940, when the American economy had not yet emerged from recession, played a role in converting it to war production. The Lend Lease Bill of March 1941 was open in admitting it was 'an Act to promote the defence of the United States'.

Those interests were clear to all in Washington: 'The United States could not afford, however, to compromise on the essential principle of breaking down the sterling bloc, for that was the key to the reconstruction of the world economy after the defeat of the Axis'.[154]

This would entail negotiations from the very first meetings between the two allies through to the Yalta and Potsdam summits and would result in the Bretton Woods agreement which established the primacy of the dollar, the GATT agreement which created a free trade zone for America and the International Monetary Fund as the world's financial policeman.

The impact of the war on America's domestic economy was to create a major restructuring of US capital which involved close collaboration between the state and big business. Much of America's wartime industrial expansion was state funded. In 1939 the entire US manufacturing plant had cost $40 billion to construct. By June 1945, $26 billion in new plant had been added to it. Two thirds of this cost came from federal funds. Just 25 corporations used up half of these government funds, General Motors being the biggest receiver. Over three quarters of this new plant was usable after the war and, deemed 'war surplus', was sold at reduced prices. This was a major transfer of state capital to private capital. Two hundred and fifty corporations acquired 70 percent of it, representing in total more than their pre-war share of US plant capacity.[155]

The war effected a giant concentration of capital into the hands of a relatively small number of firms like General Motors and Boeing which became central to America's post-war arms drive and closely intertwined with the US state.

Japan—the Pacific gamble

Japan had entered the world capitalist economy as a state monopoly capitalism at the time of the Meiji Restoration, following the state's decision to build modern industry in the face of American military threat. As such its industry and banks had always worked closely with the state bureaucracy. The onset of the world crisis reduced industrial production by 10 percent and the price of silk products collapsed. This was followed by an increase in US tariffs on Japanese goods in 1930 and a year later by America overtaking Japan as the leading exporter to China.

From 1932 Japan's ruling class, its army and navy shared a consensus that it should establish hegemony in East Asia in opposition to both the US and Russia. To achieve that Japan required control of China, naval dominance in the western Pacific and the ability to defeat the Red Army if necessary. There were deep and even bloody splits over how this might be achieved but this was an officially accepted state aim.

The occupation of Manchuria in 1931 and increased militarisation of the economy ended the recession. By 1938 industrial production was 73 percent above its 1929 figure.[156] Yet of the four major players in the Second World War Japan was still the weakest economically: 'Essentially Japan was still in the throes of industrialisation in the 1940s...' Forty four percent of the workforce was in the agriculture, fisheries and forestry sector.[157] This meant Japanese industry could not compete with the Americans.[158]

Their industrial and technological weakness was exacerbated by rivalries between the navy and the army. This meant each service demanded separate aircraft designs, placing impossible demands on Japan's aircraft industry. Because the navy refused to co-operate in provisioning overseas garrisons, the army ended the war with its own specially built aircraft carrier and a cargo carrying submarine fleet under construction! The army also refused to exempt skilled workers from conscription, adding to production problems.

These divisions were reflected in Japan's government, which produced little centralisation of the war effort. Writing of Hidecki Tojo's government A D Harvey says:

> He could resign with his whole government, but he was unable to dismiss any of his colleagues individually. He was unable to subordinate the armed forces to his control—he was not even told of the disastrous defeat at Midway for a month. He was unable to silence criticism of the government in the army, in the press, or even at public meetings.

Tojo complained that he was denied a 'dictatorial government' like, and this was his list, those of Hitler, Mussolini, Roosevelt and Churchill.[159]

A clash at the Marco Polo Bridge outside Beijing in July 1937 triggered a full scale invasion of China as the first step towards creating an 'East Asian bloc'. Japan expected an easy victory. The army minister predicted the invasion 'could be ended within the month'.[160] The Chinese Nationalist government of Chiang Kai Shek traded territory for time. Within a year Japan had one million troops bogged down in China.

The invasion of China challenged the US's 'open door' policy whereby it hoped that China would be opened up to American exports. So after the invasion of China, Roosevelt stepped up aid to Chiang Kai Shek and operated an informal trade embargo against Japan. When Japan occupied French Indochina (with the co-operation of Vichy France) America imposed an oil blockade. Japan imported 66 percent of its oil from the US.[161] Japan would initiate a war with America in December 1941 with just four months reserves of iron ore and a nine month supply of bauxite. A year before the navy had estimated its oil reserves as enabling it to fight for a year.

The mood in the country's ruling circles was summed up by its foreign minister, Teijiro Toyoda, in secret messages to his ambassadors in Berlin and Washington on 31 July 1941: 'Commercial and economic relations between Japan and third countries, led by England and the United States, are gradually becoming so horribly strained that we cannot endure it much longer. Consequently, our Empire, to save its very life, must take measures to secure the raw materials of the South Seas'.[162]

The decision to declare war was made on 5 November. The key targets were the oilfields and other raw materials of Indonesia and Malaya in south east Asia. But Japan faced an enemy, the United States, whose economy was ten times greater than its own. Japan's leading naval strategist, Admiral Yamamoto, warned: 'We can run wild for six months to a year—after that what would determine the outcome was the oil wells of Texas and the factories of Detroit'.[163]

The Japanese high command initially gambled that the attack on Pearl Harbour could cripple US naval power in the Pacific. The attack came off better than was expected by many of those involved, but it failed to destroy the American aircraft carriers which were at sea and there was no follow up attack on the repair facilities and the oil supplies. Admiral Nimitz later wrote:

> We had about four and a half million barrels of oil out there and all of it was vulnerable to .50 calibre bullets. Had the Japanese destroyed the oil it would have prolonged the war another two years.[164]

After Pearl Harbour Japan's one chance of victory lay not in seizing vast areas and inflicting major damage on the enemy (this was achieved) but also in the Americans opting for a quick showdown before their rearmament programme was in full swing. A decisive victory would give Japan time to consolidate its new empire. That crunch came at Midway in June 1942 and Japan lost its gamble.

Between 1941 and 1944 the US launched 21 aircraft carriers to Japan's five. The US fleet was supported by supply vessels which meant it could stay at sea for weeks. Their submarines had sunk half of Japan's merchant fleet and two thirds of its tankers by the end of 1944.

This loss of naval control (and air cover with the destruction of its aircraft carriers) meant that the Japanese land forces in the Pacific were largely cut off from their homeland. The raw materials Japan had gone to war for could no longer be transported back to Japan's industries. The Japanese military refused to withdraw from their far flung conquests in order to create a defensible front line.

America could afford to leave strongpoints like Singapore by 'island hopping' its way towards Japan itself. The key to the Pacific was naval power and what had been the world's biggest navy, Japan's Imperial navy, was by December 1941 ground down by the ability of American industry to carry the costs of such a war.

The fall of the Tojo government in July 1944 saw the emergence of the navy and heavy industry as the dominant faction in the Japanese ruling class. They recognised that the war was lost and began to cautiously edge towards a peace settlement.[165] The familiar fear of working class insurgency stalked the corridors of power in Tokyo as defeat loomed. By 1944 there were growing food shortages and fears of the resulting radicalisation. The former premier, Prince Konoye, told the emperor in February 1945, 'What we have to fear is not so much a defeat as a Communist revolution'.[166]

This was not idle talk. Across Asia there were signs that the Japanese armies were being infected by the growing discontent around them. A revolutionary wave was rising and it would affect the Japanese working class in the immediate post-war years.

This crisis was overcome with the aid of the Americans but the foundations of Japan's post-war economic success had already been laid. The war increased the development of Japan's giant *zaibastu* firms through state sponsored mergers, extensive use of government firms and other such state capitalist measures. This followed from the long standing policy of the Japanese state to use its capital to promote economic development and to exclude foreign interests.

By the end of the war the four largest *zaibatsu*'s industrial assets were ten times greater than their 1935 holdings. These years also saw a fundamental shift from textiles, foodstuffs and other light industries to heavy engineering and other more sophisticated activities. Heavy engineering and manufacturing grew from 38 percent of output in 1930 to 73 percent by 1942. Mergers absorbed 1,354 industrial firms in 1941-1943 alone. The Second World War and state intervention helped create the post-war Japanese economic success.

Russia—the crucible of victory

Hitler and his generals planned for a short campaign in the east. 'You only have to kick in the door and the whole rotten structure will come crashing down,' Hitler told Field Marshal von Runstedt.[167] Stalin almost played into their hands.

In 1938 Tuchachevski, who had been one of the leaders of the Red Army under Trotsky, was shot as a German spy when Stalin's terror was extended to the army. Despite being a supposed German spy his plan for the defence of Russia was maintained until the Hitler-Stalin pact extended Russia's boundaries westwards. The damage caused by Stalin's military purges cannot be overestimated: at the time of *Barbarossa* only 7 percent of army officers had any higher military education and 37 percent had not completed intermediate training.[168]

The purges affected others too: 'Between 1934 and 1941, 450 aircraft designers and aircraft engineers were arrested, of whom 50 were executed and 100 died in prison or labour camps: the survivors, including A N Tupolev, former head of the Experimental Design section and chief engineer of the Chief Directorate of the Aircraft Industry, were obliged to work in NKVD workshops'.[169]

The purges continued right up until June 1941. Many officers were released from the Gulag to take frontline positions, among them the future Marshal Rokossovskii (he survived two mock executions and emerged to take command of a mechanised corps with nine missing teeth and three broken ribs).[170]

As Russo-German relations worsened, a new plan for Russia's defence was drawn up by Marshal Zhukov. This plan was then overruled by Stalin who ordered his forces to be drawn up along the new frontier where the *Wehrmacht* overran them.[171] General Pavlov reported from the Spanish Civil War that, 'The tank can play no independent role on the battlefield'.[172] Pavlov would be shot in the first weeks of the German invasion for incompetence.

The winter war with Finland in 1940 saw huge Russian losses as 1 million men took on just 200,000 Finnish troops. Huge concentrations of infantry were sent forward without proper support to be surrounded by mobile Finnish units or butchered from well prepared defence lines.

The debacle in Finland, whose forces were only defeated by using Russia's massive firepower to crack open defensive positions, further convinced the Germans that victory in Russia would be quick.[173]

Yet Stalin was already being forced to to rebuild confidence among the officers following the Finnish war. He reintroduced the old Tsarist ranks of general and admiral in May 1940 and two months later introduced a severe disciplinary code modelled on that of the old Imperial Army.

Until 21 June 1941 Stalin refused to accept that Hitler was about to launch an invasion, despite having very precise information detailing attack plans from what was the best informed intelligence service in the world.[174] Just weeks before the German attack Zaporozhetos, head of the Political Propaganda Administration, reported:

> *The fortified districts located on our western frontiers are for the most part not operationally ready... The fortified districts are not manned by the requisite number of specially trained troops.*[175]

Until just minutes before the attack, with the sound of Panzer engines audible across the frontier, Russian raw materials continued to feed Hitler's war efforts in line with the 1939 pact.

The attack fell on Russian troops and border guards who had been refused permission to prepare their defences in case it provoked the Germans! The armoured columns raced through the Russians' linear defences. Tanks and aircraft were either destroyed by the *Luftwaffe* where they stood or simply thrown away in attacks which were ill conceived and unsupported. Infantry were detailed simply to march into the advancing Germans in a body with no artillery or armoured support.

Erickson details the state of the Russian army in June 1941: 'No reserves of spare parts or concentration of repair facilities...tractors, lorries and motorcycles were in grievously short supply', while artillery units 'faced a critical shortage of ammunition'.[176]

By October Russia had lost 62.5 percent of its coal production, 68 percent of steel output, 60 percent of aluminium production, 47 percent of its grain crops and 303 ammunition plants. In the first days of the war Stalin sent radio messages to Berlin requesting peace and approached the Japanese to act as peacebrokers. When he emerged to give his first address to the population the official rhetoric had undergone a transformation: 'Of the Party, Stalin said little; this was a "patriotic war", and his words were addressed to the Russians'.[177]

In order to survive Stalin was forced to limit the Terror and to play the nationalist card. In addition he placated his officer corps. The restoration badges of rank and epaulettes based on the old imperial designs was,

Erickson comments, 'no mere ornament, for it marked, physically and visibly, a major transition in the Red Army'.[178] Communist Party control over army units was also loosened in response to long standing complaints from officers.

But the decisive factor in stiffening the resistance of the Russians and other nationalities classed as sub-human by the Nazis was the extermination programme and mass slavery programme which came with German occupation.

As the *Ostheer* advanced deep into Russia, the Nazi rulers gathered on 16 July to discuss how the newly occupied territories would be administered. Alfred Rosenberg suggested dividing Russia into small nations, 'so as to free the German Reich of the Eastern nightmare for centuries to come'. Hitler answered that:

Small sovereign states no longer have a right to exist...the road to self government leads to independence. One cannot keep by democratic institutions what one has required by force.

He added:

While German goals and methods must be concealed from the world at large, all the necessary measures—shootings, exiling etc—we shall take and can take anyway. The order of the day is:
first: conquer
second: rule
third: exploit.[179]

Hitler had already ordered that the Geneva Convention would not apply to prisoners in the east, that any commissars (which meant any Communist Party member, intellectual or Jew) should be shot on the spot, and had threatened that Leningrad would be levelled if captured.

Alan Clark writes of the German army in Russia, 'Mass murder, deportations, deliberate starvation of prisoners in cages, the burning alive of school children, "target practice" on civilian hospitals—atrocities were so common that no man coming fresh to the scene could stay sane without acquiring a protective veneer of brutalisation'.[180]

This flowed from the Nazis' pseudo-racial theories. The Jews had to be exterminated. But the Slavs were *Untermensch*, sub-humans, who could be killed at will. This brutality affected the whole conduct of the war. There is no doubt that this and the official nationalist propaganda (as the Russians advanced into Germany it was described as 'the lair of the Fascist beast') was crucial to sustaining the Russian war effort. These words of Alan Clark carry extra weight given the author's politics:

Yet, barbarous and horrific though it was, the first impact of the Soviet armies on Germany will not stand comparison with the Nazi conduct in Poland in 1939, or in White Russia and the Baltic provinces in 1941. The atrocities of the 'Death's Head' (Totenkopf) units of the SS which systematically murdered school children and poured gasoline over hospital inmates, were the expression of a deliberate policy of terror, 'justified' by half baked racial notions, but implemented with a perverse and sadistic relish.[181]

The eventual goals of Operation Barbarossa were imprecise. By the close of 1941 German forces concentrated on capturing Moscow. They failed and their defeat brought forth a new plan from Hitler: 'He intended to smash the Russians once and for all by breaking the power of their army in the south, capturing the seat of their economy, and taking the option of either wheeling up behind Moscow or down to the oil fields of Baku'.[182]

In the event the German advance became concentrated on the River Volga at Stalingrad. The Russians led by Marshal Zhukov built up their forces and eventually launched an offensive which smashed through the German lines. A quarter of a million German troops plus Romanians, Croats and other allied formations were encircled in the ruins of Stalingrad. 'The turning point in the Second World War had arrived'.[183] The biggest tank battle the world will probably see was still to come at Kursk in the summer of 1943 and there were to be enormous losses, but the Russians had began an advance which would carry them to Berlin.

As the German threat lifted, Stalin could turn his attention to those whose loyalty he believed had wavered during the crucial months of 1941-1942. The Chechens had been brutally deported by the NKVD and their republic abolished in 1944. The Crimean Tartars suffered the same fate. Having relaxed party control over the army, Stalin now began to reimpose it in preparation for the 'purge of the heroes' which struck Zhukov and the other wartime generals.

Russia survived to virtually defeat Germany singlehanded, but it was a close run thing. The Russian ruling class were able to use their state control of industry to simplify production so that until the war's end Russian factories concentrated on basic tank designs which made repairs and replacements easier. But this concentration on arms production was only made possible by Allied, particularly American, aid.[184]

Russia would emerge from the war as the key military power in Europe: 'At the time of the Yalta conference the American generals knew that in event of a conflict with the USSR the Soviet armies would reach the shores of the Atlantic'.[185] This was also recognised by President Truman who admitted in May 1945: 'It would be open to the Russians in a very short time to advance if they chose to the waters of the North Sea and the Atlantic'.[186]

The fundamentally imperialist nature of Russia under Stalin comes out clearly in any account of the great power summit at Yalta. At a dinner hosted by Roosevelt the American official Charles Bohlen stressed America's support for the rights of small nations (this was in reference to keeping Poland out of the Russian bloc). Stalin responded '...in prim but powerful style, making absolute assertion of the rights of the "Big Three" against all the bleating of the small powers that their rights were at risk...the small must be ruled by the great, the delinquents brought to book'.[187] Later he raised the issue of Greece: 'He had no criticism of British policy in Greece, he simply wanted news of the situation...the hint was broad and crude: if the British did not break the rules, the situation in Greece would continue...'.[188]

Yet this military superpower had suffered immense damage and was economically way behind its new American rival. The strains of this military and economic competition would eventually, decades later, destroy the Stalinist system.

Stalin—bulwark against Bolshevism.

'I guess the whole world is on a leftward march,' exclaimed US Senator Vanderberg in 1945.[189] And nowhere was this more true than of Italy. Yet in Italy and elsewhere, there was a puzzle to be solved. Writing of Italy in 1945 Gabriel Kolko asks:

With red banners and power in hand 150,000 armed men disappeared overnight, and the almost morbid fears of the English and Americans proved entirely chimerical. Why?[190]

The answer lies in the policies of the Communist Party which in three crucial countries—Italy, France and Greece—dominated the Resistance. They had immense credibility because of their role in fighting fascism. In contrast the Socialists had not been able to survive the post-war repression in Italy and Greece. In France they were tarnished by the Socialist Party's involvement in the Vichy regime.[191] As Hobsbawm points out: 'Faced with a fascist takeover or German occupation, social democratic parties tended to go into hibernation...'

In May 1943 Stalin approved the dissolution of the Communist International. The spectre of 1917-1919 had hovered over all the war leaders during the Second World War. After the First World War working class unrest had erupted into revolution. That memory influenced how Hitler ran Germany's war effort. It meant that in Britain Churchill was prepared to surrender large amounts of domestic decision arrangements to Labour and the pro-Keynesian sections of his own party. It meant too

that the French ruling class in 1940, remembering recent experiences of
the 1936 factory occupations, were prepared to give way to Hitler rather
than risk another revolution. Within Russia Stalin had to lift many of the
excesses of the Terror of the late 1930s—though the extermination programme of the Nazis provided enough incentive for Russian soldiers and
partisans to fight.

Yet within Europe the collaboration of the ruling class with the Nazis,
or at best their willingness to simply wait for the Allies, meant that resistance increasingly developed its own revolutionary dynamic. In Asia
resistance in Indochina, Malaysia, Indonesia and the Philippines
inevitably combined opposition to colonialism, of either the direct kind
in the case of Britain, France and the Netherlands, or the indirect sort as
in the case of the US in the Philippines.

Much of this resistance was initially spontaneous though it increasingly became identified with the Communist Parties. Yet in Italy, France
and Greece those parties were not fully under the control of their leaderships who were in Moscow and those leaderships had to confront
massively swollen parties which might not just jump to Stalin's orders.
The Communist Parties themselves had to be brought under tighter
control as leaders like Thorez of France, Togliatti of Italy and
Zachariadis of Greece returned from Russia.

Faced with growing resistance to Nazi occupation as the Allies
approached, all three Western powers acted in the same way. Stalin was
prepared to let 166,000 Poles die in the Warsaw uprising of 1944 but
Britain's Field Marshal Alexander was acting in a similar way in 1944
when he broadcast across Italy that the Allies would not advance beyond
the Arno that winter, giving the Germans a green light to deal with the
partisans in the north.

Resistance began early on in occupied Europe. In February 1941, for
example, groups of Jews and Communists fought back and and organised strikes against the Nazis' treatment of Jews. The ranks of resistance
began to swell across Europe after Stalingrad when Germany's defeat
seemed closer. This was even true in Germany as the war ended.
Working class organisations re-emerged, their ranks swollen by new
activists. As Kolko notes of Germany in 1945:

Everywhere the Allied troops entered they found local Left committees...
running factories and municipalities which the owners and masters had
deserted, via spontaneously created shop committees and councils. Some
were old Socialists and Communists, many were new converts, but every-
where they moved to liberate concentration camp prisoners, organise food
supplies and eradicate the Old Order. For the most part they scoffed at

*regular party doctrine and talked vaguely of new forms based on a united
Left, unlike that which had helped open the door to Hitler.*[192]

In Italy the origins of the Resistance were largely a spontaneous reaction to the fall of Mussolini and the occupation of the north and centre of
the country by the Germans in the summer of 1943. In Naples the population rose up against the food shortages imposed by the Germans in
September 1943 and using the material left behind by the Italian army
drove the *Wehrmacht* from their city.[193]

By the end of 1943 there were at most 10,000 partisans in various formations. Most were simply keeping out of the way of German attempts
to conscript them as forced labour. Gabriel Kolko writes that '...partisan
formations were recruited largely from the working class and the poorer
peasantry—the origins of over half of its members in the Piedmont,
where artisans added over a tenth and students somewhat less...on the
whole it was clear that precisely those classes whom the Fascists had
muzzled after 1921 were in command of the biggest part of the armed
resistance and that the basic tensions in Italian society that had existed
before Mussolini were likely to re-emerge.'

As resistance grew, so did industrial unrest. In March 1943 in Turin
21,000 workers struck, mainly in FIAT, and the end of the year saw
further strikes in the city and in Genoa. On 25 April 1945 in Milan
60,000 workers struck and set up workers' councils to run the factories.

Similar events were unfolding in France. In the Nord and Pas de
Calais 39,000 miners struck in October 1943 and won increased wages
despite the usual arrests and deportations. Miners made up 47 percent of
those arrested in the area during the occupation, with other manual
workers making up 29 percent and the unemployed 12 percent.[194] Four
fifths of manual workers and almost one half of all resistors were in
Communist led groups.

The introduction of conscription for work in Germany swelled the
numbers of young men seeking refuge in the organisation of the countryside, the *Maquisard*. Most were not interested in resistance but they were
affected by the general radicalisation affecting France. By October 1943
the Communist FTP, the key Resistance grouping, could rely on 12,000
people across France. Beyond this there were thousands more involved
in distributing Resistance material. In the Cantal there were ten active
sympathisers for each fighter. Arms were few, however, despite Allied
promises.

All told, the Allies believed some 3 million people might aid their
invasion effort in some way. This included 800,000 workers in
Communist led unions who could disrupt transport and other services.

The Allied invasion unleashed uprisings in Paris (which was liberated
by the Resistance) and various industrial towns and cities. A nationwide

rail strike in August 1944 paralysed the country. Liberation committees took over the running of much of the country with the one in Marseilles carrying out a series of regional nationalisations.

'One state, one police force, one army', was the slogan offered by Maurice Thorez, general secretary of the French Communist Party, on his return to France in August 1944. General de Gaulle had allowed his return knowing he would enforce Moscow's line on the French Communist Party.

In Greece the Communist Party grew from 17,500 in 1935 to four times that figure by 1945, comprising 1 percent of the population and becoming the largest party in Greece. The Communist led people's liberation army, ELAS, grew from 12,500 in mid-1943 to about 50,000 by 1944 following the Nazis introduction of compulsory labour.[195] By late 1944 ELAS claimed control of three quarters of the country. Altogether 1.5 million Greeks were involved in various aspects of the Resistance movement. In July 1944 a Russian mission arrived at ELAS headquarters: 'The role of the Soviet mission to ELAS proved to be policing the unpalatable decisions already made in Moscow, deferring all and any plans for a Communist coup in Greece'.[196]

The new carve up of the world began to take shape in August 1943 when the United States and Britain vetoed Stalin's proposal for a commission of the three powers which would administer not just Italy following Mussolini's fall but Romania, Hungary and Bulgaria. The Americans and British were determined to exclude the Russians from Italy. But as Kolko writes:

> By blocking the possibility of a Soviet veto in Italy, the Anglo-Americans gave themselves a free political hand in that country but also revealed to Stalin the decisive political constraints the Americans and British were prepared to impose where their political and strategic interests were involved. Much more important, it confirmed the reality that military conquest rather than negotiations would define the political outcome of the war in Europe.[197]

Stalin now applied this principle vigorously. In Italy and Greece the British and Americans were given free hand—at whatever cost to the Communists. The Russians actively helped the British in the war with ELAS which began in December 1944.[198] On the verge of an ELAS victory the Russians and the Communist Party would insist on a ceasefire. The agreement that the Communists would be allowed to operate openly and that there would be free elections was never acted upon. Instead former ELAS fighters suffered growing persecution and assassinations which forced them back to the mountains sparking a new civil war which the Communists lost, largely because of the party's inept leadership.

Churchill would argue that the British intervention against the Greek Resistance forces was needed to deter 'radical uprisings' that 'may spread to Italy' and indeed beyond.[199]

When in August 1944 Romania signed an armistice with the invading Russian army, Stalin announced he would apply the same arrangements there as the Anglo-Americans had applied in Italy. Both Western powers were excluded from any say over the running of Romania and by extension Bulgaria and Hungary which lay on the Russians' line of advance.

In Romania the Communist Party emerged from hiding to join a government which included the remnants of the old pro-fascist dictatorship under King Michael. The Communist's ranks were 'swelled with a horde of place-seekers, collaborationists and men on the run from their Iron Guard [the Romanian fascists] past...it was one bloated with elements which only weeks earlier had manned or supported the Antonescu dictatorship—the same thugs, secret policemen and soldiers swelled with the riff-raff signed up by the Communist leadership'.[200]

In the colonial world Stalin was not in a position to directly control events. The Chinese Communist Party was already operating independently of Moscow. In China the conditions were being created which gave control to Mao Zedong's peasant armies. The nationalist leader Chiang Kai Shek had been installed as one of the 'Big Four' alongside Roosevelt, Churchill and Stalin not because of any military strength but simply as an American pawn. America continued to throw aid at Chiang despite being aware that he was little more than a gangster and of the lack of any military resistance to the Japanese by his forces.

In conversation Chiang Kai Shek was quite open about his big priorities:

For me the big problem is not Japan but the unification of my country. I am sure that you Americans are going to beat the Japanese some day, with or without the help of the troops I am holding back for use against the Communists in the North West. On the other hand, if I let Mao Zedong push his propaganda across all of Free China, we run the risk—and so do you Americans—of winning for nothing.[201]

Chiang's officers were paid by the number of troops they supposedly commanded and received food and equipment (provided by the Americans) accordingly. Most commanders were no more than warlords commanding private armies. The impact of conscription, the realities of military life plus the impact of ragged, starving bands on the countryside produced a widespread radicalisation in areas far from Mao Zedong's forces. In addition the influx of US dollars unleashed terrible inflation.

The effects were to draw the whole of China into the growing civil war and to undermine Chiang Kai Shek, despite the support given to him by Truman and Stalin.

The Japanese occupation had a devastating impact on much of south east Asia. In Vietnam they built up vast rice stocks creating famine at the close of the war. After the Japanese did away with the Vichy French colonial administration in March 1945 a political vacuum opened up. This allowed the Communist led Viet Minh to gain popular support for the first time when they launched mass raids on the rice depots. When news of the Japanese surrender came through, the Viet Minh were able to take control, beginning in the North, with just 5,000 fighters. This was 'essentially an agrarian, peasant based event'.[202] The decisive organising slogan was 'Break Open the Rice Stores to Avert Famine': 'When the Viet Minh declared a general insurrection on 12 August, days after the Japanese offer to surrender, the millions of euphoric people who filled the streets of Hanoi, Saigon and dozens of other cities also led to Viet Minh takeovers of villages and towns everywhere and transformed a numbed population into a virtually unarmed insurrectionary force'. The Viet Minh were joined by hundreds of unarmed peasants.[203]

To the south in Saigon the Trotskyists were at the forefront of a genuine working class rebellion which took control of the city. Viet Minh units arriving in the city then allowed British units to take control of the city. These rearmed Japanese prisoners who then disarmed the population and then allowed the French army to enter the city and reimpose colonial rule. In the meantime the Viet Minh had eradicated the Trotskyists. Viet Minh compliance with the British and the French was the line from Moscow. This repression opened the way for the return of French imperialism.[204] The Vietnamese Trotskyist, Ngo Van, writes that in December 1946 the Viet Minh gave up the cities and returned to the countryside to launch the guerrilla war, first against the French, then the Americans, which only ended in 1975.

In the Philippines the Japanese had ruled through the same elite who had run the islands under the Americans. This meant that a massive guerrilla army, the *Hukbalahap* (the People's Anti-Japanese Army) arose following spontaneous rural uprisings which were denounced by the Communist Party as 'extreme leftist actions'.[205] By the war's end the *Huks* had 100,000 fighters. The story of the Philippines after the Americans returned parallels events in Greece. The Communists succeeded in disarming the *Huk* units and winning their acceptance of a government dominated by the old elite, but repression triggered a rebellion which launched a civil war. Throughout this conflict the Communists were on the moderate wing of the left, urging compromise. Internal divisions on the left allowed the Americans to restore order.

Across the colonial world new movements were stirring. In India popular opposition to British rule continued throughout the war despite the British military presence (which was more concerned with suppressing the independence movement than with confronting the Japanese). In Algeria the war's end was greeted with the first major demonstrations in favour of independence which would trigger the war against France.

Was revolution possible in Europe?

The Communist Party leaders in France and Italy pointed to the Allied presence in Western Europe as the reason why revolution was not possible in 1944 and 1945. Later Thorez argued, 'With the Americans in France the revolution would have been annihilated'.[206] Paul Ginsborg in his *A History of Contemporary Italy* strongly criticises the Communists but argues that revolution was 'an impossibility'. But by 1944 the British armed forces were already shrinking in size as existing units were dissolved to make good losses in others. The Canadians had used up their pool of volunteers for overseas duties and while France was not short of men it had not the finances or means to equip them. The Americans might be less affected but war weariness was sweeping through the ranks of its forces. A New York newspaper reported from Germany at the beginning of 1946, 'The fact is that the GI's have strike fever. Almost every soldier you talk to is full of resentment, humiliation and anger'.[207] Across the Atlantic the close of the war witnessed the biggest strike wave yet seen in US history.

Demobilisation was rapid. In 1946 the British Army of the Rhine numbered just two divisions and, for a while, the Americans just one. Any Allied intervention against, for example, partisan controlled Northern Italy in support of the former fascists, collaborators and monarchists in 1945 would have been difficult to sustain, just as, following the October Revolution of 1917 domestic opposition to Western intervention in the Soviet Union had helped allow the revolution to win.

Writing of the French Communist Party in 1944, André Fontaine says that 'power was in its reach in various parts of the country'.[208] When De Gaulle requested Eisenhower to release two French divisions from the front to impose control over the vast Tolouse-Limousin area, the latter could not spare them. De Gaulle was forced to rely on Moscow and Thorez.[209]

Similarly in Greece British troops were only able to win control of Athens after Moscow and the Communist Party leaders forced ELAS to accept a ceasefire. The British and their right wing allies had nothing like the resources available if ELAS had decided to retain its control of the countryside (including the second city Salonika) by force of arms.

Some evidence about the possibility of revolution comes from Yugoslavia where the Communist led partisans defied the Yalta conventions and took power. This was not a socialist revolution led by the working class. Rather the new Tito regime replicated Russian state capitalism for its own nationalist ends. But Britain and America were powerless to intervene in 1945 just as Stalin felt restrained from invading when Yugoslavia broke free of Moscow's control.

Looking back on the close of the war the former leader of the Spanish Communist Party, Fernando Claudin, writes:

> *The possibility of revolutionary development in France and Italy was seriously threatened* [by the line of the Communist Parties]; *the position was as it would have been in Russia in the course of 1917 if Lenin's April Theses had been rejected by the Bolshevik Party. The bourgeois revolution would have consolidated itself, one way or another, but the proletarian revolution would not have taken place.*[210]

Ginsborg concludes:

> *In practice, national unity in the fight for liberation became for the Communists an objective to be placed not just above, but to the exclusion of all others. The policy of liberation first, 'progressive democracy' second, was fatally misconceived. It meant that at the very moment when the partisan and workers' movement was at it height, when the 'wind from the North' was blowing most strongly, the Communists accepted the postponement of all questions of a social and political nature until the end of the war... While the Communists postponed, in the honourable name of national unity, their opponents acted, decided, manoeuvred and, not surprisingly, triumphed.*[211]

The post-war radicalisation was largely spontaneous. Working people believed that this had been a war against fascism. They wanted to root out fascism and the old order that had collaborated with it. This feeling was mixed in with a determination that there would be no return to the horrors of the 1930s. For all their prestige in the Resistance it was not automatic that the Communists could control this movement. Paul Ginsborg argues:

> *Even among the highly politicised industrial proletariat of the northern cities it is difficult to identify a generalised revolutionary consciousness. No spontaneous attempts to create alternative organs of political power, such as soviets or workers' councils, are to be found in this period. While many*

workers looked forward to a new era of socialism (one old militant from La Spezia recalled that 'in the evenings, when we went to meetings, we talked of how to construct the socialist society, of communism and of nothing else').

Ginsborg conludes, 'It is perhaps possible to suggest that there were two dominant elements in working class consciousness at this time: a desire to reconstruct after the terrible damages of the war years and a widespread expectation of social and economic reform'.[212]

The picture painted seems right—though the liberation committees corresponded to soviet style organisations. Yet how do workers link this deep desire for revolutionary change with a concrete strategy whereby they can throw off the muck of ages to see they can take power and run society? The missing link is revolutionary organisation. What helped determine the outcome in 1945 was the strength of Stalinism and the weakness of the revolutionary left.

Revolutionaries and the Second World War

The Trotskyists entered the Second World War already weakened. In both France and the United States the Trotskyists suffered damaging splits. Added to this was Trotsky's own assassination and then the repression suffered by his followers during the war. More generally, the left felt the impact of the collapse of the French Popular Front government, the defeat of the Spanish Revolution and the harmful impact of the Hitler-Stalin pact.

Among the Trotskyists killed in the war were: Abraham Leon who was arrested in Belgium in 1944 and was murdered in Auschwitz; the French Trotskyist leader, Marcel Hic who died in the Dora concentration camp; the Austrian Franz Kascha who was executed in October 1943 for high treason and for encouraging disaffection in the armed forces; the Belgian Leon Lesoil who had led the 1932 Charleroi miners' strike and who was killed in the Neungramme concentration camp in 1942; Henri Molinier, a leading French Trotskyist who was killed in the liberation of Paris in August 1944; the Greek Pantelis Pouliopoulous who made a revolutionary speech to Italian soldiers while facing the firing squad; Henri Sneevliet, founder of the Indonesian Communist Party, and trade union leader in Holland, shot in 1942; Paul Widelin, a German Trotskyist who, in occupied France, edited the paper *Arbeiter und Soldat* aimed at German soldiers; the Italian Perre Tresso (Blasco), who was liberated from a French prison by the Resistance and then murdered by the Communists.

The tiny Trotskyist movement was a weak vessel cast adrift in stormy seas. Faced with war Trotsky was clear that it was an imperialist war but one in which ideology played a crucial role. In particular the working class's hatred of fascism meant revolutionaries had to adopt a somewhat different approach to that of 1914. Then Lenin, Trotsky, Rosa Luxemburg and Karl Liebknecht had proclaimed it was an imperialist war in which there was nothing to choose between the powers. In that situation 'the main enemy was at home'. As early as 1934 Trotsky had outlined his position on a new world war:

> A modern war between the great powers does not signify a conflict between democracy and fascism, but a struggle of two imperialisms for the redivision of the world. Morever, the war must inevitably assume an international character and in both camps will be found fascist (semi-fascist, Bonapartist, etc) as well as 'democratic' states.[213]

Flowing from this Trotsky looked back to the experience of the First World War:

> Lenin's formula, 'defeat is the lesser evil', means not defeat of one's own country is the lesser evil as compared with the defeat of the enemy country but that a military defeat resulting from the growth of the revolutionary movement is infinitely more beneficial to the proletariat and to the whole people than military victory assured by 'civil peace'... The transformation of imperialist war into civil war is the general task to which the whole work of a proletarian party during war should be subordinated.[214]

He returned to the argument in March 1939:

> The idea of defeatism signifies in reality the following: conduct an irreconcilable revolutionary struggle against one's own bourgeoisie as the main enemy, without being deterred by the fact that this struggle may result in the defeat of one's own government; given a revolutionary movement the defeat of one's own government is a lesser evil.[215]

What is crucial here is that for revolutionaries the aim must be a repeat of the October 1917 or November 1918 revolutions which took Russia and Germany out of the First World War. But if the Second World War continued from the First World War in that both were imperialist wars, there was also a break between the two. Anti-fascist ideology played a key role in September 1939, quite unlike August 1914, and the mood of the working class which resulted had to be taken into account. So in discussions with American Trotskyists in June 1940, just as France surrendered to Hitler, Trotsky explained:

Militarisation now goes on a tremendous scale. We cannot oppose it with pacifist phrases. This militarisation has wide support among the workers. They bear a sentimental hatred against Hitler mixed with confused class sentiments. They have a hatred against the victorious brigands. The bureaucracy [the American trade union leaders] *utilises this to say help the defeated gangster* [Britain]. *Our conclusions are completely different.* [216]

He returned to this at the beginning of August:

...the feeling of the masses is that it is necessary to defend themselves. We must say: 'Roosevelt (or Wilkie) says it is necessary to defend the country; good it must be our country, not that of the Sixty Families and their Wall Street. The army must be under our own command; we must have our own officers, who will be "loyal to us".' In this way we can find an approach to the masses that will not push them away from us, and thus prepare for the second step—a more revolutionary one.

We must use the example of France to the very end. We must say, 'I warn you, workers, that they (the bourgeoisie) will betray you! Look at Pétain, who is a friend of Hitler. Shall we have the same thing happen in this country? We must create our own machine, under workers' control'. [217]

Just over a week before his murder Trotsky returned to the same theme again:

It is important, of course, to explain to the advanced workers that the genuine fight against fascism is the socialist revolution. But it is more urgent, more imperative, to explain to the millions of American workers that the defence of their 'democracy' cannot be delivered to an American Marshal Pétain—and there are many candidates for such a role. [218]

And in the summer of 1940 there were even more candidates for such a role in Britain. Many working people in Britain believed that if Hitler did invade then a section of the ruling class would speedily come to a deal. And despite the rhetoric of Churchill and King George VI about resisting the Germans in the ruins of London, they would have fled. Charles de Gaulle recorded in his *War Memoirs*: 'Certainly the King and Government would have left for Canada in time'. [219]

In the dark days of 1940 when Hitler seemed set to win, Trotsky argued with those who believed that all that remained was to support Britain and its semi-ally the US and who said revolution could only return to the agenda after Hitler's defeat.

Was revolution in the face of Nazi conquest feasible?

In March 1939 Trotsky wrote in reply to those who argued defeatism
was no response in a war against fascism:

> 'Could the proletariat of Czechoslovakia have struggled against its govern-
> ment and the latter's capitulatory policy by slogans of peace and defeatism?'
> A very concrete question is posed here in a very abstract form. There was no
> room for 'defeatism' because there was no war (and it is not accidental no
> war ensued). In the critical 24 hours of universal confusion and indignation,
> the Czechoslovak proletariat had the full opportunity of overthrowing the
> 'capitulatory' government and seizing power. For this only a revolutionary
> leadership was required. Naturally after seizing power, the proletariat would
> have offered desperate resistance to Hitler and would have indubitably
> evoked a mighty reaction in the working masses of France and other coun-
> tries…the Czech working class did not have the slightest right to entrust the
> leadership of a war 'against fascism' to Messrs Capitalists who, within a few
> days, so safely changed their coloration and became themselves fascists and
> quasi-fascists. Transformations and recolorations of this kind on the part of
> the ruling classes will be on the order of the day in wartime in all 'democra-
> cies'. That is why the proletariat would ruin itself if it were to determine its
> main line of policy by the formal and unstable labels of 'for fascism' and
> 'against fascism'.[220]

Beyond that Trotsky was confident that in occupied Europe Hitler's
problems had only begun:

> It is impossible to attach a soldier with a rifle to each Polish, Norwegian,
> Danish, Dutch, Belgium, French worker or peasant. National Socialism is
> without any prescription for transforming defeated peoples from foes into
> friends…
> Hitler boastfully promises to establish the domination of the German
> people at the expense of all Europe and even of the whole world 'for one
> thousand years'. But in all likelihood this splendour will not endure for even
> ten years…
> Consequently the task of the revolutionary proletariat does not consist of
> helping the imperialist armies create a 'revolutionary situation' but of
> preparing, fusing and tempering its international ranks for revolutionary sit-
> uations of which there will be no lack.[221]

With this perspective in mind he argued:

> In order to create a revolutionary situation, say the sophists of social patrio-
> tism, it is necessary to deal Hitler a blow. To gain a victory over Hitler, it is

necessary to support the imperialist democracies. But if for the sake of of saving the 'democracies' the proletariat renounces independent revolutionary politics, just who would utilise a revolutionary situation arising from Hitler's defeat? [222]

In looking at the Second World War Trotsky started from the need to maintain independent working class organisation. He proposed building a bridge to those workers who wanted to see fascism defeated but were uneasy with their own rulers' war aims. But all of this meant little as the Trotskyists were too weak to carry them through. There were other problems too but they were largely a reflection of their weakness. Yet it was these tiny, often persecuted, bands of revolutionaries who maintained from day one of the war until its close that the Second World War was an imperialist war and that fascism could only be defeated by the means of working class struggle.

Unlike them the ruling classes of Europe had rushed to appease the Nazis until the final denouement. Unlike them the Social Democrats could, as in France, vote in the Pétain dictatorship. Unlike them the Communist Party could enter September 1939 demanding war with Germany, end the month opposing an imperialist war (though in ways which were pro-German, reflecting Stalin's alliance with Hitler) and then switch again in June 1941 when Russia was attacked. In January 1943 the writer Arthur Koestler, a former fellow traveller of the Communist Party, wrote:

... The nearer victory comes in sight, the clearer the character of the war reveals itself as what the Tories always said that it was—a war for national survival, a war in defence of certain conservative 19th century ideals, and not what I and my friends of the left had said that it was—a revolutionary civil war in Europe on the Spanish pattern. [223]

As the war ended that revolutionary civil war would emerge briefly as Trotsky had predicted. But his warnings of what would happen if Koestler's 'friends of the left' ensured it was safely bottled up again were vindicated. Fifty years on capitalism still produces wars, fascism— and the hope of revolutionary change.

Notes

1   E Hobsbawm, *Age of Extremes* (Michael Joseph, 1994), p144.
2   Both quoted in M Jones, M Foot (V Gollancz, 1994), p83. Foot, a future Labour leader, helped write the *Evening Standard*'s editorials.
3   The scale of the casualties dwarfed those of the First World War and were far more weighted to civilians. 'Deaths directly caused by this war have been estimated at between three and five times the (estimated) figure for the First World

War, and, in other terms, at between 10 and 20 percent of the *total* population in
the USSR, Poland and Yugoslavia; and between 4 and 6 percent of Germany, Italy,
Austria, Hungary, Japan and China. Casualties in Britain and France were far
lower than in the First World War—about 1 percent, but in the USA somewhat
higher'. E Hobsbawm, op cit, p43.

4   Under Margaret Thatcher ' "Winston", as she familiarly termed him, was
constantly invoked on all sides': H Young, *One of Us* (Macmillan, 1991), p400.
Thatcher not only never knew 'Winston' but went to Oxford University in October
1943 rather than taking part in the war effort and was highly unusual in joining the
Tory Club on her arrival.

5   A Horne, *To Lose A Battle; France 1940* (Penguin, 1979), p117. Marc Bloch was
shot as a resistant.

6   J Jackson, *The Popular Front in France* (Cambridge University Press, 1988),
p288.

7   A Horne, op cit, p207.

8   N Jordan, *The Popular Front and Central Europe* (Cambridge University Press,
1992), p316.

9   M S Alexander, *Soldiers and Socialists: the French officer corps and leftist
government, 1935-7*, in M S Alexander and H Graham, *The French and Spanish
Popular Fronts, Comparative Perspectives* (Cambridge University Press, 1989),
p72. Weygand took over the command of France's army prior to surrender in June
1940.

10   Ibid, p73.

11   N Jordan, op cit, p309.

12   Ibid, p280.

13   'The three authors (still concealing their identity) sold the book from barrows in
Farringdon Road and recruited friends to take turns'. Jones, p91. The manager of
the Independent Labour Party bookshop in London was visited by the police who
told him he was selling a banned book. W H Smith banned the book from its
shops in the interests of 'national unity'.

14   A Calder, *The People's War* (Granada, 1982), p100.

15   In return Attlee and Bevin of the Labour Party were given considerable control of
the internal government of Britain.

16   A Calder, op cit, p158.

17   A Roberts, *Eminent Churchillians* (Phoenix, 1995), p164. As Lord Dunglass,
Douglas Home accompanied Chamberlain to see Hitler in Munich and in the film
of Chamberlain's return can be seen standing behind him as the Tory prime
minister waved a paper from 'Mr Hitler' which promised 'peace in our time'.

18   Ibid, p164.

19   Ibid, p210.

20   Ibid, pp16-17.

21   Ibid, p310. This is part of a chapter which demolishes Bryant as a fervent
pro-Nazi.

22   N Todd, *In Excited Times* (Bewick Press, 1995), p106.

23   A Roberts, op cit, p37.

24   Ibid, p28.

25   Ibid, p40.

26   Ibid, p6.

27   Ibid, pp45-47. The German papers relating to this episiode were spirited out of
Germany at the end of the war and destroyed.

28   A Calder, op cit, p112.

29   Ibid, p160.

30   Ibid, pp158-159.

31   Ibid, p160. Priestley was stopped from broadcasting at Churchill's instigation.

32   A D Harvey, *Collision of Empires* (Phoenix, 1994), p511. Churchill would
      express a similar sentiment towards Hitler in the autumn of 1937: 'If our country
      were defeated, I hope we should find a champion as indomitable to restore our
      courage and lead us back to our place among nations'. Quoted in R Rhodes James,
      Anthony Eden (Weidenfeld and Nicolson, 1986), p136.
33   A D Harvey, op cit, p511.
34   Quoted in I H Birchall, *Bailing Out the System* (Bookmarks, 1986), p30.
35   P Ginsborg, *A History of Contemporary Italy* (Penguin, 1990), p12.
36   G Kolko, *Century of War* (The New Press, 1994), p294.
37   P Ginsborg, op cit, p40.
38   F Claudin, *The Communist Movement: From Comintern to Cominform* (Monthly
      Review Press, 1975), p409.
39   Ibid, p409.
40   Ibid, p410.
41   A D Harvey, op cit, p512.
42   G Kolko, *The Politics of War* (Pantheon, New York, 1990), p504.
43   G Kolko, *Century of War*, op cit, p283.
44   M S Alexander, 'Soldiers And Socialists: The French officer Corps and Leftist
      Government', in M S Alexander and H Graham, *The French & Spanish Popular
      Fronts* (Cambridge University Press, 1989), p70.
45   A Beevor and A Cooper, *Paris After The Liberation: 1944-1949* (Penguin 1995),
      p391.
46   P Grafton, *You, You and You!* (Pluto Press, 1981), p16. D S Lewis, *Illusions of
      Grandeur: Mosley, Fascism & British Society 1931-1981* (Manchester University
      Press, 1987), p90, quotes Churchill as writing in February 1920:
           'this movement [Bolshevism] among the Jews is not new. From the days of
      Spartacus—Weishaupt to those of Karl Marx... This world wide conspiracy for the
      overthrow of civilisation and for the reconstitution of society on the basis of
      arrested development, of envious malevolence, and impossible equality, has been
      steadily growing'.
47   D S Lewis, op cit, records visits to Mosley in a flat made up for him in an disused
      wing of Holloway jail by James Maxton, Bob Boothby and his brother in law,
      Harold Nicolson. Nicolson lobbied for Mosley's release.
48   M Beckman, *The 43 Group* (Centerprise Publications, 1990), p18. This gives a
      lively account of how the fascists were stopped.
49   A and W Scarfe, *All That Grief* (Hale and Ironmonger,, 1994), p21.
50   Ibid, p22.
51   In contrast the parliaments of Britain's dominions, Canada, Australia, New
      Zealand and South Africa, formally decided their entry into the war.
52   B Lapping, *End of Empire* (Granada, 1985), p51.
53   Ibid, p56. The powerful Indian Communist Party opposed the Quit India
      campaign as disrupting the Anglo-Russian war effort.
54   Ibid, p242.
55   Ibid.
56   Ibid, p243.
57   Ibid, op cit, p527. Amery's son John was shot in 1945 for trying to recruit an SS
      Brigade amongst British prisoners. His brother, Julian Amery, a future Tory MP,
      tried to stop the execution on the grounds that his brother was a citizen of Franco's
      Spain.
58   A D Harvey, op cit, p525.
59   A Horne, *A Savage War of Peace: Algeria 1954-1962* (Peregrine, 1979), p25.
60   Ibid, p25.
61   Ibid, p26.
62   Ibid, p27.

63   Ibid, p41.
64   See my article on Euro-Fascism in *International Socialism* 60. The German ruling
      by 1944 clearly understood that their best policy was to maintain the strongest
      possible central government over the greatest possible territory in order to ensure
      there was no working class upsurge as in 1918 and there could be smooth transfer
      of political authority.
65   L Trotsky, *Writings of Leon Trotsky 1939-1940* (Pathfinder Press, 1977), p85.
66   Ibid, p187.
67   A J P Taylor, *The Origins of the Second World War* (Hamish Hamilton, 1961).
68   Taylor, p152, even claims 'Hitler undoubtedly wished to "liberate" the Germans of
      Czechoslovakia'.
69   Both quotes, above, Foreword to 1962 edition, pp26-27.
70   A J P Taylor, op cit, p203.
71   Ibid, p107.
72   E Mandel, *The Meaning of the Second World War* (Verso, 1986), p16.
73   A Clark, *Barbarossa* (Penguin, 1966), p43.
74   C Harman, *Explaining the Crisis* (Bookmarks, 1984), p65.
75   Ibid, pp65-66.
76   T Mason, *Nazism, Fascism and the Working Class* (Cambridge University Press,
      1995), p47.
77   E Mandel, op cit, p25.
78   T Mason, op cit, p51.
79   L Trotsky, *War and the Fourth International* (10 June 1934), *Writings of Leon
      Trotsky 1933-1934* (Pathfinder Press, New York, 1975), p302.
80   G Kolko, *The Politics of War*, op cit, p251.
81   R Holland, *The Pursuit of Greatness: Britain and the World Role 1900-1970*
      (Fontana, 1991), p180.
82   G Kolko, *The Politics of War*, op cit, p195.
83   Ibid, p352.
84   Ibid, p19.
85   J Erickson, *The Road to Berlin* (Grafton, 1985), p610.
86   G Kolko, *The Politics of War*, op cit, p374.
87   J Erickson, op cit, p839.
88   G Kolko, *The Politics of War*, op cit, p561.
89   Ibid, pp540-541.
90   Ibid, pp555-556.
91   C Ponting, *1940: Myth & Reality* (Cardinal, 1990), p7.
92   Ibid, p18
93   Ibid, p19.
94   Ibid, p37.
95   Ibid, p35.
96   Quoted in R Holland, op cit, p109.
97   M Jones, M Foot, V Gollanez, op cit, p65. Lady Astor was one of the key figures
      in the pro-Nazi Cliveden Set who socialised with the German ambassador.
98   Ibid, p65.
99   Though both would qualify even more as 'far away countries of which we know
      little' which was how Chamberlain described Czechoslovakia at the time of
      Munich.
100   R Holland, op cit, p157.
100   M Jones, M Foot, V Gollanez, op cit, p75.
102   R Holland, op cit, p160.
103   A Calder, op cit, p89.
104   C Ponting, op cit, p137.
105   Ibid, pp112 and 70.

106   Ibid, p117. Holland says of the British attack on Vichy France's navy in North Africa in July 1940 'The attack at Oran meant that for the United Kingdom there could be no going back, no negotiated peace with Germany, no Vichy English-style', p170. Ponting records, 'The United States and President Roosevelt in particular were impressed by this show of determination and began to calculate that Britain might not go the way of France'—p183.

107   R Holland, op cit, p170.

108   C Ponting, op cit, p217.

109   R Holland, op cit, p631.

110   This was true after El Alamein when Rommel's *Afrika Korps* succeeded in withdrawing and in the failure to capture Caen after the initial D Day landings. The exception was the September 1944 attack on Arnhem when Montgomery tried to capture the Rhine bridge by dropping paratroops on an SS Panzer division Dutch intelligence had identified as being there and sending an armoured column 75 miles across a single road through the flat, Dutch countryside.

111   C Ponting, op cit, p221.

112   M Hastings, *Overlord: D Day and The Battle For Normandy 1944* (Pan, 1984), p23.

113   G Kolko, *The Politics of War*, op cit, p198.

114   C Ponting, op cit, p19.

115   G Kolko, *The Politics of War*, op cit, p307.

116   Ibid, p301.

117   G Kolko, *Century of War*, op cit, p28.

118   Ibid, p31.

119   A Horne, *To Lose a Battle*, op cit, p188.

120   D J K Peukert, *Inside Nazi Germany* (Penguin, 1993), p31. Peukert is quoting from Tim Mason's conclusions—see below.

121   T Mason, op cit, p109.

122   Ibid, p115.

123   Ibid, p116.

124   Ibid, p125.

125   Ibid, p123.

126   C Ponting, op cit, p124.

127   J Keegan, *A History of Warfare* (Hutchinson, 1993), p308.

128   O Bartov, *Hitler's Army* (Oxford University Press, 1992), p25.

129   G Kolko, *Century of War*, op cit, p193.

130   Ibid, p190.

131   D J K Peukert, op cit, p127.

132   A D Harvey, op cit, p548.

133   G Kolko, *Century of War*, op cit, p242.

134   Quoted in J Keegan, *Six Armies In Normandy* (Penguin, 1983), p314.

135   O Bartov, op cit, p31.

136   G Kolko, *Century of War*, op cit, p213.

137   O Bartov, op cit, p83.

138   Ibid, p96.

139   G Kolko, *Century of War*, op cit, p214.

140   G Kolko, *The Politics of War*, op cit, p316.

141   R E Sherwood, *Roosevelt and Hopkins* (Grosset and Dunlop, 1948), pp797-798.

142   This is the title of one his key essays. T Mason, op cit, pp53-76.

143   Ibid, p54.

144   Ibid, p57.

145   Ibid, p58.

146   Ibid, p68: 'Dr Karl Krauch of IG-Farben was in charge of chemical production under the Four Year Plan; 30 percent of his staff in this office came from I G-Farben'.
147   Ibid, p64. Any manager in a Russian enterprise at precisely this same time operated in a more extreme variation of this situation.
148   D Guerin, *Fascism and Big Business* (Monad, New York, 1973), p9.
149   J Keegan, *Six Armies In Normandy*, op cit, pp32-33.
150   G and J Kolko in T G Paterson (ed), *The Origins of the Cold War* (Lexington, Massachusetts, 1974), p244.
151   R E Sherwood, *Roosevelt and Hopkins* (Grosset and Dunlop, New York, 1950), pp125-126.
152   L Trotsky, *Writings 1939-1940*, op cit, p189.
153   E Mandel, op cit, p17.
154   G Kolko, *The Politics of War*, op cit, p249.
155   G Kolko, *Century of War*, op cit, p80.
156   C Harman, op cit, p68.
157   A D Harvey, op cit, pp549-550.
158   Ibid, p580.
159   Ibid, p755.
160   Quoted by G Kolko, *Century of War*, op cit, p35.
161   For an analysis which places Japan's need for oil at the centre of its war declaration see D Yergin, *The Prize* (Pocket Books, 1991).
162   Ibid, p319.
163   J Keegan, *A History of Warfare*, op cit, p375.
164   D Yergin, op cit, p327.
165   The splits in the Japanese ruling class meant they had to tread carefully in case of a military coup by the army who wanted to continue the war.
166   G Kolko, *Century of War*, op cit, p313.
167   A Clark, op cit, p70.
168   B Moynahan, *The Claws of the Bear* (Hutchinson, 1989), p79.
169   A D Harvey, op cit, p589.
170   B Moynahan, op cit, p76.
171   Thus the partitioning of Poland in 1939 did not aid Russia's defences as was argued later in justification of the Hitler-Stalin pact.
172   A Clark, op cit, p62.
173   J Erickson, *Road to Stalingrad* (Panther, 1985), p72.
174   Erickson gives detail after detail of reports reaching Stalin confirming German plans including reports from the well placed Rote Kapelle group which penetrated the German command.
175   J Erickson, *The Road to Stalingrad*, op cit, p115.
176   Ibid, pp93-94.
177   Ibid, p198.
178   J Erickson, *The Road To Berlin*, op cit, p53.
179   A Clark, op cit, p87.
180   Ibid, p225. This is brought out well in the recent German film, *Stalingrad*.
181   Ibid, p450.
182   Ibid, p221.
183   Ibid, p282.
184   Ibid, p404.
185   F Claudin, op cit, p427.
186   A Fontaine, *History of the Cold War* (Secker and Warburg, 1968), pp243-244.
187   J Erickson, *The Road to Berlin*, op cit, p647.
188   Ibid, p670.
189   F Claudin, op cit, pp311-312.

190   G Kolko, *The Politics of War*, op cit, p437.
191   The French Popular Front assembly of 1936 voted full powers to Marshal Pétain with three quarters of the Socialist deputies voting their approval. I H Birchall, op cit, p29. Another prominent collaborator was Hendrik de Man of the *Parti Ouvrier Belge* (A D Harvey, op cit, p504) while in Denmark the Social Democrats were in government for the first two years of the Nazi occupation.
192   G Kolko, *The Politics of War*, op cit, pp507-508.
193   See the chapter on the Naples insurrection in M de B Wilhelm, *The Other Italy* (W W Norton, 1988).
194   G Kolko, *Century of War*, op cit, p256.
195   Ibid, p268.
196   J Erickson, *The Road to Berlin*, op cit, p451.
197   G Kolko, *Century of War*, op cit, p272.
198   Churchill wrote on 11 December 1944 as British troops fought ELAS in Athens, 'I am increasingly impressed with the loyalty with which, under much temptation and very likely pressure, Stalin has kept off Greece.' G Kolko, *Politics of War*, op cit, p191.
199   G Kolko, *Century of War*, op cit, p299.
200   J Erickson, *The Road to Berlin*, op cit.
201   G Kolko, *The Politics of War*, op cit, p205.
202   G Kolko, *Century of War*, op cit, p347.
203   G Kolko, *Vietnam: Anatomy of War: 1940-1975* (Unwin, 1987), pp36-37.
204   N Van, *Revolutionaries They Could Not Break* (Index Books, 1995), p117.
205   G Kolko, *Century of War*, op cit, p360.
206   G Kolko, *Politics of War*, op cit, p95.
207   I H Birchall, op cit, p37.
208   A Fontaine, *History of the Cold War: from the October Revolution to the Korean War 1917-1950* (Secker and Warburg, 1968).
209   G Kolko, *Century of War*, op cit, p289.
210   F Claudin, op cit, p440.
211   P Ginsborg, op cit, p47.
212   Ibid, pp81 and 83.
213   L Trotsky, *Writings 1933-1934*, op cit, p307.
214   Ibid, p320.
215   L Trotsky, *Writings of Leon Trotsky 1938-1939*, op cit, p209.
216   L Trotsky, *We Do Not Change Our Course, Writings 1939-1940*, op cit, p253.
217   L Trotsky, *Writings 1939-1940*, op cit, p334.
218   Ibid.
219   C de Gaulle, *War Memoirs*, quoted in Roberts, op cit, p43.
220   L Trotsky, *Writings of Leon Trotsky 1938-1939*, op cit, pp209-210.
221   Ibid, p297.
222   Ibid, p297.
223   A Koestler, quoted in A Calder, op cit, p605.

Hope against the Holocaust

A review of *Social Policy in the Third Reich: The Working Class and the 'National Community', Tim Mason (Berg), £12.95, and Against All Hope: Resistance in the Nazi Concentration Camps 1938-1945, Hermann Langbein (Constable), £19.95*

ALEX CALLINICOS

There are some situations, under some regimes, where resistance is impossible. This common assumption is held particularly strongly about certain regimes—namely, those described as 'totalitarian'. In Nazi Germany and Stalinist Russia, where a dictatorial one party state ruled by a combination of police terror and ideological manipulation, the masses were too atomised, intimidated, drugged by propaganda, to fight back. Such was the picture of totalitarianism painted powerfully by George Orwell in *1984*.

In the aftermath of the East European revolutions of 1989 and the collapse of the Soviet Union it has become much harder to hold this view of Stalinism. The mass demonstrations in Leipzig, Berlin, Prague, Bucharest and Moscow gave the lie to the image of a passive, cowed populace. Historical research has shown that even at the height of the Stalinist terror in the 1930s there was considerable workers' resistance.[1]

Yet the same image persists in the case of Nazi Germany. Here it is reinforced by two myths. One is that the National Socialist regime was supported by the German working class. The other is that the Jews marched meekly into the gas chambers, not resisting their extermination.

I call these myths because the two very different books under review here refute these ideas. Both books are intellectually meticulous attempts to reconstruct histories from difficult and ambiguous evidence—since the fate of working class and Jewish resisters was frequently torture and death at the hands of the Gestapo, they had every interest in concealing their activities. One is by the most important left wing historian of National Socialism. The other is by a survivor of the Communist resistance in Auschwitz.

Tim Mason belongs to a younger generation than Edward Thompson and Christopher Hill, who played a trail blazing role amongst Marxist historians of Britain. In the 1960s and 1970s Mason played a similar role for Marxist historians of Nazi Germany.

He pioneered the 'history from below' of the German working class under Hitler. Though he was British, Oxford based and a principal animator of the *History Workshop* journal during its pioneering years, most of Mason's major work appeared in German. *Social Policy in the Third Reich* is an English translation of a book first published in Germany in 1977.

A brilliant but tormented man, Mason killed himself in March 1990. It is only now that his major work is appearing in English, edited by friends and co-workers (notably the historian Jane Caplan). *Social Policy* is in fact a much expanded version of the German original, containing an introduction and epilogue which represented Mason's tragically unfinished attempt to deal with the criticisms and unresolved questions raised by his earlier writing.[2]

The book's main title is misleading. Its subject is nothing other than the German working class under National Socialism. Mason's thesis is stark and simple. The core of the German working class—those who had been organised in unions and had supported the main workers' parties, the Communists (KPD) and Social Democrats (SPD)—did not capitulate to Nazism. They remained hostile to the regime, which had smashed their organisations through terror, and seized every opportunity to fight back. Despite the Nazi ideology of a *Volksgemeinschaft*—a 'national community' uniting German bosses and workers—the working class remained outside this community.

When exploring the class struggle under a regime which sought to repress it by police terror, definitions are vital. What acts count as resistance under these conditions? Mason distinguishes between resistance proper, a term he restricts to the 'clearly politically hostile behaviour of the adherents of persecuted organisations'—chiefly the underground activities of the KPD and (to a lesser extent) the SPD—and what he calls 'the workers' opposition':

> *Alongside the resilient agitation and organisation of the illegal groups, economic class conflict re-emerged in Germany on a broad front after 1936. This took forms which were not clearly political... Further, this struggle for the basic economic interests of the working class does not appear to have been organised in any way. It manifested itself through spontaneous strikes,*

through the exercise of collective pressure on employers and on Nazi organi-
sations, through the most various acts of defiance against workplace rules
and government decrees, through slowdowns in production, absenteeism, the
taking of sick leave, demonstrations of discontent, etc.[3]

When repression by the Gestapo made overt collective organisation
too dangerous, workers found more oblique means by which to resist.
What made these forms of struggle viable in the first place was a dramatic change in economic conditions. Mass unemployment had
demoralised the German working class, helping to create the climate in
which, Mason argues, the Nazis had been able to seize power and smash
the organised labour movement. But Hitler's rearmament drive transformed the situation. Industrial expansion created effective full
employment and indeed labour shortage: in November 1938 the labour
minister estimated the unmet demand for workers at a million jobs.[4]
Workers could use the enhanced bargaining power created by the
scarcity, especially of skilled craftsmen, to adopt a more defiant attitude
and extract concessions.

The rising workers' opposition posed a particularly acute problem for
the Nazi leadership in general and Hitler in particular. He was obsessed
by the memory of the German Revolution of November 1918. Germany
had been defeated in the First World War, Hitler believed, because of the
'stab in the back' delivered to frontline fighters like himself by the
working class at home. The conclusion he drew was that, in the future
war he was planning, it was essential to avoid demanding too many
material sacrifices of German workers. This didn't imply a benevolent
treatment of the working class—on the contrary, it was necessary also
for the Nazis to smash labour organisations to prevent another stab in the
back. Nevertheless, as Albert Speer, armaments minister and one of
Hitler's close confidants during the Second World War, put it:

It remains one of the astounding experiences of the war that Hitler wished to
spare his own people those burdens which Churchill and Roosevelt imposed
on their peoples without second thoughts. The discrepancy between the total
mobilisation of the labour force in democratic England and the sluggish
treatment of this question in authoritarian Germany serves to characterise
the regime's fear of a change in the people's loyalties... Hitler and the
majority of his political followers belonged to the generation which in
November 1918 had experienced the revolution as soldiers, and they never
got over it. Hitler often made it clear in private conversation that one could
not be careful enough after the experience of 1918.[5]

It is this fear of working class revolt which explains the failure of the
Nazi regime to mobilise women to work in war industries, in marked

contrast to the successful conscription of female labour in Britain by
Ernest Bevin, trade union leader turned minister of labour in Churchill's
wartime coalition.[6] This failure was itself part of a much more general
crisis which Mason argues gripped the Nazi regime in 1939-1940.

By 1938 it was clear that the rearmament drive was running up
against sharp material limits. The resources—not simply human but
material and financial—to sustain rearmament could no longer be found
within Germany's borders. The various factions in the National Socialist
regime were agreed that the only long term solution to this situation lay
in a war of imperial expansion. But it was also agreed that Germany was
not yet economically or militarily ready for a major war involving
France and Britain. Hitler talked about a war in 1943-1944, and wished
even then to avoid fighting Britain.

The problem facing the regime was that the growing domestic economic crisis did not allow such a relatively relaxed timetable. One wing,
represented by General Georg Thomas, head of the War Economy Office
at the Ministry of War, wanted to prepare for the coming conflict by systematic state control of the labour market—the conscription of civilian
workers to work in war industries, decreed reductions in wages, etc.
Such measures were introduced in several steps in 1938-1939, culminating in a War Economy Decree issued in September 1939, when,
thanks to a crucial miscalculation by Hitler, the invasion of Poland
brought Germany into war with Britain and France.

Yet these measures failed thanks to working class opposition:

*Despite the state of war and a 50 percent increase in the income tax for the
middle class, workers were not ready to resign themselves to even a limited
reduction of wages, to the elimination of overtime pay or to the suspension of
industrial safety regulations. The NSDAP [ie the Nazi Party], worried
because of the plebiscitary foundations of the regime, quickly made itself the
proponent of a moderate wage policy, and within a month everything had
returned to normal... The dissatisfaction and passive resistance continued,
however, until mid-November 1939, when the government saw itself forced to
make further concessions in social policy. Bonus pay (except for the ninth and
tenth hours of work) and holiday leave were restored, and this was quickly
followed by the re-enactment of most of the industrial safety regulations.*[7]

The workers' opposition, Mason argues, did not simply set limits to
what the state demanded of them at work. Fear of it was a major factor in
Hitler's decision to launch a war of rapid conquest—*Blitzkrieg*—in
1939-1940. The adoption of such a strategy was by no means inevitable:
even after the outbreak of war in September 1939 an accommodation
might still have been found with powers whose governments—above all

Neville Chamberlain's in Britain—were reluctant to wage an all out conflict with Germany.

A war of expansion and conquest would, however, provide the resources to build up German military strength without pursuing the politically dangerous course of squeezing the working class too hard. The economies of conquered countries could be plundered to sustain the war effort.

War, continuous war, war as an end in itself, became the way out of an insoluble domestic situation. 'In terms of economic and domestic policy, the conduct of war has become the precondition of continuing to prepare for war.' Mason seizes on a phrase of Hitler's—'the idea of a "flight forwards" (*Flucht nacht vorn*)'—to sum up this strategy: endless military expansion as a way of escaping the class contradictions which National Socialism had been unable to abolish.[8]

This thesis—that Hitler's war strategy had its roots in the class struggle within Germany itself—was the aspect of Mason's work which attracted the most criticism. The long epilogue to the English edition of *Social Policy* is largely devoted to a response to his critics.[9] Mason, though qualifying and refining his arguments, basically stands by them. He also defends, in the face of changes of historiographic fashion, his use of a class perspective in analysing the National Socialist regime (here he is ill-served by Ursula Vogel, who in her introduction declares that these changes have made Mason's approach obsolete).[10]

It is clear that his use of the tools of class analysis is more than a matter of intellectual method, but reflects a political commitment. One of the admirable characteristics of Mason's work is the moral passion that informs it. He spurned the pose of a neutral scholar. 'If historians do have a public responsibility,' he wrote at the end of his most influential intervention in German historical debates, 'if hating is part of their method and warning part of their task, it is necessary that they should hate precisely'.[11]

Mason was a scrupulous historian, whose arguments were based on the most careful scrutiny of archival evidence, yet one is never left in any doubt about the driving force behind his work—the effort to recover the life and struggles of a working class confronted with the most brutal and barbarous of capitalist regimes. It is very good to have this classic work available in English.

With characteristic honesty Mason admits that there were certain obstacles that his historical writing could not overcome—in particular, he was unable to confront directly the Nazis' biological racism and the policies of extermination to which it led. 'I have always remained emotionally, and thus intellectually, paralysed in front of what the Nazis did and what their victims suffered,' he confesses.[12] As he concedes, the failure to address this central aspect of National Socialism imposes distinct limits to his exploration of German society under Hitler—limits which any attempt at a more comprehensive class analysis would have to overcome.

One source on which such an analysis can draw is Hermann Langbein's remarkable history of resistance by the most vulnerable and abject of the Nazis' victims, the inmates of the concentration camps. Langbein speaks from direct personal experience. A member of the Austrian Communist Party in the 1930s, he fought in the Spanish Civil War, took refuge in France after the Republic's defeat, and, like many other Spanish veterans, was sent to a concentration camp after the German conquest of France in 1940. Sent first to Dachau, he was later, as a Jew, transferred to Auschwitz. There he was a leading member of the Combat Group which sought, on an internationalist basis, to resist the SS even in the inmost circle of Hell.

Langbein's aim is to confront what he calls 'a distorted stereotype of the concentration camp victim. When younger people meet survivors they often cry out in bewilderment: "Why did you let yourself be led to slaughter like sheep?"'[13] This stereotype is one that is sometimes reinforced by historians. Perhaps the greatest single historical study of the Holocaust, Raul Hilberg's *The Destruction of the European Jews*, tends to minimise the degree of resistance to their murder mounted by the Nazis' victims. And the predominant image of the Holocaust—lines of prisoners being herded from railway sidings straight into the gas chambers—probably lends plausibility to such attitudes. For how in such conditions *could* the victims have fought back?

In fact we know that even at the very final moments of the extermination process acts of resistance did take place. In October 1943 what the Auschwitz commandant Rudolf Höss called a 'wild shoot-out' took place when prisoners in the undressing room attached to one of the gas chambers seized guns from the guards and chose to die fighting.[14] But in order to understand how far more extensive and well organised forms of resistance were possible we need to understand the nature of what the Buchenwald survivor David Rousset called the *univers concentrationnaire*—the world of the concentration camps. It is one of the great strengths of Langbein's book that he carefully analyses the conditions which some inmates took advantage of in order to fight back.

In the first place, there were different kinds of concentration camp. The first were established immediately after the Nazi seizure of power in January 1933 in order to house primarily political prisoners—members of the KPD and SPD, dissident clergy, Jehovah's Witnesses, and so on—and 'asocials' (chiefly habitual criminals and sex offenders). Chief among these camps were Dachau, Buchenwald and Sachsenhausen. The

Nazi conquests between 1939 and 1941 vastly expanded the camp population with Jews, Poles, Russian prisoners of war, Resistance fighters and so on. As this happened the number and size of the camps increased, and their functions changed to include supplying some of the forced labour on which the German war economy came to depend. The SS Economic-Administrative Office (WVHA) became an economic empire in its own right. By 1944 it controlled 20 fully fledged concentration camps and 165 satellite labour camps clustered around them.[15]

There was, however, a third category of camp—the six killing centres established in occupied Poland in 1941-1942 to implement the Final Solution. It was here, at Auschwitz-Birkenau, Kulmholf, Treblinka, Sobibor, Majdanek, and Belzec, that the full scale extermination process —murder by assembly line—took place. Some camps played more than one role. Thus Auschwitz was both a killing centre and a labour camp. Strategically placed at a main junction of the Central European railway system, Auschwitz had functioned since the late 19th century as a labour exchange where Prussian landowners could pick up cheap Polish farm workers. It seems to have been selected by SS chief Himmler as a labour camp soon after the Nazi conquest of Poland in the autumn of 1939, and was later expanded into the vast factory of death where at least one and a half million people were murdered.[16] It continued to play an economic role—thus its largest subsidiary camp was at Monowitz, where IG Farben's Buna Works manufactured artificial rubber.

The conflicting imperatives of extermination and production introduced a major tension into how the camps were run. This was reflected in the bureaucratic struggle between two sections of the SS. The Reich Main Security Office (RSHA), from where Adolf Eichmann organised the Final Solution, wasn't interested in the economic contribution camp inmates could make—at most they saw work as a means of what Nazi leaders called 'extermination through labour'. The WVHA, on the other hand, wanted a relatively stable and efficient workforce, and thus instructed camp commandants in the winter of 1942-1943 to cut mortality rates among prisoners sharply.[17]

The Nazis' need for the prisoners' labour could never be counted on. The driving force behind the Final Solution was never economic but reflected the drive by SS fanatics with Hitler's backing to seize the opportunity offered by German military triumphs to implement a central theme of Nazi ideology—the elimination of 'inferior' races, above all the Jews. Mason points out:

Among the first Polish Jews who were gassed in the extermination camps were thousands of skilled metal workers from Polish armament factories. This was in the autumn of 1942, at the turning point in the campaign against the Soviet Union, which was to increase still further the demands made by the **Wehrmacht** *on the German war economy. The army emphasised the irrational nature of this action in view of the great shortage of skilled labour, but was unable to save the Jewish armament workers. The general who made the formal complaint was relieved of his post.*[18]

Nevertheless, the prisoners were able to take advantage of the conflicts within the Nazi bureaucracy over how much effort should be made to conserve the camp labour force:

Since the instructions to lower the mortality rate were primarily directed at the SS doctors, some of whom could, on the basis of their profession, more easily be persuaded at least to limit the mass murders, the resistance movement in several camps attempted to influence physicians who were there on duty in SS uniforms.[19]

That this effort met with some success—by the summer of 1943 the mortality rate at Auschwitz (among those prisoners not selected for extermination immediately on arrival) had fallen to 3.5 percent, from over 20 percent the previous winter—was made possible by another crucial feature of the camps. Particularly after the outbreak of war, the camps began to expand enormously, so the SS alone could not run them. They had to rely on a whole system of trusties—the capos. Himmler explained in 1944:

These approximately 40,000 German political and professional criminals...are my 'non-commissioned officer corps' for this whole kit and caboodle... The moment he [a prisoner] *is made a capo, he no longer sleeps where they do. He is responsible for getting the work done, for making sure that there is no sabotage, that people are clean and the beds are of good construction... So he has to spur his men on. The moment we are dissatisfied with him, he is no longer a capo and he bunks with his men again. He knows that they will kill him during the first night... Of course, we can't do it with the Germans alone, and so we use a Frenchman as a capo in charge of Poles, a Pole as a capo over Russians, playing one nation off against another.*[20]

As Himmler makes clear, this whole system rested on tactics of divide and rule. From the start of the camps, the SS sought to give ordinary criminals power over political prisoners (a similar method was used in the Stalinist gulags), and the system evolved from there. It was an enormously corrupting arrangement: in the appalling conditions of the camps it was all to easy for individual prisoners to seize the marginal advantages offered by the status of capo and become the instrument of brutal, even fatal, punishments inflicted on his or her fellows. But where the prisoners organised to take advantage of the system—especially as the expansion of the camps forced the SS to give non-Germans, and even Jews, positions of responsibility—they could use it to defeat or blunt the Nazis' aims. This was particularly true in the camp hospital and the work assignments office, where prisoners employed in clerical duties could often save lives by altering lists for particular labour details, camp transfers, etc.

Achieving these goals—like resistance generally—depended on organisation. The professional criminals had to be driven out of their positions. Langbein describes what he calls 'the battle between Reds and Greens' (political prisoners wore red triangles, criminals green ones), for 'the actions of the prisoners' self-government was a matter of life and death for innumerable people'.[21] The conditions of the camps were designed to atomise the prisoners and set them against each other. Therefore it was those who came to the camps with some tradition of collective organisation and struggle—particularly if they came there together, in relatively large groups—who provided the Resistance with its basis. Members of the KPD and other Communist Parties, of the SPD, of the Polish Socialist Party (PPS), Spanish Civil War veterans—these were the kind of people who were best equipped to adapt and resist. The Jehovah's Witnesses, though they did not actively fight back against the Nazis, also had an extremely fine record of courageous refusal to violate their religious beliefs by engaging in war work.

The camps became vast depositories of different nationalities. The SS sought to exploit national differences in order to control the prisoners. Sometimes this worked, to some extent at least. The KPD group which ended up running Buchenwald has sometimes been accused of German nationalism. Initially prisoners' organisation at Auschwitz was dominated by Polish army officers who adopted extremely chauvinistic attitudes towards other nationalities, notably Jews and Russians. But once PPS activists took over the organisation they established close links both with Polish Resistance groups operating in the neighbourhood and with German and other Communists. In general, it is extraordinarily impressive how, in an atmosphere in which the Nazis' racist ideology and manipulative techniques encouraged prisoners to emphasise the differences among them, they were able, in camp after camp, to create internationalist Resistance organisation. Undoubtedly the traditions and the connections provided by the European labour movement played a crucial role here.

What did resistance achieve? It didn't stop the extermination of nearly 6 million Jews and millions of others. The sheer overwhelming physical power of the Nazi state over its victims ensured that the killings went on to the very end. When the Russian army drew near to Auschwitz in the winter of 1944-1945, the Combat Group simply lacked the military strength to prevent the SS transferring most of the prisoners to other camps, even though they knew that many would die either on the forced march from Auschwitz or in the new camps.

Nevertheless, some prisoners did rebel, taking up arms against the Nazi butchers. Russian prisoners did at least twice—at Flossenberg in May 1944 and Mauthausen in January 1945. So too did Jewish members of the *Sonderkommandos*, the special details of prisoners assigned to assist with the extermination process, at Treblinka in August 1943 and at Auschwitz in January 1945. And at Sobibor in October 1943 the 600 remaining inmates rose up, killed their guards and broke out—some 50 or 60 succeeded in escaping.

Langbein underlines the significance of these actions: 'During the period of the concentration camps' existence, Jews killed SS men in Treblinka, Sobibor, and...Auschwitz'.[22] The participants in these actions were generally in hopeless situations: *Sonderkommando* members knew they were bound to die as part of the SS's efforts to conceal the evidence of their crime. This was especially true in camps which were being wound up, such as Treblinka, Sobibor and Auschwitz were when the risings took place.

But there were other forms of resistance as well. Staying alive was one. The camps were designed to demoralise and humiliate their inmates. 'As a rule, a person who had lost their inner fortitude was no match for the harsh living conditions of a camp.'[23] *Any* form of organisation—not necessarily anything political, but merely giving a music recital, staging a play, or giving a lecture—could help give people the will to live. Then there was saving other people's lives. Prisoners in positions of responsibility in the camp offices and hospitals could rescue people from death—though all too often they were in the tragic position of deciding *who* would live or die, rather than saving life altogether.

There were also possibilities of sabotaging the Nazi war effort, particularly as the camps became extensions of the German arms industry. At Dachau the works assignments office would send unskilled prisoners to do expert work in arms factories. One Russian prisoner at Mauthausen who worked in the Messerschmidt factory would throw the rivets for airplane wings into the latrine and replace them with rivets that didn't fit. And numerous prisoners escaped—to save their own lives and in many cases to take part in Resistance groups outside the camps.

The price of these actions could be appallingly high. Those defying the SS would suffer torture and execution as a matter of course. Open defiance—for example, escape—was usually punished by the execution not simply of the culprits themselves if they were caught but of their workmates. The 'political department'—the SS secret police unit within each camp—would frequently conduct mass arrests to break Resistance organisation, exacting the most terrible revenge. And yet, in the immense diversity of forms documented by Langbein, resistance went on. He writes:

> *When our Combat Group there* [at Auschwitz], *which had many failures, was able to influence the destiny of the camp, we knew that we were no longer mere objects in that '**univers concentrationnaire**', in the hermetically sealed world created by the SS in which its misanthropic ideology about members of a master race and persons not worthy of living was to achieve an absolute triumph. We knew that we would not allow ourselves to be broken and would knowingly incur additional risks to pass muster before ourselves as active subjects.*[24]

Both Langbein's book and Mason's show how, even in the worst possible conditions, it is possible to fight back. But they also carry a warning. The German working class did not rise up against a regime that imposed on it far worse hardships than it had suffered between 1914 and 1918. Mason suggests that one reason why the Second World War did not end in a repeat of the revolution of 1918 was the divisions created by the employment in German industries of 7 or 8 million foreign conscripted workers from occupied Europe.[25] The outright slavery suffered by concentration camp prisoners was the most extreme form taken by these divisions. A divided working class may find itself impotent in the face of racist terror. This is a lesson we must learn.

Notes

1   See, for example, D Filtzer, *Soviet Workers and Stalinist Industrialisation* (London, 1986).

2   See the special issue of *History Workshop*, no 30 (1990), devoted to Mason. A collection of Mason's most important essays, *Nazism, Fascism and the Working Class* (Cambridge, 1995), edited by Jane Caplan, has recently been published.

3   T W Mason, 'The Workers' Opposition in Nazi Germany', *History Workshop*, 11 (1981), p120.

4   T W Mason, *Social Policy in the Third Reich* (Providence, 1993), p185.

5   Quoted in ibid, p32.

6   T W Mason, 'Women in Germany 1925-1940', in *Nazism*, pp197-203.

7   T W Mason, *Social Policy in the Third Reich*, p252.

8   Ibid, pp261-262.

9   See also R Overy, 'Germany, "Domestic Crisis" and War in 1939', *Past and Present*, 116 (1987), the comments by D Kaiser and T Mason, and Overy's reply to them, *Past and Present*, 122 (1989), and T W Mason, *Nazism*, chs 1, 4, and 9.

10   U Vogel, 'General Introduction', in T W Mason, *Social Policy in the Third Reich*, ppxiv-xv. Compare the section of Mason's 'Epilogue' devoted to class, ibid, pp284-294.

11   T W Mason, *Nazism*, p230.

12   T W Mason, *Social Policy in the Third Reich*, p282.
13   H Langbein, *Against All Hope* (London, 1994), p2.
14   Ibid, p280.
15   R Hilberg, *The Destruction of the European Jews* (New York, 1985), p225.
16   I Traynor, 'Death and its Detail', *Guardian Weekend*, 21 January 1995.
17   H Langbein, *Against All Hope*, p16.
18   T W Mason, *Nazism*, p73.
19   H Langbein, *Against All Hope*, p17.
20   Quoted in ibid, p26.
21   Ibid, p37.
22   Ibid, p301.
23   Ibid, p316.
24   Ibid, p393.
25   T W Mason, *Social Policy in the Third Reich*, pp331-369.

Is the media all powerful?

CHRIS NINEHAM

It's the Sun Wot Won it.
The *Sun*'s analysis of the 1992 general election

Britain doesn't need the KGB, we've got the BBC.
Tony Benn[1]

It has become fashionable to argue that as the end of the millennium approaches we are slipping into a media controlled nightmare:

> *The average American household now watches television roughly seven hours a day...and the soap opera stars receive thousands of letters a week in which the adoring faithful confess secrets of the heart which they dare not tell their wives, their husbands, or their mothers... The individual voice and singular point of view disappears into the chorus of corporate consciousness... in place of an energetic politics, we substitute a frenzied spectacle, and the media set the terms of ritual combat upon the candidates who would prove themselves fit to govern.*[2]

Politicians and political commentators everywhere are obsessed with the media. Bill Clinton's aides are trying to recruit sympathetic radio talk show hosts in the belief that right wing radio was the key to the recent Republican landslide.[3] The Italian political elite is still in awe of Berlusconi's media influence. 'TV is everywhere,' one expert commented recently. 'In the last decade it has literally hypnotised Italians'.[4] Meanwhile American Republican Newt Gingrich is proclaiming that the new cable technology is the basis of a revolutionary new 'hyper-democracy'.

But this obsession runs deepest on the left. The British Labour Party has been fascinated with the media for years. The leadership have used the notion of an all powerful media as a key justification for shifting the party to the right. Kinnock spent the best part of the 1980s hounding socialists out of the party and ditching radical policies claiming this would make the party 'media friendly'. By the 1992 election shadow ministers were complaining that media consultants were actually setting the party's agenda. When Labour lost in 1992 Kinnock predictably blamed 'the Conservative supporting press'.[5] Since Blair, 'the media's choice', has taken over, he has been wining and dining the media moguls and his colleagues have been loudly welcoming the commercially led 'communications revolution'.[6]

Their argument is simple. If the media corporations are all powerful, then it is only sensible to mould policy to the media's whims and throw out all principles and all ambition for change. This has been the path taken by the Labour Party and a good deal of the left internationally over the last ten years. The consequence in Britain is that working people no longer have a parliamentary party that even talks in terms of basic working class demands for cheap housing, improved benefits, or comprehensive education.

Meanwhile, those who look for fundamental change are hampered by the suspicion that it is impossible to compete with the media corporations for the hearts and minds of the mass of the population.

That is why it is vital that socialists challenge the often unspoken assumptions of the media pessimists: that the media is always the main source of people's information and understanding about the world, that people religiously believe all it says, and that the mass media itself, the factory for ruling class ideas, can never be disrupted.

Ownership

The class which has the means of material production at its disposal, has control at the same time over the means of mental production.[7]

The British ruling class has always taken the media very seriously. Since the earliest days of capitalism it has sought to establish effective control. During the 19th century the capitalists fought hard to destroy a popular radical press that was a strong focus of working class organisation. In 1836 radical London based newspapers had a readership of more than 2 million. Even the government admitted that the circulation of the

radical papers exceeded that of the 'respectable' press.[8] Papers like the
Northern Star, the *Poor Man's Guardian* and *Reynold's News* were
crucial to organising and generalising the Chartist movement. 'On the
day the newspaper the *Northern Star*…was due', one activist wrote, 'the
people used to line the roadside waiting for its arrival, which was para-
mount to everything else for the time being'.[9] As early as 1819 one MP
complained:

> *These infamous publications…inflame working people's passions, and
> awaken their selfishness, contrasting their present condition with what they
> contend to be their future condition—a condition incompatible with human
> nature, and with those immutable laws which Providence has established for
> the regulation of human society.*[10]

After failing to muzzle the radicals with the libel laws the establishment turned to taxation. In 1819 publications subject to the stamp duty
were redefined to include political periodicals to ensure, in the words of
Lord Castlereagh, that 'persons exercising the power of the press should
be men of some respectability and property'.[11] The attempt failed as
workers responded to higher newspaper prices by pooling resources. In
the heightened political atmosphere of the 1830s union branches, clubs
and political associations financed the collective purchasing of papers.

Ironically, it was the repeal of the stamp duty that finished off the
radical press. Mid-19th century free marketeers realised that the popular
press was a potential money spinner for business investors. Aware of the
rising capital and operational costs in popular newspaper publishing in
the US, they realised that free market processes would favour wealthy
entrepreneurs and drive the impoverished radicals out of the field. The
repeal of press taxes, declared Milner-Gibson, president of the
Association for the Promotion of the Repeal of the Taxes on Knowledge,
would create 'a cheap press in the hands of men of good moral character,
and of respectability, and of capital'.[12] Leaving aside the question of
moral character, Milner-Gibson proved to be right. Against the background of the political demise of the Chartists, spiralling capital costs
and advertisers' distaste for working class papers were enough to break
the radicals and ensure the supremacy of a popular capitalist press which
was 'a police of safety and a sentinel of public morals'.[13] By the late 19th
century the royalist and pro-imperialist *Daily Mail* was Britain's number
one daily.

Concentrated capitalist ownership of the press was well developed by
the beginning of the 20th century. By 1910 three companies controlled
67 percent of the circulation of the daily metropolitan press.[14] In Britain
today four companies control 85 percent of all daily and Sunday news-

paper circulation. Of the national press, only the *Guardian* is owned by a company which does not have major commercial interests outside the media.[15] The development of broadcasting presented a different kind of problem for the ruling class. The technical nature of radio-limited wavelengths and the need for a national infrastructure for transmission pointed to the need for state involvement. The new medium had massive reach, and state control must have had its attractions for a ruling class that felt shaky in the period of massive working class militancy after the war. Too obvious state control, however, would have weakened broadcasting's credibility. The notion of a broadcasting 'corporation' gave the BBC the illusion of independence from the government, and from the capitalists. As Reith, the BBC's founder, said during the general strike, 'The cabinet want to be able to say they did not commandeer us, but they know they can trust us not to be really impartial'.[16]

Far from being independent, the BBC has always been run by governors directly appointed by the government. In the Thatcher years a spate of appointments led to a level of direct Tory influence at the top of the BBC that shocked even the director general at the time, Alisdair Milne. When he complained to the Home Office, 'They said that No 10 was quite clear in its view that the board should be as she wanted it. There is no doubt in my mind at all that she wanted to Thatcherise the board'.[17]

Even if not always so politically partisan, the board is always selected from amongst society's elite. A 1980s survey showed that out of 85 recent BBC governors more than half had business or upper civil service backgrounds. Only six were trade unionists.[18] In any case, the government holds the purse strings:

> In 1935, when broadcasts by the communist Harry Politt and the fascist Oswald Mosley were planned, the Foreign Office was not prepared to tolerate a communist on air. But nor did it want to be seen to issue a direct prohibition (as a government is entitled to do under the BBC Charter). Instead the Postmaster-General reminded Reith that the license fee was shortly due for renewal, and the government made it quite clear it would not countenance any mention of its own interference. Both broadcasts were abandoned without any reference to government pressure.[19]

So called 'independent' broadcasting has always been owned by big business. The government's 1988 white paper on broadcasting declared that 'clear rules will be needed which impose limits on concentration of ownership and on excessive cross media ownership in order to keep the market open for newcomers and to prevent any tendency towards editorial uniformity or domination by a few groups'.[20]

But, in fact, since the 1990 broadcasting act Central has merged with Carlton, Meridian has acquired Anglia and Granada has taken over London Weekend Television. Carlton now has a 15 percent share in Good Morning Television, a 50 percent stake in London News Network and a 36 percent stake in Independent Television News. Regulations were suspended for satellite ownership, making a complete mockery of the government's commitment to limiting cross media ownership. Rupert Murdoch's Sky television now dominates British satellite.[21]

The situation is little different elsewhere in the world. Berlusconi's domination of the Italian media is legendary. In Germany Leo Kirch presides over 40 media companies including Europe's largest distributor of films and TV programmes, Germany's main film production company and Springer, Germany's biggest newspaper house.[22] Everywhere the media industry is well integrated into the wider capitalist economy. In Brazil 63 percent of TV sets are tuned in to market leader TV Globo at any given time. Globo, which makes all five top rated programmes in Brazil, is a business empire, with interests in computers and telecommunications as well as shares in financial, real estate, mineral and manufacturing companies.[23]

Meanwhile, media moguls like Murdoch, Berlusconi and Henry Luce with Warner Brothers have created corporate structures and media systems that span continents. Times-Warner, by 1989 the biggest media corporation and valued at $18 billion, has bases in Latin America, Asia, Europe and Australia, and employs over 340,000 staff. In 1990 it modestly changed its motto to, 'The world is our audience'.[24]

Media studies

Left wing commentators have always tended to equate media monopolies with unlimited social control. When the mass media first became a subject of study in the 1930s, academics were in awe of the media's power because of its novelty, and because some believed mass media had played a key role in the rise of fascism. On the reformist left Adorno and Horkheimer in Germany concluded that what they called the 'culture industry' was moulding the masses' subjectivity with mechanical standardisation, in the process creating a population ripe for fascist ideas. Mainstream academic studies developed what has come to be called the 'hypodermic' theory of media effects, not much more sophisticated than a theory of brainwashing.

After the war the academic consensus shifted. A whole range of studies in the 1940s and 1950s stressed differences in the way that media 'messages' were received and understood. Sociologists pointed to studies showing that the average member of the media audience 'reacts not merely as an isolated personality but also as a member of the various groups to which he belongs and with which he communicates'.[25] These conclusions were based on the first systematic attempts at audience research and clearly constituted a step forward from the crude brainwashing or 'hypodermic' model. Social class, gender, political affiliation and 'sub-cultural formations' were all found to influence the way individuals received information from the media.[26] However, in the hands of sociologists like Shils and Bell these conclusions were used to build a rosy Liberal pluralist view of American democracy that contributed to the Cold War offensive against the left. In this increasingly influential model American democracy functioned, in an albeit imperfect and pragmatic way, as an 'open society'. Questions of media ownership were sidestepped by concentration on the mediating influence of a host of primary groups—the family, the church, trade union branches or a local business community—and by a model of 'competition for opinion: that institutional arrangement for arriving at political decisions in which individuals acquire the power to decide by means of a competitive struggle for people's votes'.[27]

This pluralistic view of opinion formation prevailed in academia until sometime in the 1960s. In the words of Stuart-Hall, 'It was not, however, destined to survive the testing times of the ghetto rebellions, campus revolts, counter-cultural upheavals and anti-war movements of the late 60s'.[28] In the late 1960s and early 1970s the notion of 'ideology' returned to the debate. 'Critical' social theorists began to argue that, rather than simply 'reflecting' a pre-existing social consensus, the media was part of 'producing' it. The return of ideology to the debate was welcome, and amongst the flood of 'radical' or 'critical' media studies that came out of the 1970s and 1980s there is a good deal that is useful. But media studies was based in the universities and colleges and its key exponents, such as Stuart Hall, James Cullan and Tony Bennet, were, like most academics, inclined to exaggerate the role of ideology in society. Many of these writers were influenced by Marx, but rather than using Marx's sophisticated grasp of the interplay between social structure and human activity and consciousness in society to develop an understanding of both the strengths and weaknesses of ruling class ideology, they argued that Marx had simply underestimated the importance of 'the non-coercive aspects of power'.[29]

For support they looked particularly to the work of French structuralist Louis Althusser, and a distorted reading of the work of Italian revolutionary Antonio Gramsci. Althusser completely broke the link, essential to Marxism, between economic development and ideas in society, arguing that ruling class ideology operated 'autonomously' of other social factors. What was needed therefore, was patient exposure of ruling class ideas from within the 'ideological state apparatus'. This was a consoling notion for academics who could now claim that their academic research was their 'revolutionary practice' (or praxis, as they pretentiously called it).

The work of Italian revolutionary Antonio Gramsci was more selectively plundered. Gramsci had pointed out (as had both Lenin and Trotsky) that workers need to create an independent pole of attraction in society to gain enough social leverage—hegemony as he called it—to take power. In developing this analysis, Gramsci stressed the complexity of 'civil society' and the need of workers to gain influence and hegemony through a range of institutions. Media studies academics took up Gramsci's stress on 'the central role which the superstructures, the state and civil associations, politics and ideology, play'[30] to justify their inflated view of the importance of the media.

Both these strands of thinking removed class struggle from the picture. Ideology for the post-Althusserians was coded into language itself, and therefore undetectable to the masses. Only a handful of enlightened academics could penetrate the seamless world of ideological illusion. Gramsci's writings were used, or abused, to justify arguments for taking up influential positions within the media, and making 'tactical' alliances with just about anyone. Work that had started out as a critique of the capitalist media had become an attack on Marxism, a rejection of the possibility of change.

For all the obscurity of much of their reasoning, many of their political conclusions were straightforward. They recognised the stubbornness of bourgeois ideology and the necessity to fight for 'hegemonic positions' within civil society. But many media academics either succumbed to postmodernist apathy or joined the Labour Party. There many of their ideas were used to bolster the new realists against anyone who still talked about 'class struggle'.

Unfortunately, most of the academics who have tried to challenge the pervasive pessimism within media studies have fallen back on pure subjectivity. Writers like Morley and Fiske have once again stressed the fact that different groups or individuals produce their own meanings from the same text. These diverse responses are presented as a form of resistance to dominant ideology. Morley and Fiske want to centre the production of meaning back on the individual as a means to reassert the possibility of human resistance to what Fiske calls 'the power bloc'. But because there is no notion of class in their analysis and no attempt to explain the relationship between 'ideology' and 'reality', they allow no possibility for the emergence of a coherent or united movement that could challenge 'the power bloc in reality'. Resistance could only be local: 'It is in micro-politics that popular control is most effectively exercised'.[31] The danger is that by simply stressing people's ability to interpret the media for themselves, we end up with a postmodern view of communication in which meaning depends entirely on the receiver, the complete opposite of the Althusserian notion of an all powerful ideology—but equally unhelpful.

'Interactive' cable technologies have raised new questions. Fringe sections of the American right were the first to claim that they can help to take power away from a remote political elite, and win it back for the people. 'Today's spectacular advances in communications technology open, for the first time, a mind boggling array of direct citizens' participation in political decision making'.[32]

In Britain Labour media experts have taken up these wild claims: 'The electronic revolution could significantly alter the effectiveness of UK democracy by ensuring that ordinary people could constantly access information and input their views using new technology'.[33]

The new communications technology is theoretically exciting. But it is not in itself going to democratise anything. Would it give us access to information currently withheld? Will it give us more *power* over decision making? Will it put us in direct contact with anyone we can't already get on the phone? The information superhighway would no doubt be put to good use in a socialist society. But the problem with our present 'democracy' is not that we don't have adequate communications technology. Our parliamentary representatives already know from the polls that the majority oppose privatisation, health cuts and the recent huge pay rises for the rich. The problem is they are *socially* and *politically* tied to the establishment and we have no control over them.

The 'left' media analysts approach the media in isolation from wider society. The fact that they overestimate the media's power leads them either to pessimism or a naive confidence in the 'revolutionary' potential of new communications technology. Either way they do not get to grips with the complete relationship between the media and public opinion and the changing, contradictory nature of media 'effects': the fact that long accepted attitudes propagated in the media can suddenly be questioned on a mass scale, or that different sections of society are more critical of the media than others, or even that the same individual will happily go along with certain media prejudices, but reject others.

Media academics overstate the media's influence because they are remote from the majority of the population. And because of the increasing rightward shift in intellectual attitudes in the last 15 years they have little theoretical understanding of how real challenges to ruling class ideology can arise.

Influence

Just because 18 million people have their sets switched on, it doesn't mean they are watching.
Robbie Coltrane[34]

Does the media shape our lives? The standard rationale for the current media obsession is that the 'communications industries' are playing a more and more important role in our lives. In addition, many on the left argue that current levels of media monopoly and concentration are unprecedented.

Neither is necessarily true. The number of media systems and the number of global media consumers has increased in the last 20 years. Consequently, the level of investment worldwide in the media has rocketed.[35] But the impact on the daily lives of ordinary people in countries with an established mass media is another matter. The idea of a 'communication society' hooked together by the Internet and interactive cable services is itself still very much a media myth. Most families can't afford Sky Sport, let alone a computer linked to the Internet. A recent survey published in the *Guardian* showed that in fact people in Britain are watching less TV of all kinds than they did a few years ago.[36] The reach and influence of the tabloid press are also exaggerated. Only one third of the electorate in this country regularly reads a Tory paper (including the so called qualities)[37] and of those who read the *Sun* only 38 percent voted Tory in the 1992 election.[38]

Of course the mass media does provide the bulk of entertainment and leisure time activity for millions of people, particularly working class people, around the world. But this is not because we are all media dupes. The fact is TV and the tabloids are the cheapest and most accessible entertainment available. A 1985 survey revealed widespread dissatisfaction with the quality and choice of TV programmes and suggested that viewers would switch off the TV 'given the opportunity to participate in a more enjoyable activity'. Another survey, this time by Sahin and Robinson in 1974, found that TV viewing was regarded as one of the least enjoyable pastimes. 'Once again', it concluded, 'viewing emerges as the most expendable or least important of daily activities'.[39]

Most people are not naive or uncritical consumers of the media. People often buy tabloids for entertainment, not news. For that they rely on TV which is regarded as much more reliable.[40] Even there cynicism is growing. A 1993 Gallup survey published in the *Daily Telegraph* showed that only 6 percent of the population thought politicians were truthful on the TV and radio![41]

And despite the patronising attitude of editors and schedulers there is a popular hunger for worthwhile media production. Though a good deal of 'highbrow' output is off-putting in form and content, 'quality' dramas like *Boys From the Black Stuff, The Singing Detective* and *Middlemarch* regularly attract audiences of many millions. The tough investigative journalism of *World in Action* currently has average ratings of more than 7 million, and the *Mirror* was closest to challenging the circulation of the *Sun* when it was most fearlessly exposing the Tories in the early 1980s.[42]

There is no doubt that the media is dominated by big business. But it has been throughout the century. There were in fact more non-Tory newspapers available at election time in 1992 than at any time in the previous decade.[43] As early as 1922 four press barons, Lords Beaverbrook, Rothermere, Camrose and Kemsley, dominated the newspaper industry.[44] In 1961 some 89 percent of national daily circulation was owned by the three leading corporations, higher than the figure in 1985.[45] And yet Labour has managed to win seven elections this century. Recent research into voting intentions shows that owning the media is one thing, controlling the hearts and minds of the population is another matter altogether.

Voting intentions of newspaper readers

	Conservative	Labour	Lib Dem	Other	Swing*
Daily Express	48%	31%	18%	3%	18%
Daily Telegraph	48%	33%	18%	1%	23%
Daily Mail	41%	38%	18%	3%	24%
Times	40%	39%	18%	3%	24%
Sun	22%	59%	15%	4%	23%
Today	18%	60%	20%	2%	27%
Independent	15%	63%	18%	4%	18%
Daily Star	16%	71%	11%	2%	16.5%
Daily Record	8%	68%	5%	19%	9.5%
Daily Mirror	8%	81%	10%	1%	15%
Guardian	5%	80%	11%	4%	18%
None	21%	57%	18%	4%	21.5%

*Swing from Conservative to Labour, compared with 1992 general election. *Source: MORI*

In fact, research into the last two elections makes Labour's claim that the media has kept them out of office look threadbare.

William L Miller's exhaustive study of the 1987 election concludes that, although the tabloid press had a marginal influence (both in favour and against Labour), 'TV coverage had surprisingly little impact on party credibility' and 'only had a small influence on the public's issue agenda'.[46] In the third week of the campaign TV coverage shifted its emphasis 'massively' onto the question of defence. According to Miller's research, the public recognised that the *media* debate had shifted but the public's own concern with the defence issue only increased slightly. Throughout the campaign unemployment remained a vital issue for the electorate but was barely touched upon by the media.[47] Miller came up with one other important finding: media influence is greatest amongst people with little political involvement or commitment:

> *The media set the agenda for only a part of their audience: those highly reliant on a particular news source, those low in political involvement and information, and those who are relatively inattentive to politics generally—in short, those who are marginal to politics.*[48]

And 'the influence of the tabloid press was particularly strong on those voters who denied being party "supporters" even when they had a party preference'.[49]

Evidence from the most extensive survey of the 1992 election showed that the *Daily Mirror* had more of an impact on the electorate than the Tory press (Labour did after all increase its vote on 1987) and that Labour's vote actually went up amongst readers of the Tory tabloids. Without making any judgement on the long term influence of the media, the writers of *Labour's Last Chance* concluded, 'Neither the *Sun* nor any other of the pro-Conservative tabloids were responsible for John Major's unexpected victory in 1992'.[50]

Dennis McQuail, who has collected and analysed material from a wide range of campaigns has come to a strikingly similar conclusion about media propaganda in general: 'There is evidence that the lack of a strong disposition either way and a condition of casual attention may be most favourable to the success of mass propaganda'.[51]

The evidence suggests that Labour massively overestimates the influence of the media on elections. It also implies that Labour's policy of moving towards the centre ground, shedding both activists and identifiably working class policies that create some enthusiasm, actually increases the media's ability to influence the outcome of elections.

If specific media campaigns have a limited impact, doesn't the media influence general behaviour and attitude in more subtle and subliminal ways? There is a widely held belief, for example, that the barrage of stereotypes and negative role models in soap opera, adverts, magazines and pulp romances are key to shaping women's role in society generally.

The media treatment of women *is* a disgrace. Recent statistics show that men appear twice as often as women in light entertainment, drama and adverts on TV and, more tellingly, the proportion of men over 30 on TV outnumbers women by three to one.[52] Judging by the new accept-

ability of the 'use' of women's bodies in ads and in programmes like
Baywatch or *The Word*, improvements made in the way women are represented on TV are being rolled back. While it continues to treat women
as objects of sexual desire, the media is still littered with tired stereotypes of women as monogamous and emotionally dependent 'carers'.

In fact the representation of women bears little relation to the reality.
Massive changes have taken place in women's lives in the last 50 years.
During the Second World War millions of women were conscripted into
the labour force to replace absent men. Their lifestyles and expectations
changed dramatically, the rate of births to married women fell, and the
rate of illegitimate births and divorces soared.[53] Nearly a million women
joined unions and thousands took strike action for equal pay. These mon-
umental changes were barely referred to in much of the media. Gillian
Murphy's study of contemporary women's magazines shows they 'still
depicted courtship, marriage and motherhood as a girl's main aim in life
and ignored topics arising from the increased part women played during
the war'.[54]

Since the 1960s widespread availability of contraception has allowed
a new sexual freedom, and women have been drawn back to work in
large numbers—by the 1990s they made up more than half the workforce. The nature of the family and sexual behaviour have changed
dramatically, most women have a series of relationships during their
lives, and the number of single parent families has rocketed.[55] These
changes have not brought liberation for women, far from it. The ruling
class now want women to go out to work *and* to be the 'caring' centre of
the family. But they are real changes. The media has half heartedly
responded to these trends—often with hostility—but it has played no
part in making them happen. As always, changes in women's lives have
been a response first and foremost to the social and economic needs of
the system.

In the light of the evidence, the most convincing model of media
influence is that suggested by Raymond Williams's argument that the
media plays a complete ideological role which older institutions like the
church can no longer fulfil. Rather than directly manipulating opinion or
behaviour he argues that, by airing controversies and anxieties, the
media attempts to reorientate people in a world of accelerating social and
economic change. The media, in other words tries to provide 'safe'
frameworks of family, parliament and national community through
which people can interpret a divided and disturbing world. At the same
time, simply by running a commentary on the decisions of the powers
that be, the media helps to foster the illusion of an 'open' society.[56]

Williams cleverly exposes some of the more subtle media tricks: the
way linked political, social and economic issues are separated into dis-

crete news 'items'; the way TV can 'normalise' the most momentous events by inserting them into a predictable and endless flow of pictures; and the way ultra-respectable newscasters in their well ordered studios try to reassure us that however bleak things may seem out there, they, and by implications the establishment itself, are in control.

Williams underplays the more direct and conscious ideological ploys of the media—the attacks on the left, the racism and sexism—but the great strength of his analysis is that he recognises the media doesn't create social trends, but responds to them and tries to incorporate them into a world view that doesn't threaten the status quo. But even Wllliams exaggerates the media's role. He underestimates the role of politicians and trade union leaders in propping up the creaking institutions of the nation, he fails to see that capitalism survives as much because of the alienation of the population as through any positive conviction, and he doesn't recognise that the social and economic change he talks about can lead to explosions which blow apart the media's precious notions of family values, gradualism and national community.

Ideology versus experience

Consciousness does not determine life, but life consciousness.
Karl Marx[57]

Even some Tories are aware of the limits of ideology. This is Tory deputy chairman John Maples in his 'secret memo' to the party:

> *Privatisation has not been popular... Very few people think we are out of recession... There is a feeling of powerlessness and insecurity about jobs, housing, health service. business, family values, crime etc and no vision about where we are heading... What we are saying is at odds with their experience, which leads them to conclude that we are 'out of touch', lying...[58]*

All ideology has to contend with people's experience of the real world. Even at the height of Thatcher's influence in the 1980s most people did not completely swallow the Tories' line. The government, broadly supported by the media, tried to convince us that class was a thing of the past, that 'greed was good' and that low inflation and low taxation were the ultimate virtues. We were sceptical. The annual British *Social Attitudes Survey* showed that throughout the 1980s workers continued to believe the notion not just that we lived in a class society, but that 'there is one law for the rich and another for the poor'. Most people also consistently supported the idea of a one pence tax increase if the proceeds went direct to the NHS.[59] More recently government ministers

and 'independent experts' alike have gone blue in the face insisting that
we are experiencing an 'economic recovery'. High street retail figures
show we remain unconvinced. We have our own 'economic indicators',
wage slips, shop prices or layoffs at work. And no amount of propaganda
is likely to convince us that such first hand evidence is wrong.

There are plenty of studies of the media that analyse the different
'readings' that individuals from different social groups make of media
output. But because these studies treat their subjects as passive consumers, they don't take us very far. At their worst some of these studies
reproduce stereotypes themselves. One report concludes that:

> *News and current affairs, as well as much documentary and adventure fiction
> output—such as war films—were designated as masculine and avoided by
> many of the women. The genres which they most readily related to were quiz
> shows—especially those with a domestic, familial theme—movies with a
> 'fantasy' content, and, most notably, soap operas.*[60]

Others end up glorifying pulp culture. Janice Radway's *Reading
Romance*, very influential in media studies, goes as far as to celebrate
escapism as a form of women's resistance. 'By the social act of reading
romance, women signal a time out from their domestic and caring
labour; and by taking up romances in particular with their omnipresent
androgynous hero capable of nurturing woman herself, they deny the
legitimacy of patriarchal culture in which such men are hard to find'.[61]

The point is not to just identify different responses to media ideology,
but to discover how it can best be resisted. That is why class is so important. Class is not just the central division in society, it is the main source
of oppositional ideas. David Morley's report on the way different groups
interpreted one edition of the *Nationwide* current affairs show concluded:

> *It is the shop stewards that spontaneously produce by far the most articulate,
> fully oppositional reading of the programme. They reject the programmes
> attempt to tell us what 'our grouse' is and its attempt to construct a national
> 'we'. This group fulfils the criteria of an oppositional reading in the precise
> sense that it redefines the issues which the programme presents. Its members
> are critical of what they see as significant absences in the discussion of eco-
> nomics. More than that, however, their critical reading also involves the
> introduction of a new model, outside the terms of reference provided by the
> programme: at one point they explain **Nationwide**'s implicit 'theory' of the
> origin of wealth—in terms of classical economics—then explicitly move on to
> substitute for it a version of the labour theory of value.*[62]

Class is decisive first of all because of workers' economic position in society. The experience of being at the wrong end of a system of wildly unfair distribution makes it obvious that there's a gulf between ideology and reality. Nothing is going to convince a worker at Telecom or ICI or British Gas that they live in a classless society when their boss earns their monthly wage in a day. The day to day experience of work makes things even clearer. Most work is repetitive and oppressive, and though the contract of employment is legally a 'free' one, every time the boss haggles over a pay rise, tries to lengthen the working day or cut the workforce, workers are confronted with evidence that their contract with their employer is a contract with an enemy, not an equal. The fact that workers everywhere sooner or later try to organise into trade unions to defend their conditions shows that the experience of work under capitalism always leads to some consciousness of exploitation.

The current mood of revolt against the establishment identified in John Maples' memo shows that for workers everyday existence in a crisis ridden system can lead to deep distrust of ruling class propaganda. But individuals' experience of exploitation doesn't mean they *automatically* throw off all ruling class ideas at once. In his memo John Maples points out that, although the majority of the population are sick of the Tories, some still have 'right wing views on crime and immigration, deep disapproval of "scrounging" on social security…deep fear of loony lefties' and 'distrust of politically correct, liberal minded "do gooders".' There may well be an element of wishful thinking here, but there is no doubt that it is possible to hate the boss, be a union member at work, and still accept some of the ruling class's backward ideas about society in general.

Under capitalism workers always hold in their heads contradictory ideas about society. As Gramsci put it, 'The active man of the masses works practically, but he does not have a clear, theoretical consciousness of his actions, which is also a knowledge of the world in so far as he changes it.' So there are 'two sorts of consciousness', that 'implicit in his actions' and that, 'superficially explicit, which he has inherited from the past and which he accepts without criticism'. Gramsci goes on, 'The unity of theory and practice is not a given mechanical fact, but a historical process of becoming'.[63] Whether workers see themselves as atomised individuals competing in the market for houses and jobs, and are therefore vulnerable to ruling class ideas, or whether they see themselves as part of a class united by common interests depends crucially on whether they have experience of collective action in the real world.

Capitalism periodically forces workers to take this kind of action to defend their conditions, and this is the second reason for Marxists' insistence on the importance of the working class. It is not simply that workers have the collective power to fight back effectively, but that in the process of fighting back workers dramatically change the ideas they hold about society. In 1968 dockers from east London marched to parliament in support of the racist Enoch Powell who had been sacked from the Tory front bench after his notoriously bigoted 'rivers of blood' speech. The dockers' action was supported by some other groups of workers and some dockers came close to beating up anti-Powell demonstrators. Much of the left drew gloomy conclusions:

> *In Britain very many trade unionists have more sympathy with the police force and racialism than with student demonstrators. The only work stoppages in recent times which were meant politically were the racialist demonstrations of dockers and meat packers in support of Enoch Powell... Can it be that the most effective militant workers in Britain are to the right of the powerful Conservative Party?*[64]

Yet in the years that followed, British workers were involved in a series of huge struggles against the ruling class, culminating in the miners' strike of 1973 which brought down the Tory government. The London dockers were central to this wave of resistance and in 1972 organised a strike which led to a massive demonstration to Pentonville jail forcing the release of five of their number who had been imprisoned for picketing offences. The outlook of the dockers changed so much in this period of struggle that by 1977 they sent their banner and a large contingent to support the Grunwick strikers, a group of Asian women who were fighting for union recognition at a factory in west London. The dockers were joined by postal workers, car workers and miners who travelled from Yorkshire to support their fellow workers.

As well as changing workers' ideas, the strike wave of the early 1970s gave them the confidence to take on the media. On the first evening of their unofficial strike in 1972:

> *Dock stewards turned their attention...to Fleet Street, knowing that if they could shut the papers they would have a massive and immediate impact. But the initial response was cool. The papers appeared the next morning, and played down the significance of the jailings, trying to kill the dockers' campaign with silence. The following day docks stewards visited virtually every father and mother of chapel (shop steward) in Fleet Street, aided by leading print union activists. At last they met with some success. Within two days Fleet Street was closed down.*[65]

In the next few years of heightened struggle, socialists and activists in many different industries went one step further and set up their own rank and file newspapers. They wanted to drive the struggle forward by giving a voice to the most militant workers. By 1973 there were at least 20 such papers, amongst them papers produced by and for miners, bus workers, teachers, building workers, dockers and journalists.[66]

Even at the top of the unions there was a feeling that media lies had to be tackled. The following motion from the ACTT (the TV and cinema workers' union) was passed unanimously at the 1975 TUC congress. Despite the bureaucratic language, the anger shines through, and so does the conviction that anti-union propaganda could be effectively countered:

> Recognising the over-simplification and distortion which characterises the manner in which the majority of the media discuss and report economic issues and aware that this over-simplification and distortion frequently expresses itself in savage attacks on the objectives and methods of trade unions engaged in free collective bargaining, Congress calls on the General Council to instigate the production on a regular and ongoing basis of a counter-critique, deliberately written to correct and counteract the distortions of the media and to provide for shop floor trade unionists a straightforward and effective refutation of anti trade union propaganda.[67]

Faced with this level of suspicion and hostility throughout the working class movement it is clear that the media on its own was not capable of heading off the wave of militancy and restoring 'order'. For that the ruling class had to rely on the political and industrial leadership of the movement itself. The role of the British trade union leaders, the Labour Party and the Communist Party in heading off working class militancy in the mid-1970s has been analysed in detail elsewhere.[68] All three groups in different ways helped to disorientate the militants, enforce the Social Contract and ensure that in the end workers paid for the crisis.

In this situation sections of the media started to change tack, recognising aspirations for change, even occasionally supporting strikes, but working to channel bitterness into the 'safe' hands of union leaders and the Labour Party. At the same time, they led a witch-hunt of rank and file militants. No doubt the media reinforced reformist ideas, but its attempt to witch-hunt the left was not decisive. The influence of the Communist Party and the much smaller revolutionary groups grew in this period. The problem was that the Communist Party, which dominated the shop stewards' movement, offered no political alternative to that of voting Labour.

It was the domination of reformist ideas inside the working class movement and the lack of a credible revolutionary alternative that was the key to ensuring the safety of capitalism in the 1970s, not simply the media. Recent events in Italy have shown once again that mass action can transform the political climate—whoever runs the media. Last year academic commentators were complaining of Berlusconi's unshakeable hold over the country's imagination: 'TV is the breeding ground of a new dictatorship, stable and appealing... able to condition people's lives even in their own homes'.[69]

The fears of many on the left in Italy increased when legislation forced the PDS to give up control over RAI 3, its once loyal TV station. But despite his continued domination of the Italian media, at the end of last year Berlusconi's influence evaporated under the pressure of a general strike and the biggest demonstration Italy has ever seen.[70] As if to rub home the point that a mass movement can break the hold of the most powerful propaganda, Italian trade unions produced a sticker that was to be seen on almost every lapel on one of the huge demonstrations, 'Look Berlusconi, we are your audience.'

Marxists' stress on class and class struggle does not mean ignoring discrimination or oppression. Sexism and racism need to be challenged wherever they arise. But time after time it is during mass struggles that prejudice is most thoroughly broken down. The crucial role played by women in the Great Miners' Strike of 1984-1985 forced miners to change sometimes backward attitudes. By the end of the strike women were treated as equals in the struggle and the naked pinups that had been run in the union's Yorkshire paper disappeared by the popular demand of men and women. Anyone who believes the power of the media cannot be bucked should note that it was media lies that inspired many of the women to organise in the first place. Isabell helped start a women's action group at Yorkshire Main colliery:

> *It started because I couldn't stand the TV making out that the wives weren't behind their men. I was so angry and frustrated for a week that in the end Brian* [Isabell's husband] *took me round the wives of some other militants in the pit. Ten of us sat up half the night talking about what to do and five of us decided to go and picket Thoresby in Nottinghamshire that night. Brian made* **my** *snap for a change! And he made us a banner. We called ourselves an action group because everyone says they support the miners but we want to be active.*[71]

The experience of the strike did more than just overcome sexual prejudice amongst the men. Many of the women involved gained a new pride as they discovered their abilities to organise, speak in public and defend the picket line. Even more important, both women and men began to question the key institutions of a society that had openly turned against them, the police who arrested pickets, the courts that convicted them, and the press which lied about picket line violence. As one miner's wife explained, the power of the press had evaporated:

> *I have lost faith in the newspapers I once read. The **Sun** and the **Daily Mirror** are banned from this house now. They are banned from most homes in this village. They have told lies, half truths and peddled propaganda.*[72]

Class is the central contradiction in capitalism that no amount of ideology, however sophisticated, can completely hide. Workers are most vulnerable to ruling class propaganda when they are passive and demoralised, though even then most remain sceptical. But when workers start to fight back in large numbers, the class nature of ideology becomes obvious. Then workers start to throw off ruling ideas and look for new ideas that can take their struggle forward.

Inside the media

How does the ruling class try to ensure it gets *its* message across in the media? For most of the left, it's automatic. Ownership equals control: 'money and power are able to filter out the news fit to print, marginalise dissent, and allow the government and the dominant interests to get their messages across to the public'.[73]

In fact it is not that simple. The media employs real people living in a messy world. Establishment control relies on a delicate balance between intervention and wider social determinants. The state and media managements are prepared to intervene directly. When necessary, they censor programmes, plant stories, rig statistics and bribe journalists. In his recent book about Scargill, *The Enemy Within*, Seumas Milne points out that a number of national industrial correspondents are in regular contact with M15, and that there was a direct intelligence input into the the 1990 Maxwell funded media campaign against Scargill.[74] In 1985 it emerged finally that M15 had been routinely vetting recruits to the BBC.[75] Censorship is widespread, particularly at times of 'national crisis'. During the General Strike in 1926 no representative of organised labour was allowed on air. Even Ramsay MacDonald was banned.[76] During the Second World War the BBC was told not to include the Internationale in the popular Sunday evening concert of Allied national anthems[77] and during the Gulf War an absurd list of pop songs were banned from the air, as were pictures of soldiers 'in agony or severe shock' or patients 'suffering from severe disfigurements'.[78]

Censorship continues in 'normal times'. There are more than 40 documented cases of programmes on Northern Ireland being cut or banned outright since 1988 alone.[79] At least five *Panorama* programmes on subjects as diverse as Tory party funding, fraud in Westminster Council and arms trading with Iraq have been pulled, delayed or cut in recent years.[80] When *The Cook Report* set up a sting operation on parliamentary lobbyist Ian Greer Associates, which showed the lobbyists believed they could 'deliver' Michael Portillo and John Major for commercial interests, the programme sank without trace.[81]

The government also uses backroom pressure to ensure media chiefs stay in line. After one meeting with top BBC officials about coverage of the Falklands War, MPs who had been present were telling tales of 'blood on the walls' and 'roasting them alive'. One of them, Alan Clarke, bragged, 'It is good for people in these sort of positions to be roughed up...it's quite funny, those sort of self satisfied creeps on big salaries and fixed contracts, when they have a nasty time'.[82]

However, if the media is too obviously controlled or manipulated, it can become fairly useless for the ruling class. In Eastern European countries, for example, before the upheavals at the end of the 1980s, state run broadcasting was regarded as a joke. People either ignored TV and radio altogether, or where possible tuned into foreign stations. In Italy Berlusconi's blatant control of large sections of the media became a focus for opposition: in the words of BBC correspondent David Walter, 'Berlusconi's domination of the media, which was such an asset to his campaign, has now become a liability'.[83]

The strength of the media in many 'advanced' countries is that it *appears* to be 'free', 'independent', 'neutral' or at least 'balanced' when it is really none of those things. Direct censorship and state control have to be used sparingly if this illusion is to be maintained. Instead the ruling class rely on a number of other mechanisms to ensure their values and priorities prevail.

The market

We have seen how market forces historically concentrated ownership and control of the press into the 'safe' hands of big business. The market continues to strangle dissident voices. In the 1980s a group of well known radical journalists tried to launch an 'alternative' national weekly called *News on Sunday* to challenge the agenda and perspective of the established press. Despite the backing of various trade union leaders and sections of the Labour Party, the paper failed. Though the editorial board made generous political concessions, they failed to raise the kind of investment capital from big business necessary to compete with the media giants.

Advertising and the growing practice of media sponsorship provide useful extra discipline when necessary. An article in the *Economist* on the American media explains the process: 'Projects unsuitable for corporate sponsorship tend to die on the vine...stations have learned to be sympathetic to the most delicate sympathies of the corporations.' The journal cites the case of public TV station WNET which lost its contract with Gulf and Western 'as a result of a documentary called *Hunger for Profit* about multinationals buying up huge tracts of land in the Third World'. Gulf's chief executive wrote to the station saying that producing the documentary 'had not been the act of a friend', and that the programme was 'virulently anti-business, if not anti-American.' The *Economist* concluded, 'Most people believe WNET would not make the same mistake today'.[84]

Institutional filters

Chomsky describes how the internal organisation of media institutions amounts to a kind of permanent, institutionalised censorship:

> ...conformity is the easy way, and the path to privilege and prestige; dissidence carries personal costs that may be severe, even in a society that lacks such means of control as death squads, psychiatric prisons, or camps. The very structure of the media is designed to introduce conformity to established doctrine. In a three minute stretch between commercials, or in 700 words, it is impossible to present unfamiliar thoughts or surprising conclusions with the argument and evidence required to afford them some credibility. Regurgitation of welcome pieties faces no such problem.[85]

The journalists' agenda is set not just by their own newsroom but by a whole range of ruling class institutions that 'produce' news. The best research on this process is from America. Woodrow Wilson's Committee on Public Information noted that 'one of the best means of controlling news was flooding news channels with facts'.[86] In 1979-1980 the US airforce (in an interlude of openness since closed down) revealed that its PR exercises included 140 newspapers, 3,200 news conferences, 50 meetings with editorial boards and more than half a million news releases.[87] The late 1970s saw a massive increase in state and corporate spending on PR. By 1983 the US Chamber of Commerce had a PR budget of $65 million. It is estimated that the corporations in America employed 150,000 professionals as political and media lobbyists:[88]

> They provide the media organisations with facilities in which to gather; they give journalists advance copies of speeches and forthcoming reports...they write press releases in usable language, and they carefully organise their press conferences and 'photo opportunity' sessions.[89]

The ruling class bureaucracies also use their control of access to news as a means of disciplining journalists. The Gulf War was an extreme case because the authorities seemed to have such complete control over the flow of information. Accreditation was only given to journalists who promised to be obedient. All reports had to be approved by the army and journalists were not to travel to the combat zone unattended. The few brave souls like Robert Fisk who tried to do a bit of independent reporting were treated as outcasts by the authorities and the rest of the press pack. One *London News* editor admitted that it was desperation to keep on the right side of the military authorities that persuaded news organisations to pull reporters out of Baghdad at the start of the war.[90]

But in fact similar kinds of discipline are at work all the time. In Britain the 'lobby system' allows 'acceptable' journalists access to 'unattributable' information from 10 Downing Street. More informal access to high level briefs can only be earned by unquestioning loyalty. During the Falklands War, for example, Thatcher gave exclusive briefings to an 'inner circle' of Tory news editors.

Privilege

Even the best media commentators tend to miss the way class and privilege help to keep media workers 'loyal'. Trade unionists in the media have always found professionalism and snobbery a problem. In 1907 one NUJ pioneer, Frank Rose, vented his frustration in a letter to the *Clarion*:

> *If the average journalist will shed the silly notion that he is a superior sort of special creation, and accept the bitter fact that he is just a working man, he will make it easier... He can put as much professional side on as he chooses, but he will keep going down industrially until he substitutes common sense for vanity.*[91]

In the first half of the century many journalists were drawn from the upper ranks of society. During the First World War soldiers complained of the upper class attitude of the 'gentlemen of the press': 'They would visit the front now and then, as many staff officers did, but it could only be as afternoon callers from one of the many mansions of the GHQ, that haven of security and comfort. When autumn twilight came down on the haggard trench world, of which they caught a quiet noon day glimpse, they would be speeding west in Vauxhall cars to lighted chateaux'.[92]
For the average war correspondent it was all a kind of sport:

> *Through his despatches there ran a brisk implication that the regimental officers and men enjoyed nothing better than 'going over the top'; that a battle*

was just a rough jovial picnic, that a fight never went on long enough for the men.[93]

Many journalists reporting on the the October Revolution of 1917 in Russia were so upper class they simply couldn't understand what was going on. As the *Times* admitted 35 years later:

The idea of a campaign in the interests of the majority of workers was so foreign to Wilton [their correspondent] *that he never understood it... More unfortunately still, the idea was equally foreign to Steed* [the foreign editor], *Dawson* [the editor], *Northcliffe* [the proprietor].[94]

Things have changed, but privilege still helps to keep the journalists in line. This is how one explains the mentality of a colleague on the *Sun*: 'He knew, and others like him knew, that life on the *Sun* might have its repugnant side...but it also pays more bills than any other job he is likely to get. His spinelessness, and the apparent cynicism and indifference of the *Sun*'s journalists to that sewer they are daily asked to swill, has a connection with his bank balance'.[95]

Most journalists are still recruited from outside the working class and, at least in the national media, paid way over average wages. A producer on national TV for example can expect to earn at least £30,000 a year. Senior broadcasters earn over £100,000. Consequently, they tend to inhabit an establishment world, rubbing shoulders with lawyers, City dealers and politicians, and often barely coming into contact with workers. The distinction between the personal, professional and political often becomes blurred. Robin Oakley, the BBC's chief political correspondent, for example, recently went on holiday with Tory Lord Archer aboard the latter's yacht. One of the leader writers for the *Daily Mail* is a chief adviser to Lady Porter.[96]

The crucial point here is not simply that such proximity encourages party political bias (although it undoubtedly does), but that top journalists share general ruling class assumptions about the world. They are impressed by officialdom: 'reporters operate with the attitude that officials ought to know what it is their job to know. In particular, a news worker will recognise an official's claim to knowledge not merely as a claim, but as a credible, competent piece of knowledge'.[97] They see economic affairs from the perspective of the stock exchange, not the dole queue. They analyse NHS 'reforms' with the eye of the trust administrator, not the nurse on the ward or the patient on the waiting list, and, most important of all, the range of political opinion that they are prepared to consider begins and ends at Westminster.

Charles Curran, a former BBC director general, may have thought he was being ironic when he admitted that 'the BBC is biased in favour of parliamentary democracy',[98] but in fact his comment neatly sums up one of the ruling class's key ideological manoeuvres. A 'bias in favour of parliamentary democracy' is in fact crippling to objective reporting, because what little debate there is in parliament does not begin to reflect the reality of most people's lives. Unlike the population at large, the Westminster parties are united in their confidence in British justice, their respect for the royal family, and their belief in market forces. Parliament seems like an alien world to most of us, and yet any opinions not represented there are regarded as beyond the pale by the news media.

The 'bias in favour of parliamentary democracy' allows journalists to disguise the very strong class line that they take at times of crisis. They link parliament with 'the people' to create a fictional consensus which they use to marginalise dissenters. Research by the Glasgow Media Group in the 1970s showed again and again how striking workers were treated as troublemakers, while directors who had closed down whole factories forever were unfortunate victims of circumstance.[99] Reporting on last year's signal workers' strike was particularly misleading. Journalists obediently and uncritically spouted Railtrack's line and repeatedly interviewed scabs. The media barely mentioned that Railtrack had promised to sack any strikers who spoke to the press and helped give the impression of 'a drift back to work' towards the end of the dispute, when in fact the total number of scabs never exceeded 70.[100]

Far from being 'independent' from Westminster and Whitehall, the media is locked into a mutually supportive role with parliament and with the political establishment. Journalists' obsession with the parliamentary process allows them to ignore the fact that there is political life outside Westminster, that most of the decisions that affect our lives are in fact taken elsewhere in corporate executive meetings, in quangos or in Whitehall. The result is that 'balance' extends only across the narrow spectrum from Major to Blair. The media largely colludes in concealing the world of the boardroom, the civil service or the CBI—where real decisions are made. Meanwhile the views and experiences of millions of ordinary people are hardly ever sought by journalists who are encouraged to regard themselves as part of an elite, and who often unthinkingly accept that role.

None of this means, however, that the media simply churns out pure ruling class propaganda. Just as media commentators ignore the contradictions in society as a whole, they miss the possibility for conflict and contradiction in the media itself The media has to bridge the gulf between ruling class ideas and people's experience. Straight lies normally make bad propaganda. The media has to partially 'reflect' people's experiences, even if in a distorting mirror.

Different types of media play different roles. Raymond Williams has argued that the specific ideological role of the press is to deal with the controversy and anxiety caused by social change through the rapid transmission and discussion of news'.[101] The press does help to 'normalise' alienating experience and to popularise 'safe' and cynical responses to a turbulent world. But at times of ideological ferment this can be a difficult trick to pull off. In the 1980s the Tory tabloids confidently pushed a right wing populism and attacked the left. Today even the *Sun* has lost its way. Some of its more notorious journalists have left the paper. Those who remain are finding they have to reflect working class resentment against the establishment. Most of the time they frame attacks on the government in terms of their bungling incompetence, but recently even they have been running editorials condemning handouts to the rich.

The 'qualities' are partly used to pass information and opinion within ruling circles. This means they do carry some accurate information. The *Financial Times* is often the most reliable source of information about strikes apart from *Socialist Worker*.[102] The broadsheets can also be a forum for airing differences within the ruling class. As divisions have deepened, embittered groups and individuals like the Al Fayeds have used the pages of the press to attack and expose others, in the process deepening the sense of crisis itself.

The local press deals with issues that local people know about. Although editors try and concentrate on official openings or beautiful baby contests, when it comes to a local strike or a campaign against cuts they often have to be supportive in their reports, if not the editorials. And because they are less remote, local papers are more open than the rest of the media to popular pressure. A Yorkshire journalist witnessed popular pressure in action during the miners' strike of 1984-1985:

Police had viciously attacked a picket of a scab's house and badly hurt a number of miners and their wives and even children. I knew some of the victims personally and they made me promise to report events as they had happened. I suggested they go down to the paper's offices themselves to make sure. They thought that was a good idea, so they marched into the building demanding that the police's brutality was reported, and promising to picket the place if it wasn't. I got a grilling from the editor, but he ran my story next day, on the front page, verbatim![103]

The main ideological function of broadcasting is forging the illusion of national unity. Sir Michael Swann, then chairman of the BBC, told the Annan committee in 1976:

An enormous amount of the BBC's work [is] *in fact social cement of one form or another. Royal occasions, religious services, sports coverage, and police series, all reinforce our sense of belonging to our country, being involved in its celebrations, and accepting what it stands for.*[104]

Though placing itself in close association with the establishment and centres of power, broadcasting has to seem 'unofficial'. To be effective it has to make concessions to change and sometimes even voice criticism of the establishment.

Early broadcasting assumed a basic confidence in national institutions. In the Empire Day broadcast of 1935 a mother was heard explaining to her daughter, 'The British Empire, Mary, is made up of one big family.' Mary asks, 'You mean a family like ours, mummy?' and mother replies, 'Yes darling, but very much larger'.[105] In its first years BBC TV concentrated heavily on national ceremonies. Outside broadcasts of the trooping of the colour, the coronation, the cup final or the national exhibition were, in the words of Jonathan Dimbleby, 'the most valued jewel of the BBC television crown'.[106]

These visual, ritual displays of national corporate identity were never criticised on air. The accompanying news service was restrained and formal, avoiding anything contentious. By the early 1960s, however, the BBC had to change tack sharply. The Suez crisis and the Profumo affair had raised serious questions about the political and moral standing of the British ruling class. Commercial TV was appealing over the BBC's head to a newly prosperous and confident working class with programmes that reflected working class life and a brash, journalistic approach to national news.

The BBC responded with programmes like *Tonight* and *That Was The Week That Was* which accepted divisions in society and tried to define themselves as on the side of the audience and against the powers that be. Satire became fashionable and its target was the establishment. A *TW3* sketch looking back over 1962 summed it up as 'a year in which principles went by the board. A year of incompetence. A year of mendacity. A year of lying'.[107]

Since the royal family started to implode in the late 1980s broadcasting has had to play down national ritual and now tries to construct a sense of communal identity around pop culture and soaps. Soaps have dealt with issues some of the establishment would rather have kept under wraps. The *Sun* periodically attacked *Eastenders* through the 1980s for its positive portrayal of gay characters, for example.[108] And soap producers take care to employ some writers from working class backgrounds. One of them, Jimmy McGovern, has pointed out that management filter out anything that might offend the advertisers. Despite being set in Liverpool, *Brookside* barely mentioned the miners' strike or the rebellion of Liverpool council in 1984-1985.

At times of social struggle, however, broadcasting has had to incorporate some genuinely radical voices. In 1969 LWT hired the French Maoist Jean-Luc Godard to make *British Sounds*, an experimental documentary about the need for revolution in Britain, though the film was later banned. At the BBC a few left wingers like Jimmy McTaggart, Tony Garnett and Ken Loach had a chance to make some more challenging drama in the *Wednesday Play*. Plays like *Lena O My Lena* and *Cathy Come Home* presented a shockingly real picture of working class life and raised searching political questions about poverty and class.

For broadcasters the balance is always a delicate one. They have to please their political and commercial masters, while maintaining the illusion of independence. They have to seem to be abreast of change without ever encouraging it. As Ken Loach said about his years directing at the BBC:

> *The reaction from the BBC was split... On the one hand they liked the fact that we were getting good audiences and winning some public interest, but they were also very nervous...about their relationship with politicians and beyond them.*[109]

The outcome of this balancing act can be unpredictable. The aim is to promote confidence in our 'open society' and to resolve controversy within the boundaries of 'common sense'. But broadcasters have not been able to hold back change. They haven't been able to restore confidence in national institutions as one by one they have been discredited. And just occasionally they produce programmes like *Cathy Come Home, Death on the Rock* or *Spitting Image* at its best, which confirm or deepen the public's feeling that things are very wrong.

Increased concentration and commercialisation can sharpen the contradictions inside the media. Commentators, however, play down the potential conflict between the media's commercial and ideological roles:

> *Making money is not incompatible with indoctrination...the purpose of the 'entertainment' industry, in its various forms, may be profit; but the content of its output is not by any means free from ideological connotations of a more or less definite kind.*[110]

In fact market forces *can* conflict with the ideological role of the media. While at a time of real danger they will pull together, most of the time individual capitalists do not necessarily put the overall interests of their class before those of their own business, and in the media this can cause special problems. While competition for advertising and investment discourages 'anti-business stories', the associated competition for ratings or circulation has encouraged the press to expose sleaze and attack Major. Though this has not created the Tories' problems, it *has* helped to generalise the Tories' crisis. There is no doubt, for example, that the *Daily Mirror*'s campaign to keep the pits open in 1992 helped to mobilise support for the NUM's massive demos. At a time when the press itself recognises that 'the image of politicians, the monarchy, and even the judiciary' has 'never stood so low',[111] stories that expose the authorities simply make good copy.

The ruling class itself is aware of the dangers of allowing market forces free reign in the media. That is why there is a debate about deregulation in broadcasting. Free market Tories see the media primarily as a money spinner, and so support privatisation. Others do not trust the private sector with the BBC's unifying ideological role, currently defined in terms of reflecting 'all the dimensions of both popular and minority culture that make us different as a nation'.[112] The recent unpredictable behaviour of the press, the growing power of Murdoch, and the antics of Berlusconi in Italy must have underlined their fears.

The drive for profit in the media creates another more serious problem for the bosses—class struggle in the media itself. The transformation of the media into a central, highly profitable sector of the world economy has led to the rapid introduction of new technology and to a whole series of attacks on the conditions of media workers. Working life for journalists has become more repetitive, routine and stressful, and less well rewarded. Despite their privileged position, journalists are being treated more like workers than ever before. The resentment this causes can combine explosively with the political nature of a lot of journalists' work.

When the *Mirror* introduced new management as part of its shift to the right in 1992, there was uproar amongst staff. Paul Foot, who was involved, described what happened:

> *Montgomery, the new managing director, came from Murdoch. Everyone was frightened for their jobs and conditions, but also fearful that the editorial line might change—we were comfortable with Stott* [the current editor]. *We had an enormous meeting in the newsroom and voted 360 to two not to work with Montgomery. The place was packed and there was a tremendous atmosphere— we were all fired up by the huge miners' demonstrations that had happened that week. We occupied the newsroom until we thought they could never get next day's paper out.*[113]

Unfortunately, persuaded by editor Stott (who was soon sacked), they left too early, and a lightweight *Mirror* appeared the next day.

In 1985 journalists took political strike action with more success. The BBC had attempted to ban a *Real Lives* programme featuring Republican Martin McGuinness. The National Union of Journalists called a 24 hour protest strike and won almost total support from broadcasters. The *Times* reported, 'The walkout by journalists and technical staff represented the most serious industrial action ever undertaken in British television, and attracted more support than has ever been won by a pay claim or a call for conventional industrial action'.[114]

On the very day of the strike the BBC announced the programme would be broadcast with minor amendments.

Other media workers have often used collective power to challenge the worst excesses of ruling class propaganda. Unofficial political action by Fleet Street print workers helped spark the off the General Strike in 1926. A lockout of the miners had caused anger across the country, and when the *Daily Mail* tried to run an editorial calling trade unionists unpatriotic and disloyal, the printers refused to print it. The government used this as an excuse to call off negotiations and the TUC had to call the strike.[115] The fact that the printers were so central to the strike forced the NUJ to vote to join it, even though the union was not at the time affiliated to the TUC. More recently, during the miners' strike of 1984-1985, printers at the *Sun* refused to print a front page carrying a picture of Scargill that made him look as if he was giving a Nazi salute. Later they forced their management to carry an NUM reply to a particularly scurrilous article about the strike. In October 1993 technicians and production staff at the BBC threatened to walk out if Nazi Derek Beackon was included in a planned round table discussion of a local election called *After Millwall*. The programme went ahead without Beackon.[116]

Trade union organisation limits the proprietors' power and encourages everyday journalistic independence. Put bluntly by one journalist, 'I can't tell the editor to fuck off if I haven't got a union behind me'.[117] The best investigative journalism of the 1970s relied partly on strong organisation. The Insight Team at the *Sunday Times* that exposed the thalidomide scandal and investigated Bloody Sunday was headed by John Barry, who was also father of chapel. They were well organised: 'The chapel met regularly, and if members didn't like something the editor was saying or doing, they would haul him in and tell him to explain himself'.[118]

In the 1980s the Thatcherites attacked 'restrictive practices' in the media, claiming that union derecognition would promote freedom of expression, and a more pluralistic press. In fact, since the defeat of the print unions at Wapping in 1986 we have seen the opposite, what an ex-editor of the *Independent* called 'a return to the industry's ugly past, dominated by proprietors inebriated with the power that newspaper ownership is thought to bring'.[119] After a brief flurry of new titles, monopolisation has increased since Wapping, and there has been a dramatic lowering of standards, not just in the trash tabloids, but in the *Mirror* and the *Sunday Times*. Strong unions gave journalists some confidence to fight their corner, and as Roy Greenslade, one time *Mirror* editor, pointed out, they also held back monopolisation. Unions 'regulated proprietors', he said:

> to preserve jobs...[they] *did all they could to ensure that no newspaper gained an advantage over another... The threat of industrial action restricted papers in their printing and distribution arrangements.*
>
> *This uneasy preservation of the status quo didn't stop the concentration of titles in fewer and fewer hands. But it did significantly slow down that movement, not least because it was difficult to extract the level of profits necessary to wage all out war on rivals.*[120]

Protest and the media

The revolution will not be televised.
Gil Scott-Heron[121]

There is a widely held view on the left that the media can always marginalise or criminalise mass protest, and that a 'softly softly' public relations approach to the media is the most effective.

This is wrong precisely because the media does have to relate to the real world. To a journalist a PR campaign is just another fax or press conference. Campaigns that involve lively mass protest, however, can actually make news. Individual demonstrations and strikes are sometimes blacked out by the media, but sustained protest and widespread strike action cannot be completely overlooked. M11 campaigners won regular and sometimes sympathetic coverage for their militant protests in 1994 and the miners' fight against pit closures dominated the news agenda in October 1992. When the miners' struggle was wound down by the TUC, however, and turned into a lobbying campaign, pit closures were hardly worth a mention on the news. Last year striking signal workers won regular coverage by disrupting the trains. Much of the coverage was hostile, but given the public's general distrust of the media and their general support for anyone who takes on the Tories, that hardly mattered. At a time of growing discontent any coverage of protest, even hostile coverage, spreads the word and builds support.

TV pictures can sometimes speak louder than words. The voice track of reports on last summer's demonstration against the Criminal Justice Bill that ended in Hyde Park in London were full of references to 'a handful of troublemakers' and claimed that police action was a response to attack. The pictures caught the reality: repeated and brutal police baton charges on overwhelmingly peaceful demonstrators. Most people believed their eyes, not their ears. The media started to change its tune, and even the *Independent on Sunday* timidly condemned police violence.

Despite gloom on the left about the growth of global media systems, they too have helped spread struggles. News of the Russian Revolution in 1917 took weeks to filter out. Most British papers didn't even have a correspondent there, and when they did, reports were easy to censor. The *Times* maintained 'a dark silence', and other papers carried no real reports, confining themselves to repeating the claim that the Bolsheviks were on the brink of collapse.[122]

But in the modern world Gil Scott-Heron may well turn out to be wrong. Nowadays images of demonstrations, strikes and insurrections from Tiananmen Square to Bucharest, from Trafalgar Square to Haiti, are bounced instantly around the world's satellite systems. Governments around the world try to limit the flow of information and images into their countries, but international signals are somewhat harder to control. After the massacre of a pro-democracy march in Thailand in 1992:

The military regime ordered all Thai TV channels to operate strict censorship on all footage of bloodshed. However, Bangkok's fast growing business elite with their Motorolas and their satellite dishes saw the real story, courtesy of BBC TV, CNN and Japanese NHK. Within 24 hours their VHS tapes recorded from the satellite channels were being sold like hotcakes on the still blood-stained streets of Bangkok.

In short, the old techniques of mind control and censorship were rendered useless as the new technology of mobile phones, fax machines, and video were deployed to disseminate information, counter government lies, monitor troop movements and organise further protests and demonstrations.[123]

Protest and struggle in the outside world are also the key to building the confidence of trade unionists and socialists within the media to organise and challenge management's agenda. It was during the wave of working class action in the late 1960s and early 1970s that journalists first really learnt to fight. A series of disputes at IPC in London and on local papers led to the first national NUJ strike in 1978. That strike of 8,000 local journalists, which involved bitter mass picketing across the country, showed that in a period of militancy journalists can become politicised and fight not just for better conditions, but for a better media: 'The fight was for wages, but it got massive support because everyone hated the exploitation of young journalists, the petty meanness of many politically unpleasant characters (the true fathers of Thatcherism) and the lack of care about journalistic standards that ushered in the era of the freesheet'.[124]

Media and war: the case of Vietnam

The history of the media coverage of the Vietnam War throws more light on the relationship between media coverage, protest and ruling class policy. Left and right took opposing views of the media's impact on the war: 'The general view among the military was that it was the nightly showing of television pictures from South East Asia which undermined popular support in America for the Vietnam War'.[125]

For radical commentators Herman and Chomsky, however, 'Media failure to report the facts when they were readily available in 1968, and to investigate them further when they were undeniable, by late 1969, contributed to the successful deception of the public, and to the continuing destruction'.[126]

What was the real picture? Daniel C Hallin's detailed study of the media throughout the war shows that for the first few years 'the Kennedy administration successfully managed the news in order to minimise public knowledge of the growing US role in Vietnam'.[127] The government soon ran into trouble, however. As more and more troops were committed, the casualties started to mount, and the body bags started returning. This was difficult to hide. The authorities could not use censorship, because this was a secret 'undeclared' war. Paradoxically, they felt introducing censorship would reveal the scale of involvement. Although the media remained ideologically tame, its commercial commitment to the drama of war led to some graphic coverage. 'First they were satisfied with a corpse,' Richard Lindley, a British television reporter, said. 'Then they had to have people dying in action'.[128]

As the death toll mounted, reporters on the ground started voicing some of the troops' frustrations and criticisms of the campaign. Although these were tactical gripes, they 'provided the basis for the emergence of differences'.[129]

On the whole, however, the voluntary ideological line held until the Tet Offensive in 1968. Then real doubts started to be sounded in the media in the context of a changing political situation: declining morale in the army, the growth of the anti-war movement, and divisions within the administration—'with officials divided and communication channels within the administration inoperative, the media became a forum for airing political differences rather than a tool of policy'.[130]

It was still a very limited forum, that 'remained open primarily to official Washington, despite the rise of political protest'.[131] The anti-war movement was still vilified, even by supposedly liberal media figures. Reports of demonstrations were introduced with outrageously loaded throwaway lines like, 'Meanwhile, Hanoi was having paroxysms of joy over the demonstration in this country over the war in Vietnam,' or, 'While Americans fight and die in Vietnam, there are those in this country who sympathise with the Vietcong'.[132] Despite the fact that they represented a rapidly growing section of the population, anti-war activists were almost never given a platform by the media:

> *Their fate was frequently like that of a demonstrator at a campaign rally for Democratic vice-presidential candidate Edmund Muskie in 1968. Muskie had offered demonstrators a deal: if they would stop heckling, he would let them select a representative to address the crowd for a few minutes. Their representative appeared on TV for perhaps five seconds, long enough to say, 'We're here to make our voices heard.' Then the story cut away and returned to its major theme.[133]*

But the important thing was that dramatic scenes of anti-war demonstrations did make the TV, and reports, however hostile, made the front pages. On 16 October 1967, for instance, when anti-draft demonstrations were held around the country, CBS led its broadcasts with a series of four film reports from different parts of the country.[134] As Todd Gitlin commented, 'The journalistic premium on clash and theatrics was wrestling with the journalists' political interest in moderation'.[135]

Fired up by the US government's growing involvement in Vietnam, the widening of the draft, and the inspiring resistance of the North Vietnamese people, the anti-war movement grew dramatically. By April 1965 some 400,000 people were demonstrating in New York, 100,000 in Washington and 75,000 in San Francisco. In the San Francisco Bay area a 'stop the draft' week saw attacks on thousands of demonstrators by police with clubs and guns.

Hatlin argues that it was only after sections of the ruling class came out against the war—Eugene McCarthy stood as a peace candidate in the New Hampshire primaries in 1968—that 'the openly condemnatory tone of early television coverage' vanished, and 'the standards of objective journalism were applied to all forms of protest'.[136]

But as he himself suggests, the anti-war demonstrations, combined with the mass uprisings in the ghettos of a string of American cities, had helped ensure that 'dissent in general, inside and outside the "system", had become a political issue by the Nixon period'.[137] And, crucially, it was the growing protest that had finally convinced key sections of the ruling class to come out against the war. In March 1968 President Johnson heard from a 'senior advisers group' which 'quietly let him know that the establishment—yes, Wall Street—had turned against the war... It was hurting the economy, dividing the country, turning the youth against the country's best traditions'.[138]

The story shows that the authorities cannot always use the media to mould opinion or contain mass protest in a simple and straightforward manner. Censorship was judged impossible, and though military information was hard to get hold of, the nightly instalment of blood and horror on TV gave weight to the moral stance of the anti-war campaigners. Meanwhile, despite editorial gloss, pictures of their demonstrations helped to build the movement, and the use of the media by the establishment as a forum for debate inevitably generalised doubt and discussion. It was the armed people of North Vietnam and the protesters in the US who 'lost' the war for America, but the media unwillingly helped.

The Western ruling classes tried to 'learn the lessons' of Vietnam. After the war the BBC's Robin Day commented in a lecture to a US military institute, 'One wonders if in future a democracy which has uninhibited television coverage in every home will ever be able to fight a war, however just...blood looks very red on a television screen'.[139]

Since then, in the Falklands and the Gulf, governments and the military have tried to take control of war coverage. The results have been mixed. Censorship succeeded temporarily in hiding much of the bloody reality of both conflicts. But, particularly in the Gulf War, and partly thanks to anti-war campaigners, the existence of censorship became public knowledge. This helped to politicise the war and build opposition to it at home, especially in the media: more than 1,000 media workers attended a series of meetings in central London to discuss and organise opposition to censorship and the war.[140] The best study of the media during the Falklands campaign shows media co-ordination was incompetent: 'There were conflicts inside the Ministry of Defence, inter-service rivalries...unco-ordinated actions by civilian and military censors in the field, not to speak of a lack of clarity over the role of Number Ten in co-ordinating news management'.[141] At first, the authorities wanted to be very selective about which correspondents could sail with the fleet, but, 'faced with an outcry from the national press and Downing Street, eventually places were allocated to all the national dailies, the quality Sundays, the Press Association and regional news representatives, as well as BBC and ITN'.[142] Compared to Vietnam, these were short small scale wars, but nevertheless, despite the shameful attempt at military 'news control', the reality of combat was not completely hidden. Reports came through of the slaughter of Iraqi civilians in the Amiriya bunker by allied bombers and the loss of *HMS Sheffield* in the Atlantic. In reality, the authorities were lucky. If there had been more Western casualties the news would have got out. If the Gulf War had continued after the shocking images of carnage on the Basra road had been published, the steadily growing anti-war protest might have mushroomed.

The media in revolution

The dramatic images of armed insurgents bursting into the studios of the Romanian TV station in 1989 illustrated just how powerless the 'non-coercive wing of the state' can be when confronted with a popular uprising. But the experience of the Portuguese Revolution of 1974 and the May events in France in 1968 tells us more about the media's role during full scale workers' revolt. In revolutionary situations the relationship between workers and the media is turned on its head. Where in pre-revolutionary times the media tried to influence the workers, now workers struggle to influence and control the media. When workers succeed in taking over, media institutions can be turned into beacons of revolutionary democracy.

Though it failed to hold on to power, a revolutionary movement of workers and soldiers in Portugal forced out Caetano's dictatorship in 1974, and began a period of mass working class mobilisation. In the turmoil of an open battle for class power, the media became a crucial battleground of the revolution. Media workers both identified with the rest of the class and recognised that they had special responsibilities.

Workers at the *Republica* newspaper kicked out the management and started running it themselves. The democracy they set up was thorough-going. A message of support from workers at the *A Capital* paper read:

Information cannot be left in the hands of journalists alone. ALL workers must participate and we must protest any elitist manoeuvres.[143]

In fact the first workers' co-ordinating committee, elected by and answerable to all 174 workers at the paper, was composed of four print workers, three office workers, two from the dispatch department, one proofreader, one driver and one press operator. This committee had day to day editorial control and initially contained no journalists because, in the words of one eyewitness, 'most of the journalists now working for the paper are new and it is felt that they should have more time to prove their support for the editorial aims of the paper since they were not present during the struggle to keep it as a broad paper of the workers'.[144]

But *Republica* workers were not interested in controlling the paper for themselves. As their manifesto made clear, they wanted it to be an instrument of democracy at the service of the working class as a whole. 'We declare to all Portuguese workers that we are fighting for control over the press by the working class. We declare that the working class should interfere in decisions related to the production of social communications and their distribution'.[145]

In a revolutionary situation this was not just rhetoric. The debates and struggles that led to the issue of the manifesto and the takeover of the paper involved thousands of workers. On one crucial night in May 1975 a debate took place between the occupying workers and various representatives of workers' parties that turned into a spontaneous mass meeting:

> *Towards midnight the TV and representatives of other papers were let in. An impromptu debate began from the windows to...a background of jeers, sloganeering and applause from the large crowd in the street... Although it was raining hard, the night was warm. The debate continued till 6am.*[146]

Workers at *Republica* and Radio Renacensa found novel ways of making the media a vehicle for popular democracy. Radio Renacensa technicians, for example, set up microphones on demonstrations and rallies so that the slogans and speeches could be heard across the country. In a similar way media workers in Poland during the period of workers' uprising in 1980-1981 organised live broadcasts of negotiations between workers' leaders and the authorities.

During the French 'events' of May 1968 millions of French workers were involved in demonstrations and occupations in the biggest general strike in European history. Once again discontent inside the media exploded, and workers themselves tried to take control of sections of the media, and place them at the service of the struggle.

A few days after the great united worker-student demonstration of 13 May, members of the film technicians' union, who were on all out strike, called together film technicians, directors, actors and students to discuss what they could do. More than 1,000 people responded. A new organisation, the Estates General of Cinema, was set up, born, in the words of its own programme, 'of a popular movement of opposition and struggle against the economic, social and ideological order—that of capital protected by the state apparatus'. Its main aims were:

> *...the destruction of the monopolies and the creation of a nationalised industry; workers' control and a method of production not governed by the*

*law of profit; the abolition of censorship; and the linking of cinema and tele-
vision 'independent of the political and financial powers'.*[147]

The situation in France did not allow completion of this programme,
but the experiment was begun. New film groups were set up, working in
collaboration with occupying workers, finding ways of using films as
weapons in the class struggle:

*It is urgent that we become aware of the absolute need to place in the service
of the revolution all the means at our disposal. We must support the strikers.
Films must be projected in the factories.*[148]

New methods of distribution were organised to ensure that films
would be projected in 'factories and firms, schools and universities,
youth clubs and cultural centres, ships, trains, aeroplanes and other
means of transport and mobile projection units created in suburban and
country areas'.[149]

In a few weeks of revolutionary enthusiasm workers had begun the
task of transforming and democratising the film industry. They had
shown that, far from being an insurmountable block to social change,
under workers' control the media can become a mobilising focus for the
revolution.

Conclusion—who's influencing who?

*Politicians move willingly onto the journalists' agenda, the two engage in
light-hearted or more serious banter...and the wider electorate looks on in
bafflement.*[150]

The media is not all powerful. The more passive we are the more influence it has, but its control is never total. And when workers start to fight
back, they can reject outright even its more general assumptions. But in
the meantime the attitude of the leadership of the Labour Party and the
trade unions plays into the media's hands and the media, in turn, strives
to influence the Labour Party's aims and methods. A tame Labour Party
serves two purposes for the media. First the media point to the Labour
Party as proof of its claim that we live in a pluralistic society, that there
is political choice. Second, because Labour accepts the basic priorities of
national capitalism, private property, the rule of law, the need for immigration controls and so forth, it allows the media to construct the notion
of consensus, to present society as fundamentally united.

Meanwhile, the constant efforts of Labour and trade union leaders to
distance themselves from militancy and dissuade workers from taking on

the Tories through mass action encourages the very passivity on which Tory ideas can thrive.

But even in Labour's own terms, the new realist drive for respectability in the 1980s was a disaster. The more Labour moved to the right, the more the media attacked them, and the more confidently it supported the Tories. Even in 1992, when Kinnock had scrubbed every mention of 'socialism' from the manifesto and promised not to tax the rich, the *Sun* baited him on election day with the headline, 'Will the last person leaving the country if Kinnock is elected please turn out the lights'.

By throwing out all vision of social change the party lost the enthusiasm and activism of most of its followers. From a high point of one million in 1952, membership shrunk to less than 200,000 by the end of the 1980s, only a small proportion of them active.[151] By offering no real alternative to Thatcherite values it implied there were none, and so encouraged cynicism and despair. No wonder then, that despite the media's obsession with the middle class vote, it was largely amongst workers that Labour failed in 1992:

> Exit polls indicated that Labour had underperformed amongst three crucial groups: older women, young men and, most telling of all, its own 'core vote'. Labour won a smaller proportion of the votes of the unemployed than in 1987. It also lost support among council tenants and people on low incomes.[152]

Blair and his supporters are no doubt congratulating themselves on the recent improvement of their media image. Murdoch's *Today* now supports them and most of the other papers are at least polite. But has it been worth it? To win grudging acceptance Labour has shamefully capitulated to the media and adopted the agenda of the right wing press wholesale. While the rest of us are enjoying the death throes of the Tories and their discredited free market dogma, Tony Blair is distancing himself from comprehensive education and concentrating his energies on abolishing Clause Four.

And no one should believe the press will stay friendly to Labour. In fact it is not primarily Labour's move to the right but the unpopularity and incompetence of the Tories that has shifted the media. Outcry and protest over the NHS, the poll tax, pit closures, VAT on fuel, and successive privatisations have forced the Tories onto the defensive, and forced the media to distance itself from them. But the Conservatives are the natural party of the ruling class—while most of the media is relatively polite to Labour now, things can change very fast.

From the revolutionary wave at the end of the First World War to the mass struggles of the 1960s and 1970s every major period of economic and political crisis this century has thrown up mass movements that have shaken the certainties of the capitalist order. Rather than craving respectability and accommodating to media prejudices, socialists need to do two things to counter the media's influence. First, encourage and support any struggle against oppression and exploitation, and second, use our own independent media—socialist leaflets, papers, literature—to expose the media's lies and bring together all those who want to see real change. Most of the time a revolutionary paper will only attract a minority, precisely because it makes no compromise with prevailing ideas. When workers move into action on a big scale again, however, it can reach and influence millions.

Notes

Thanks to John Rees, Paul Foot, Mike Haynes, Des Freedman, Colin Sparks and Jim Aindow for their advice and suggestions.

1   Tony Benn was quoted by Ken Loach on *Face to Face*, BBC2, 19 September 1994.
2   From L H Lapham's introduction to M McLuhan, *Understanding Media: The Extensions of Man* (MIT, September 1994).
3   *Independent*, 5 January 1995.
4   Quoted on *The Berlusconi Late Show*, BBC2, 26 September 1994.
5   A Heath, R Jowell and J Curtice (eds), *Labour's Last Chance—The 1992 Election and Beyond* (London, 1994), p44.
6   See for example the interview with Chris Smith in the *Guardian*, 12 December 1994, in which he says, 'The information superhighway has the potential to be a revolution on the scale of the printing press,' and, 'The superhighway must act to the benefit of the population as a whole'.
7   K Marx and F Engels, *The German Ideology* (Lawrence and Wishart, 1989), p64.
8   J Curran and J Seaton, *Power Without Responsibility: The Press and Broadcasting in Britain* (London, 1988), p12.
9   Ibid, p19.
10   Ibid, p12.
11   Ibid, p12.
12   Ibid, p26.
13   Ibid, p26.
14   R Negrine, *Politics and the Media in Britain* (London, 1989), p72.
15   National Council for Civil Liberties, *Censored—Freedom of Expression and Human Rights* (London, 1994), pp48-49.
16   R Negrine, op cit, p130.
17   S Barnett and A Curry, *The Battle for the BBC—A British Broadcasting Conspiracy?* (London, 1994), p20.
18   S Hood, *On Television* (London, 1985), p55.
19   S Barnett and A Curry, op cit, p13.
20   National Council for Civil Liberties, op cit, p53.
21   All statistics, ibid, pp54-55.

22   *Guardian,* 12 November 1994.
23   J Curran and M Guretvitch (eds), *Mass Media and Society* (London, 1990), p124.
24   J Curran, M Guretvitch and J Woollacott (eds), *Mass Communication and Society* (London, 1977), p76.
25   P F Lazerfeld and P L Kendall, 'The Communications Behaviour of the Average American', in W Schramm (ed) *Mass Communications* (Urbana, 1994).
26   J Curran, 'The New Revisionism in Mass Communication Research, a Reappraisal', in *European Journal of Communication* (Sage, 1990), p150.
27   T Bennett, 'Theories of The Media, Theories of Society', in M Guretvitch, T Bennett, J Curran and J Woollacott (eds), *Culture, Society and the Mass Media* (London 1990), p40.
28   S Hall, 'The Rediscovery of Ideology, The Return of the Opposed in Media Studies', in ibid, p60.
29   S Hall, 'Culture, Media and The Ideological Effect', in J Curran, M Guretvitch, J Woollacott (eds), op cit, p334.
30   Ibid, p334.
31   J Fiske, 'Popularity and the Politics of Information', in P Dahlgren and C Sparks (eds), *Journalism and Popular Culture* (London, 1992), p60.
32   R Wright in *Time,* 23 January 1995, p51.
33   G Allen (shadow minister for media, broadcasting and the superhighway) in the *Guardian,* 24 February 1995.
34   Quoted in the *Independent,* 20 October 1994.
35   There are some useful figures in A Sreberny-Mohammadi, 'The Global and Local in International Communications', in J Curran and M Guretvitch (eds), op cit, p118-138.
36   *Guardian,* 23 January 1995.
37   A Heath, R Jowell and J Curtice, op cit, p58.
38   Ibid, p56.
39   Both quoted in C Lodziak, *The Power of TV—A Critical Appraisal* (London, 1986), p133.
40   In 1985 62 percent of Britons quoted TV as their main source of news and 23 percent the press. See R Negrine, op cit, p1.
41   *Daily Telegraph,* 13 September 1993.
42   *Middlemarch* peaked at 5.7 million, *Boys From the Black Stuff* at 4.7 million, *The Singing Detective* at 3.4 million (all figures from the BBC broadcasting research department).
43   A Heath, R Jowell and J Curtice, op cit, p26.
44   J Curran and J Seaton, op cit, p48.
45   Ibid, p48.
46   A Heath, R Jowell and J Curtice, op cit, p55.
47   W L Miller, *Media and the Voters: The Audience, Content and Influence of the Press and TV at the 1987 General Election* (Oxford, 1991), pp164-165.
48   Ibid, p165.
49   Ibid, p136.
50   Ibid, p198.
51   D McQuail, 'The Influence and Effects of the Mass Media', in J Curran, M Guretvitch and J Woollacott (eds), op cit (London, 1977), p79.
52   S Hood (ed), *Behind the Screens—The Structure of TV in the Nineties* (London, 1994).
53   *Socialist Review* 183, March 1995.

54   G Murphy, 'The Socialisation of Teenage Girls', in J Curran, A Smith and P
      Wingate, *Impacts and Influences—Essays on Media Power in the Twentieth
      Century* (London, 1987), p216.
55   For a discussion of changes in women's lives and the family, and the forces
      that mould them, see L German, *Sex, Class and Socialism* (London, 1989),
      especially the chapter 'The Family Today', pp43-60.
56   The argument is best presented in R Williams, *Television, Technology and
      Cultural Form* (London, 1974).
57   K Marx and F Engels, op cit, p64.
58   *Financial Times*, 21 November 1994.
59   All figures from R Jowell, S Witherspoon, L Brook, *British Social Attitudes
      Survey 1986/1987* (London).
60   S Moores, 'Texts, Readers and Context of Meaning', in P Scannell, P
      Schlesinger and C Sparks (eds), *Culture and Power, a Media, Culture and
      Society Reader* (London, 1992), p147.
61   L Van Zoonen, 'Feminist Perspectives in The Media', in J Curran and M
      Guretvitch (eds), op cit, p44.
62   D Morley, *Television, Audiences and Cultural Studies* (London, 1988), p117.
63   A Gramsci, *The Modern Prince* (London, 1957), pp66-67.
63   *Black Dwarf*, 12 May 1968, quoted in C Harman, *The Fire Last Time: 1968
      and After* (London, 1982).
67   Glasgow University Media Group, *Bad News*, vol 1 (London, 1976), p235.
68   See C Harman, op cit.
69   *The Berlusconi Late Show*, BBC2, 26 September 1994.
70   D'Allema spoke on the evening of the October strike, ending his speech by
      saying, 'The workers' struggle gives us [the PDS] strength.' Quoted in
      L'Unita, 15 October 1994.
71   Quoted in A Callinicos and M Simons, *The Great Strike—The Miners' Strike
      of 1984-5* (London, 1985), p178.
72   Quoted in *Socialist Review* 91, October 1986.
73   E S Herman and N Chomsky, *Manufacturing Consent: The Political Economy
      of the Mass Media* (New York, 1988),p2.
74   S Milne, *The Enemy Within—MI5, Maxwell and The Scargill Affair*
      (London, 1994).
75   J Curran and J Seaton, op cit, p300.
76   Ibid, p128.
77   Ibid, p157.
78   *Socialist Review* 176, June 1994, p7.
79   Listed and described in L Curtis and M Jempson, *Interference on the
      Airwaves: Ireland, the Media and the Broadcasting Ban* (Campaign for Press
      and Broadcasting Freedom, 1993), pp63-91.
80   S Barnett and A Curry, op cit, pp226, 169, 162 and 164.
81   *Index on Censorship*, March/April 1995 (Writers and Scholars International),
      p68.
82   S Barnett and A curry, op cit, p21.
83   *Index on Censorship*, September/October 1994 (Writers and Scholars
      International), p35.
84   N Chomsky, *Necessary Illusions: Thought Control in Democratic Societies*
      (London, 1989), p8.
85   Ibid, p10.
86   Ibid, p67.
87   E S Herman and N Chomsky, op cit, p20.
88   Ibid, p21.
89   Ibid, p22.

90   M Rosenblum, *Who Stole the News? Why we can't keep up with what's happening in the world and what we can do about it* (Wiley, 1993), p153.
91   Quoted in C J Bundock, *The National Union of Journalists: A Jubilee History, 1907-1957* (London, 1957), p4.
92   P Knightley, *The First Casualty, From Crimea to Vietnam—The War Correspondent As Hero, Propagandist and Mythmaker* (Harvest, 1975), p98.
93   Ibid, p99.
94   Ibid, p146.
95   Quoted in *Socialist Review* 95, January 1981.
96   *Guardian*, 20 November 1994.
97   N Chomsky, op cit, p8.
98   Quoted in *Socialist Review* 175, May, 1994.
99   Glasgow University Media Group, op cit, ch7, 'Down to Cases', contains useful examples of the media's treatment of strikers.
100   *Socialist Review* 180, November 1994.
101   R Williams, op cit.
102   It was, for example, the *Financial Times* that revealed at the end of the strike that only 70 signal workers scabbed during the dispute.
103   From a personal interview on 20 February 1995 with a local journalist in the region who wishes to remain anonymous.
104   J Curran, A Smith and P Wingate, op cit, p172.
105   Ibid, p163.
106   Ibid, p167.
107   Ibid, p170.
108   *Observer*, 19 February 1995.
109   S Hood (ed), op cit, p196.
110   R Miliband, *The State in Capitalist Society* (Quartet 1973), quoted in M Guretvitch, T Bennett, J Curran and J Woollacott (eds), op cit, p144.
111   Editorial in the *Observer*, 30 October 1994.
112   S Hood (ed), op cit, p47.
113   From a personal interview with Paul Foot.
114   Quoted in L Curtis and M Jempson, op cit, p56.
115   C J Bundock, op cit, p100.
116   A brief account of these events is given in Bulletin No 2 of Media Workers Against The Nazis.
117   From a personal interview with Paul Foot.
118   Ibid.
119   *Guardian* Media Section, 27 June 1994.
120   Ibid.
121   Gil Scott-Heron, *The Revolution Will Not Be Televised* (Arista, 1978).
122   P Knightley, op cit, pp149-152.
123   *Index on Censorship* September/October 1994, p46.
124   From the *Journalist*, the official paper of the NUJ, January 1989, p9.
125   D E Morrison and H Trumber, *Journalists at War, the Dynamics of News Reporting During the Falklands Conflict* (London, 1988), p169.
126   E S Herman and N Chomsky, op cit, p259.
127   This is from P Schlesinger's summary of Hallin's research in P Scannell, P Schlesinger and C Sparks (eds), op cit, p298.
128   Quoted in P Knightley, op cit, p410.
129   P Schlesinger in P Scannell, P Schlesinger and C Sparks (eds), op cit, p298.
130   D C Hallin, *The Uncensored War: The Media and Vietnam* (Oxford, 1986), p187.
131   Ibid, p201.
132   Ibid, p193.

133   Ibid, p200.
134   Ibid, p192.
135   Ibid, p194.
136   Ibid, p197.
137   Ibid, p197.
138   C Harman, op cit, p175.
139   P Knightley, op cit, p411.
140   *Socialist Review* 175, May 1994.
141   D E Morrison and H Tumber, op cit. Here their findings are summarised by P
        Schlesinger in P Scannell, P Schlesinger and C Sparks (eds), op cit, p301.
142   Ibid, p301.
143   P Mailer, *Portugal: The Impossible Revolution* (Solidarity, 1977), p231.
144   A Wise, *Eyewitness in Revolutionary Portugal* (Spokesman, 1975), p47.
145   From *Radical America*, vol 9 no 6, p65.
146   P Mailer, op cit, p228.
147   S Harvey, *May 68 and Film Culture* (London, 1980), p27.
148   Ibid, p28.
149   Ibid, p25.
150   Steve Richards from the *Guardian,* 12 December 1994.
151   C Kimber, 'Bookwatch: The Labour Party in Decline' in *International
        Socialism* 61, Winter 1993, p128.
152   R Heffernan and M Marqusee, *Defeat From the Jaws of Victory* (London,
        1992), p142.

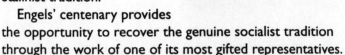

How the West was won

A review of C Milner II, C O'Connor, M Sandweiss (eds), **Oxford History of the American West** (Oxford University Press, 1994) £30.00/$39.95

PETER MORGAN

Introduction

There are many images of the American West. It is a land which has been inhabited for some 30,000 years, but it is the most recent history on which our images of the West are based. This is not surprising—the West's transformation from a predominantly hunter-gatherer society into one of the most important regions of the Pacific Rim and the world capitalist system has been phenomenal.

There are various reasons for this transformation. Hollywood leads the way in presenting the right wing view which tells of the cowboys, Davy Crockett characters, who, as strong and self reliant individuals, carried the fight for white America into new and hostile territories. But there is another history of the 'Wild West' which is captured marvellously in the book *The Oxford History of the American West*.[1] This tells of ruthless expansion and exploitation, as the West witnessed the conquering and decimation of the Native American population by the newly arrived Europeans. The book then describes the emergence and development of a capitalist system which is more brutal and oppressive than that which it replaced.

The impression often given is that this was a land of vast spaces, a natural wilderness largely uninhabited, where the native population was uncivilised, unable to adapt to changes to the environment and incapable of resisting the intrusion by the new settlers. Nothing could be further from the truth. Parts of the South West of America were inhabited by the Acoma and the Pueblo Indians who occupied what is now known as Arizona and New Mexico. California was home to the Modocs, the Maidus and the Pomo Indians. The Pacific North West was rich in farming areas and timber and many communities flourished—such as the Eyaks, Tlingitis and Haidas. The Plains were occupied by the Lakola and Cheyenne Plains people (who first encountered white people in the early 18th century), and these were later joined by the Kiowas and the Comanches. And the largest Native American nation of the modern American period was the Dine, known as the Navajos, who were scattered over a large portion of North America.

The conquest of these people by the Europeans brought changes to their way of life. Not least of these were the many diseases that the Europeans brought with them. In California the native population was reduced by at least half—from 300,000 to 150,000 between 1769 and 1821; along the Pacific North West 'the destructive force of smallpox, tuberculosis, malaria, and other diseases hit various Native American groups in epidemics that ran their course in a year or two'.[2]

But despite the effects of war, disease and disruption of the Native American way of life, the contact with the Europeans brought other more positive changes to their existence. Farming, for example, was greatly enhanced by the introduction of many new crops. By adopting many of these new crops the Indians enriched their economy and their diet. Trade with the Europeans opened new ways of life for the Native Americans, a point made by Leacock in her examination of the Monagnais-Naskapi of Quebec.[3]

The relationship between the new Europeans and the native population wasn't static as shown in the first section of this book entitled 'Settlement'. The Native Americans learnt to speak European languages. The European people had a more advanced economy. They had better technology and more sophisticated weapons, and were more experienced at warfare. But they encountered resistance—often in the form of prolonged and bloody wars (the Pequot Wars of 1637 to 1638, the Anglo-Powhatan Wars) or in the form of smaller, more localised battles. However, for the real conquest of the American West and the beginnings of capitalist expansion we need to look east. When you examine the carve up of America some 300 years ago, its capitalist culture today is no surprise.

The Dutch, British and French all realised the potential for the advancement of capitalism in America and the profits that this could bring. By 1606 James I committed the crown to the colonisation of North America which was to be divided by the Virginia Company (in practice two companies).

The Dutch were interested not so much in the land but in the trade values of the commodities, especially in the fur trade. And the French also saw the emergence of the cities as the key to development. They left a trail of cities from Montreal to Detroit, St Paul to Kansas City; they established New Orleans in 1718 and St Louis in 1764.

Thus there was a clash between the new and old ways of life, between two economies that could not live harmoniously side by side. The development of capitalism was to destroy all that was put in its way—the pursuit of profit was to rip asunder the old ways of existence. But how did the new ruling class facilitate the development of the new system?

The National Legislature passed two of the most important laws in the history of westward expansion. The Ordinance Acts of 1785 and 1787 meant the division and selling off of large tracts of land at extremely cheap prices for the developing capitalists. Large areas of land were surveyed, thousands of acres at a time, grouped into regions and then sold off, sometimes for as little as nine cents per acre. Once an area had 60,000 inhabitants, they could then petition for statehood and establish their own legislator. It was, as Elliot West notes, the ideal geometry for wheeling and dealing and encouraged the search for profit. Public auctions were held where speculators scrambled over each other as they sought vast tracts of land to develop.[4]

The Native Americans, although formally protected in Clause Three of the Ordinance, were actually forced from the lands they had occupied for hundreds of years. As West states:

> We shall protect the Indians and their ancestral lands, the government promised, and we shall lay out the means, step by step, for that land to be sliced up, cleared by the axe, and broken to the plough, then laid over by the English common law, and parliamentary republicanism... A policy that could make such promises, all within the same pair of documents, had moved beyond contradiction to schizophrenia.[5]

There was no limit to the greed from the new capitalists. An infamous, but not untypical, transaction occurred in 1795, 'when a bribed Georgia legislature sold more than 35 million acres reaching to the Mississippi for half a million dollars, or just over a penny an acre'.[6] Over the coming decades there were enormous profits to be made from the development of such land.

Improvements in the transportation network, as the new capitalists saw the benefits of developing an extensive canal system, led to increases in the urban population. In Indiana and Ohio the population mushroomed from just over 50,000 in 1800 to over 2 million by 1840 (from 1 percent of the nation's population to 14 percent). New canals brought great opportunities for trade because cattle and manufactured goods could be transported easily.[7] The 'canal counties' prospered and were crucial to the economic development of the region at the time. Cattle trading flourished in the old South West. Profits were high as cattle was transported to the West Indies and cities along the Atlantic coast. And many towns turned towards the manufacture of goods that couldn't be brought over primitive roads.

Westward expansion was now part of an expanding capitalist economy, emanating from Europe and the Atlantic coast. It was an area instantly desirable for squatters, wealthy landlords and capitalists alike. War was launched with ferocity against many of the Native American tribes, and government policy was dictated by the needs of profits. By the mid-19th century the US had solidified its military and political domination as the tide of white migration grew, and the market economy took hold on the towns—it was the solid basis needed for the capitalist expansion of the West.

Expansionism

The expansion of the United States beyond its western frontier is the story of the development of American capitalism by a capitalist class which saw the enormous potential for profits. It is also the story of the emergence of an industrial working class whose history is often neglected, yet is every bit as militant as that of the working class in Europe.

Throughout the 19th century the US government proceeded to extend its domination over the West by acquiring land. The Native Americans continued to resist, forcing the US government to change its policy from outright warfare to the removal of Native Americans to reservations, predominantly west of the Mississippi. But for this to proceed, the US government had to have a legal right to large areas of the American West.

The US government proceeded to purchase large tracts of land often at minimum prices. The Louisiana Land Purchase of 1803 (purchased from the French government) stretched along the Mississippi from (what was to become) Louisiana in the south to the Canadian border at North Dakota. It was a huge area covering thousands of square miles, rich in mineral reserves and potential profits. This enormous acquisition of land doubled the territory of the United States at a stroke.

What followed was an unprecedented period of land seizure and annexation:

On 14 May, 1804, an era of American exploration and expansion began...
Through purchase, treaty annexation, and war, the federal government added
extensive territory beyond the original Louisiana Purchase.[8]

America went to war with Mexico, which resulted in the annexation of Texas in 1845. It was a war that was unpopular in parts of the east, with demonstrations by Irish workers in New York, Boston and Lowell against the annexation of Texas. During the war itself some 9,207 soldiers deserted from the US army. As the war veterans returned home, the speculators moved in to buy land warrants given by the government to the soldiers. As Howard Zinn explains:

Many of the soldiers, desperate for money, sold their 160 acres for less than
*$50. **The New York Commercial Advertiser** said in June 1847, 'It is a well*
known fact that immense fortunes were made out of the poor soldiers who
shed their blood in the revolutionary war by speculators who preyed upon
their distress'.[9]

The Treaty of Guadalupe Hidalgo was signed in 1848 by which the Americans took half of Mexico at a cost of $15 million. The Texas boundary was set at the Rio Grande, and California and New Mexico were ceded. Later on Britain gave up Oregon and Russia 'sold' Alaska.

There was also the 'slight' problem of what to do with the Native Americans. Initially the Indian Bureau was part of the Department of War. However, the government saw the effectiveness of the reservation policy as a means to pacify the resistance of the Native Americans. It led to the annihilation of many Native American tribes, which is mentioned by Milner although he doesn't go into the full scale of murder and genocide that was to characterise the ruthless expansion of American capitalism. The US government's policy against the Native Americans was, as Zinn explains, absolutely central to their economic ambitions:

Indian removal was necessary for the opening up of the vast American lands
to agriculture, to commerce, to markets, to money, to the development of the
modern capitalist economy. Land was indispensable for all this.[10]

Between the discovery of gold in California in 1848 and the discovery of 'black gold' (oil) in Texas at the turn of the century, the American West was transformed from a largely agricultural economy into a modern urbanised capitalist economy. Minerals were discovered and transport and communication continued apace which helped develop and accelerate the economy. As Bryant argues in his excellent chapter, 'Entering The Global Economy', 'Capitalism emerged as the prevailing force in world history by the 19th century and as the all pervasive aspect of American life, especially in the West'.[11]

Mining was one area in which huge fortunes could be made. Each discovery of new minerals saw a rush of prospectors in pursuit of rapid gain—California saw its population expand from 14,000 when gold was discovered in 1848 to 250,000 by 1852. Waves of pioneers also swept into Nevada, Idaho, Montana and Dakota territory seeking gold and silver. The huge investment in mining meant, 'The trade surplus generated by the western mining companies encouraged the expansion of credit and brought the United States into the mainstream of the world economy'.[12]

But there was also a transformation in the mining economy itself as the individual prospector was rapidly replaced by the wage labourer as mining companies and other capitalists moved in.[13]

For this new class of labourers life was hard, monotonous and dangerous. It was insecure employment. The wages were low and the workforce highly mobile. As Bryant states:

> *Mine owners in the West, not unlike those who controlled mines in the East, the United Kingdom and continental Europe, moved slowly, if at all, to install safety devices and open air vents to improve timbering... The absence of concern for the welfare of the workers could be found throughout capitalist economies in the 19th century.*[14]

An itinerant or floating workforce became the norm and there was often discrimination against Chinese and immigrant workers. All the ingredients were there for class conflict.

Miners formed their own federation called the Miners Protective Association which sought better wages, shorter hours and safer conditions. Soon the ideals and demands of the federation were taken up by thousands of miners throughout the West. In Idaho in 1892 miners struck for recognition, and seven were killed fighting the troops. Within a decade the Western Federation of Miners (WFM) was formed and had 50,000 members. It fought to stop intervention by the military in disputes: '...they [the WFM] would serve as the starting point for the more militant Industrial Workers of the World...and Idaho won settlements for better wages and safer working conditions under the leadership of the future militant William "Big Bill" Haywood'.[15]

The West was being integrated into the world capitalist system through better transport and communication networks.

As early as the 1850s, California had entered a global capitalistic economy. Trade with Asia heightened demands for an overland route to the West coast.[16]

The answer to these demands was to come from the development of the rail network across America. The construction of the east-west rail link was one of the greatest subsidised capital investment projects by the American government in the 19th century. It was also to generate enormous profits for a small number of companies both east and west; it helped oil the wheels of capitalist development in America in the second half of the 19th century; and it was one of the greatest financial scandals in the history of Congress.

The Pacific Railroad Act proposed to construct the Central Pacific Railroad from San Francisco across California to the Sierra Nevada, enter Nevada and go eastward to meet a line beginning at the Missouri River. Thousands of workers flooded to the project—particularly Irish and Chinese labourers. They laid four lengths of rail per minute:

But the object was not to construct the best or more efficient route but to move quickly, at the least expense. The trackage was not ballasted with rock, the bridges were often flimsy and the ties were generally untreated and frequently of poor quality.[17]

Despite the short cuts the expense was enormous and initial government loans failed to meet even the minimum of costs (or, more importantly, generate enough profits). Thus the rail companies had to secure more government funding—to secure it they resorted to bribery and theft.

The Union Pacific Company started in Nebraska and built west. It received 12 million acres of free land and $27 million in government bonds, and created a bogus company to raise more funds. The other rail company, the Central Pacific, started on the west coast and went east. They spent $200,000 in bribes in Washington to get 9 million acres of free land. They also convinced President Abraham Lincoln that the Sierra Nevada began near Sacramento, so that the federal subsidy was $48,000 per mile, not 16 dollars. To top it all, both railroads used twisting routes to get even more subsidies from the towns they went through.

There was also a human cost to this story. In 1889 records of the Interstate Commerce Commission showed that 22,000 rail workers were injured or killed in the construction of this railroad.[18] But with the completion of the transcontinental rail lines the west coast ports grew in importance as links in an expanded trade network. By 1900 the West was linked to all areas of the United States, Mexico and Canada, and also had access to the trade routes of Latin America and Europe:

> *Indeed, the urbanisation of the West reflected the coming of the railways, with cities as diverse as Dallas, Los Angeles, Tacoma and Denver largely owing their existence, and their growth, to the presence of railways tapping their hinterlands. The detractors of the railways decried their 'capricious' rate making, corrupt financial activities, and political involvement, but the iron and, later, steel rails gave the region the transportation base necessary to form a viable segment of the world economy.*[19]

The opening of the rail line gave a great boost to capitalist expansion in the West. The expansion of mining and the increasing urbanisation of the American population brought demand for lumber. By the 1880s firms from New England, the Great Lakes and San Francisco began to secure the right to large tracts of land for lumbering :

> *The completion of the Northern Pacific meant that the lumber from the Northwest could be shipped to the Plains states to compete with the Chicago lumber market. The days of the lumber giants began.*[20]

Other areas of the economy expanded and developed as the result of government intervention. There were huge investments in banking and agriculture—the 1880s were known as the 'Golden Age of American Beef'. But all this expansion was done at a cost—some of it mentioned above with the appalling conditions of workers forced to labour for long hours, in unsafe conditions for poor pay.

But the growth of capitalism also created a concentrated, disgruntled workforce. Karl Marx wrote to a friend in America that nowhere else in the world was class conflict—'the upheaval most shamelessly caused by capitalist oppression'—taking place with such speed as in California.[21]

Colorado, for example, experienced a period of 'thirty years war' between 1884 and 1914 as miners fought their bosses by rioting and the use of dynamite. The Western Federation of Miners (WFM) mentioned above were at the forefront against the repressive mine owners. At Cripple Creek the WFM representative killed 13 strikebreakers with the use of dynamite. At Ludlow the Rockefeller controlled Colorado Fuel and Iron Company fought against the United Mine Workers and, with the use of the militia, killed 13 women and children: 'Enraged by the tragedy, hundreds of miners and their sympathisers roared across the mining counties in a spasm of property destruction that ended only when federal troops were sent in by President Woodrow Wilson to restore order'.[22]

Other areas suffered similar upheavals. The miners of Coeur d'Alene of Northern Idaho fought back against the mine owners by dynamiting their costly machinery. The state governor called in the troops and martial law was declared. In Los Angeles at the turn of the century two American Federation of Labour militants blew up the *Los Angeles Times* building, killing twenty people, in protest at the company's fierce open shop policy. But the public outcry and backlash against this bombing set the union back.

These struggles went hand in hand with the arrival of thousands of immigrants to America. Despite their great poverty[23], many easterners were drawn to the West. Kathleen Conzen in her chapter on 'A Saga of Families' documents much of the migration that occurred at this time as many families took all they possessed to what they saw as a new, better future. And as Allan Bogue notes in his chapter 'An Agricultural Empire':

> *For most westering Americans, the decision to emigrate involved the vision of a verdant farm and a thriving family. Land was the lure. Settlers learned of the agricultural possibilities of the West in myriad ways. Land speculators advertised their western holdings within handbills, pamphlets and newspaper stories... Eastern newspapers featured letters from the West, sometimes from former residents happily re-established on the new frontier.*[24]

In 1889-90 six new states, all in the West, entered the Union (United States)—Washington, Montana, North and South Dakota, Idaho and Wyoming. And in 1890 the US Census Bureau announced that the frontier had been closed—that is, there no longer existed a boundary to move beyond and to explore new territory.

Transformation

For the West, the 20th century has been a century of striking contrasts—between an explosion of investment and economic expansion which created enormous rewards for a few, and a growing and, on many occasions, fighting working class whose labour built this expansion and who quite rightly fought on many occasions to share in what was theirs.

At the beginning of the century the West's economy was still heavily dependent on the massive reserves of natural resources. In the mineral industry some 90 percent of America's reserves were located in the West. But natural sources of energy, such as coal, faced a new rival when in January 1901 a wildcat driller named Captain Anthony Lucas discovered an enormous oil field in Beaumont, Texas, which spewed forth oil at such pressure it took six days to cap and control. As the oil gushed into the Texan sky it was proclaimed as the eighth wonder of the world. Oil frenzy gripped Texas and California, a frenzy not seen since the discovery of gold 55 years earlier:

> *Speculative mania seized all parts of the state. Petroleum was eventually found under more than half the counties of Texas, and it replaced cotton as the primary contributor to the state's economy. Petrochemical production became the state's largest manufacturing industry. From hundreds of small companies, three eventually emerged to dominate the Texas oil industry: Gulf, Texaco and Humble (now part of Exxon, the modern name for Standard Oil of New Jersey).*[25]

And California was not far behind with new discoveries made almost every year through to the 1920s:

> *A speculative frenzy gripped southern California as production in the state soared from 5 million barrels in 1900 to 15 million barrels in 1914, and that was only the beginning. From the San Joaquin Valley to Santa Barbara and Los Angeles, new finds gave rise to...industrial giants like Union Oil of California and Standard Oil of California—now Chevron—which was originally only one more part of John D Rockefeller's giant Standard Oil monopoly. Between 1901 and 1940 California ranked first among American oil producing states for 14 years... Oil refining became the state's chief manufacturing industry, and the man-made harbour at San Pedro became one of the nation's chief oil-shipping ports.*[26]

Oil discovery and production were to put the West Coast at the heart of one of the most important parts of the capitalist system for decades to come. But how was this 'black gold' to be transported to the various parts of the globe? Here we witness the beginnings of enormous state spending and intervention which were to be features of industrial capitalist economies in the 20th century. 'Uncle Sam' was to become more active than the 'pioneers' of the 18th and 19th century could have imagined.

The Panama Canal was begun in 1905 and opened in 1914 at a cost of $365 million—federal money had done what private money couldn't. The canal improved access to the Pacific and the Atlantic and to all the great markets of the world. By 1919 the federal government had helped the West increase its share of national petroleum production from 29 percent to 68 percent.

Aided by access to the Panama Canal, timber production in the West grew from 10 percent to 35 percent of the nation's timber industry.[27]

War was good for the West. The First World War brought unparalleled demands for the West's resources—both oil and timber production increased rapidly. Agricultural production reached record levels, ship building in the Pacific Northwest expanded at a pace not seen before, and in 1916 William E Boeing founded a small company that eventually became the world's major manufacturer of passenger aircraft.

But it was the Second World War that proved to be greatest stimulant to the West's economic transformation. Schwantes explains:

> *No event in the 20th century, not even the great depression or the New Deal, brought more dramatic economic changes to the West than World War Two.* [28]

In 1937 the aircraft company Lockheed built 37 planes. Between 1941 and 1945 they produced 18,000. Uncle Sam poured billions of dollars into shipbuilding in California with employment in the San Francisco shipyards expanding from 4,000 to 260,000. At the peak of production the yards stretching from San Francisco Bay to the Columbia River launched a new ship every ten hours.

Employers were desperate for labour. One Boeing official said, 'We hired anybody who had a warm body and could walk through the gate'.[29] Boeing's workforce reached 55,000 during the peak of wartime production, 46 percent being women. Nearly a quarter of a million blacks, many from the South, moved west during the war in search of work. Many ended up working in the shipyards of Los Angeles, Oakland, San Francisco and Richmond.

The Second World War produced an economic boom in the West and it laid the foundation for the expansion of military spending that was to continue after the war ended, 'In a real sense,' argues Schwantes, 'World War II never ended'.[30] The levels of federal expenditure in the war industry continued after the carve up of the world by the superpowers. In fact, it was this territorial division that created the third great war of the 20th century—the Cold War—which continued the boom, expansion and transformation of the West's economy:

> *From the 1940s through to the 1980s, federal investment in science, defence, reclamation, and highways all combined to further industrialise and urbanise the West. The rising tide of federal investment in sophisticated military and aerospace technology was especially pronounced in southern California, in the urban Southwest and Texas and around Puget Sound... Cold war fears kept many of the West's defence plants busy, notably those of the aerospace giants, Boeing, Lockheed and Douglas, all of which manufactured jet aircraft, intercontinental ballistic missiles, and space equipment. In the 1960s, shortly after the National Aeronautics and Space Administration [NASA] was organised, the federal agency spent 50 percent of its funds in California.*[31]

The significance this level of state and defence spending had on the US economy as a whole was considerable. As Chris Harman has explained elsewhere[32] the amount of expenditure on arms produced a boom in the American economy and the West was the main beneficiary. It led some to argue that the problems of the cyclical capitalist crisis of booms and slumps had been eradicated. As the 20th century progressed, however, this idea was blown apart as the American economy was hit by the slump in the world economy in the 1970s.

The older mineral industries were particularly badly affected by a slump that was to last into the 1980s. The West suffered its most severe economic recession since the 1930s, the working class being at the sharp end. Nevada suffered its worst slump in mining in 40 years. Arizona produced 60 percent of all the copper in the US, but when foreign copper flooded the market in the 1970s the Arizona mines were decimated, closures shook the economy and thousands were thrown on the dole. It was a story that was repeated throughout much of the West as the American economy went from boom to bust, recession dawned and the 'American dream' became, for millions, a living nightmare.

Even the defence industries suffered. There was much talk about a so called peace dividend after the end of the Cold War but instead of making the transition towards 'civilian' production, many defence industries closed down and cut back. It was estimated that the closure of the Davis-Monthan air force base in Tucson would cost 10,000 jobs and precipitate a mass exodus of 15,000 people. As Schwantes states:

> *For California, which as recently as 1989 had received almost one-fifth of all federal defence contracts, the road to peace would obviously require some very painful adjustments... In the late 20th century, the region's natural-resource-based economy left a distinctive signature on the land in the form of abandoned mines, sawmills, and once bustling towns that had withered or disappeared.*[33]

Much of the American working class, not just those in the West, suffered during the 1980s as the Reagan years took their toll. As Sharon Smith points out, close to 40 million Americans have no health insurance cover whatsoever. The US now ranks twenty-second in infant mortality rates internationally, 'so that by the end of the 1980s, while the US was still the richest nation in the world, by a number of measurements it was also among the most unequal, leading among major industrial countries in the gap between the richest and the poorest fifths of the population'.[34]

Much of that poverty is to been seen on the streets of the massive metropolitan cities that are now a feature of the American West. As *The Oxford History of the American West* shows, the growth of the city has been essential for the growth of the American capitalism—its economic expansion would not have been possible without a steady and concentrated supply of labour—a dramatic feature of 20th century American capitalist expansion. The growth of cities led to a growth of trade.

Los Angeles is the heart of the important Pacific Rim. The volume of imports and exports through Los Angeles and Long Beach tripled between 1970 and 1990. California is second only to New York as America's banking and financial power. Governor Jerry Brown in the late 1970s referred to his state as 'the Pacific Republic of California'.

The growth of Los Angeles is remarkable. Fuelled by federal funding Los Angeles grew from a town of 5,165 at the turn of the century to the metropolis of the 1990s. The federal government aided this development with the construction of the largest dam in the world—the 726 foot high dam in Black Canyon on the Colorado River. The 'Boulder Dam' became the supplier of much of the electricity for the city of Los Angeles and the surrounding area. The Los Angeles aqueduct was completed in 1913 and carried water 233 miles from the mountains.

The level of government investment used to develop the cities of southern California was enormous, and for many workers it was a cheap place to live: 'No matter whether the original source was local, state or federal, the capital that had been invested...made it possible for Californians to enjoy astonishingly cheap water in the midst of desert landscapes that had never known before such abundance'.[35] It also demonstrates the extent to which the forces of production have enabled man to develop the earth's natural resources to satisfy the needs of millions of people.

Thousands of workers now flooded to the city of Los Angeles and its surrounding cities in the search for work. Mike Davies describes the population explosion[36] and the social polarisation[37] which accompanied it in his book, *City of Quartz*. High levels of insecurity and poverty, combined with years of systematic racism and discrimination against a predominantly 'immigrant' population, created a ferment of anger that burst with such a dramatic impact onto the world stage in 1992.

But the Los Angeles riots are only the most visible example of a working class taking to the streets. The American West may have led the world in the development of the forces of capitalism, but, as this book illustrates, it has also given us some fine examples of working class resistance that rank alongside many of the greatest struggles of our time.

The IWW, or Wobblies as they became known, were born out of the struggle of the Western working class, although they did not limit their struggles to the West. But they particularly appealed to those who worked in the brutal conditions among the West's camps and mills. At a time when the main national trade unions targeted skilled white labour, the IWW emphasised the solidarity of all workers—men and women, black and white, and Asians who were usually shunned because of their willingness to take low wages.

And the success of organising in the West made recruitment in the east easier—union membership rose from 40,000 in 1916 to 100,000 in 1918.

At the beginning of the century there was a large army of itinerant workers which numbered millions.[38] The IWW fought to organise this group of workers through the Agricultural Workers Organisation (AWO) in 'one big agricultural union' which sought to limit the hours of work, improve wages, win free transportation on freight trains and replace job by job arrangements with collective bargaining.

> By the end of its second year of existence, the AWO could raise the demand that all hiring be done either through IWW halls or IWW delegates on the job site. De facto picket lines stretched hundreds and hundreds of miles, for any would be harvest hand without a red card was likely to be ejected from freight cars by IWW militants...the consensus was that workers without an IWW card were really scabs.[39]

Even when the bosses sought to recruit black labour, as they did in 1916 when they planned to bring 30,000 black workers from the South to crush the AWO in the lumber areas of Texas and Louisiana, the IWW met such a challenge head on: 'Thirty thousand Negroes will come and 30,000 IWW's will go back. The red card is cherished as much, and its objectives understood as well by a black man as a white.'

The transformation of the economy and the rapid industrialisation of the West led to many working class battles. In February 1919 Seattle was gripped by a general strike as 60,00 workers shut down the city and it became known as the Seattle 'four day revolution'. The single most important strike of the 1930s and one of the most important in the West's working class history was the great maritime strike of 1934 when the International Longshoremen's Association challenged the hated 'shape-up' whereby the longshoremen turned up at the docks in the morning hoping to be selected by the company foreman for a day's work. Some 3,500 longshoremen quit work, went on strike and were quickly joined by dockers from various marine unions. From Seattle to San Diego the ports were strikebound and a three day general strike saw 127,000 workers out in solidarity. In San Francisco in July 1934 pitched battles erupted between police and strikers, but the workers held firm and won most of their demands, including the end of the 'shape-up' system.

'The widespread militancy among urban and rural workers in the 1930s', argues Deutsch, 'laid the foundation for the civil rights and farm workers movements in the 1960s'.[40] A five year strike by Filipino grape farm workers near Delano, California, (against the advice of their leaders) led to considerable gains for low paid, poorly organised farm workers throughout the West. It was a strike that spread a 'grape boycott' to over 100 US and Canadian cities. The boycott was so popular it forced Senator Robert F Kennedy to publicly support the strike and, with his wife, raise funds for the farm workers.

In 1994 Las Vegas hotel workers went on strike in recognition of their union. Up until the Second World War Las Vegas was nothing more than a dusty railroad town. But with a workforce that worked long hours, was badly paid, worked in poor conditions and was badly organised, Las Vegas grew into the gambling centre of the West. By the 1980s gambling accounted for 32 percent of all Nevada jobs, with another 25 percent in related employment—thus the gambling workers were central to the Nevada economy and in 1994 they had the confidence to flex their muscles, despite being a traditionally weak group of workers.

Conclusion

There has been an attempt throughout the 20th century to reinterpret the past and popularise the romantic image of the West to try and hide many of the brutal excesses of capitalist expansion.

There is much therefore in this book to recommend—the wonderful illustrations, in black and white and colour, and each chapter has an excellent comprehensive bibliography. A fascinating chapter on 'The Visual West' by Brian Dippe looks at how artists have interpreted the West, 'The Literary West' by Thomas Lyon examines how writers have portrayed the West through fiction. There is also a wonderful chapter on the history of Alaska and Hawaii, which only became states in 1959, but whose indigenous population suffered treatment as harsh and as brutal as the early Native Americans.

The *Oxford History* uncovers the hidden history of the West, like the black 'buffalo cowboys' who rode with the US cavalry, or of the 5,000 or more black cowboys who herded cattle and who, in 1880, constituted a quarter of the total cowboy population. We are also introduced to the Asian-Americans whose labour was vital to 'conquering' the frontier. They were central to the construction of the Central Pacific Railroad but were deliberately excluded from the famous photographs which celebrated the joining of the transcontinental line at Utah. This book reminds us of the brutal history of the Native Americans who are popularly confined to being mere supporting players in the Westerns, useful for Hollywood in that they help highlight the 'superiority' of the white culture and way of life.

This history is more enlightening than that which has been popularised by Hollywood. It is to be found in the struggles of the Mexican-American pecan shellers on strike in San Antonio, Texas, in 1938 against the introduction of mechanisation, when they fought to preserve jobs worth $3 an hour for a 54 hour week,[41] or the workers organised in the Building Trades Council in San Francisco who, from the 1890s until after the First World War, 'were the dominant force in the economic, political and social life of San Francisco...who frightened businessmen in Los Angeles'.[42]

The history of the West in the 20th century is full of such examples—the fight for gay rights in California, the struggle against the Vietnam War on the campuses, the urban ghetto uprisings of 1964 and 1965 (notably the Watts riots in Los Angeles), the growth of the Black Panthers in the East Bay area in the 1960s; the fights by the American Indian Movement when in 1969 they occupied Alcatraz Island in protest. We owe a great debt to the resistance of the Western working class, and for the history and experience they have given us.

Despite the glamour of Hollywood, Beverly Hills or the beaches of southern California, the burgeoning trade of the Pacific Rim or the make it rich quick visits to Las Vegas, the impact of the 20th century on the West has been to create a working class that is now more disillusioned than ever before, with the level of class polarisation at its starkest and where workers come together both at work and in the cities in numbers not even dreamed about before. The remarkable thing about the transformation of the West is that we can quite confidently say that when the workers rise again—as surely they will—they will wield a power more fearsome than ever before in their history.

Notes

1   C A Milner II (ed) et al, *The Oxford History of the American West*, (Oxford, 1994), hereafter referred to as *OHAW*. Each quote/reference taken from this book is named by author, title, and then chapter number.
2   P Iverson, 'Native Peoples and Native Histories (Ch 1,*OHAW*), p27.
3   Leacock states: 'To the Indians, the trade opened up a source of new and more effective tools and weapons, of cloth which did not have to be tanned and worked, and of foods which could be more readily transported and stored. However, it demanded an unending flow of furs, and trapping fur-bearing animals began to displace the hunting of the large game in the Indian economy. Within a few generations the Indians near the earliest trade centres around Quebec had become dependent upon trade goods as the mainstay of their existence.' E B Leacock, *Myths of Male Dominance*, (London, 1981), p36
4   E West, 'American Frontier' (Ch 4, *OHAW*), p125.
5   Ibid, pp125-126.
6   Ibid, p126.

7   R Ranson, 'Public Canal Investment and the Opening of the old North West' in D
     Klingaman et al, *Essays in Nineteenth Century Economic History*, (Ohio Press,
     1975). In 1815 the West sent about one fourth of its 100,000 tons of agricultural
     exports to the East—all of it by canal. Fifteen years later western shipments to the
     East had risen to over 500,000 tons, or 60 percent of the total exports from the
     region.
8   C Milner, 'National Initiatives' (Ch 5, *OHAW*), p156.
9   H Zinn, *A People's History of the United States*, (Longman, London, 1980), p166.
10   Ibid, p125.
11   K Bryant, 'Entering the Global Economy (Ch 6, *OHAW*), p196.
12   Ibid, p198.
13   Ibid, p200. In California, for example: 'The gold rush in California created wealth
     for the few and labour for the many. When the output of gold reached 80 million
     dollars in 1852, the economy of the region had been transformed. Demands for
     goods and services made San Francisco a city with merchants, bankers, ship
     owners, freighting firms, and manufacturers competing for a share of the wealth.
     Clipper ships sailing round the Horn could not deliver enough clothes, shovels,
     nails, mercury, and other necessities. The urbanisation of northern California
     initiated a pattern to be found across the west... The California gold rush set in
     motion the economic maturation of the West.'
14   Ibid, p208.
15   Ibid, p208.
16   Ibid, p209.
17   Ibid, p216.
18   See H Zinn, op cit.
19   K Bryant, op cit, p224.
20   Ibid, p226.
21   Quoted in R Brown, 'Violence' (Ch 11, *OHAW*), p400.
22   Ibid, p411.
23   N Ware, *The Industrial Worker* (Chicago, 1990), p37.
24   A Bogue, 'An Agricultural Empire' (Ch 8, *OHAW*), p285.
25   C Schwantes, 'Wage Earners and Wealth Makers' (Ch 12, *OHAW*), p435.
26   Ibid, p435.
27   From C Abbott, 'The Federal Presence' (Ch 13, *OHAW*).
28   C Schwantes, op cit, p452.
29   Ibid, p453.
30   Ibid, p455.
31   Ibid, p455.
32   The theory of the Permanent Arms Economy explained how post war arms
     spending created an economic boom in the major economies,
     'This expenditure of vast quantities of surplus value on arms had a peculiar effect
     on American capitalism, as was already clear in the course of the war. The amount
     of surplus value remaining in the hands of private capital after the state had taken
     its share of arms was actually higher than before, the organic composition of
     capital tended to fall and the rate of profit rose.' C Harman, *Explaining the Crisis*
     (Bookmarks, 1987), p79.
33   C Schwantes, op cit, p464.
34   S Smith, 'Twilight of the American Dream', *International Socialism* 54, p15.
35   W Cronon, 'Landscapes of Abundance and Scarcity' (Ch 17, *OHAW*), p620.
36   'Stretching from the country club homes of Santa Barbara to the shanty towns of
     the colonias of Ensenada, to the edge of Llano in the high desert and the Coachella
     Valley in the low, with a built up surface area nearly the size of Ireland and a GNP
     bigger than India's—the urban galaxy dominated by Los Angeles is the fastest

growing metropolis in the advanced industrial world.' M Davies, *City of Quartz* (London, 1992), p6.

37   'Social polarisation has increased almost as rapidly as population. A recent survey of Los Angeles households income trends in the 1980s suggests that affluence (incomes of $50,000 plus) has almost tripled (from 9 percent to 26 percent) while poverty ($15,000 and under) has increased by a third (from 30 percent to 40 percent).' Ibid, p7.

38   C Schwantes, op cit, p438.

39   S Bird et al, *Solidarity Forever: An Oral History of the Wobblies* (London, 1988), p32.

40   S Deutsch et al, 'Contemporary People/Contested Places' (Ch 18, *OHAW*), p650.

41   Ibid, illustration, p650.

42   C Schwantes, op cit, p442.

Bookwatch: China since Mao

CHARLIE HORE

Since Mao Zedong died in 1976, China has changed out of all recognition. Throughout the 1980s the Chinese economy grew at an average annual rate of over 10 percent—one of the highest growth rates anywhere in the world. Parts of the Chinese countryside, in particular the areas of Guangdong province close to Hong Kong, have experienced what amounts to a full scale industrial revolution. And a large part of this growth has been fuelled by China's reintegration into the world market—China is now the eleventh biggest trading nation in the world.

Under Mao the economy had stagnated, and many of the gains that had been made since 1949 were wiped out, first in the Great Leap Forward of the late 1950s, and then in the Cultural Revolution. Far and away the best book to read on Mao's economic strategy and why it necessarily failed is Nigel Harris's *The Mandate of Heaven*,[1] an excellent socialist analysis of the limitations of state capitalism. Most other books written on contemporary China in the 1960s and 1970s are marred either by uncritical repetition of state propaganda, or a simple inability to get any hard facts. The works of Simon Leys are some of the very few exceptions, giving a devastating account of the Cultural Revolution, and the intellectual and spiritual poverty of official culture in the 1970s.[2]

The new leadership that took over in 1978 shared Mao's aim of building a strong industrial economy capable of competing with the rest of the world. They junked Mao's economic strategy for the simple reason that it had failed to deliver the goods. Their new strategy of the 'four modernisations', introduced by Deng Xiaoping in 1978, had essentially two strands: reducing direct state control over the economy in favour of 'market socialism', and taking China back into the world market to gain export markets and state of the art technology.

In the villages the communal fields were broken up, and each family was given plots of land to plant as they saw fit. A certain proportion of the crop had to be sold to the state, and taxes paid in cash or crops—everything else they produced was theirs to consume or sell on the open market. In the cities day to day control of the factories was devolved to the managers and local officials. After meeting state quotas and paying taxes, they could sell the rest of their output on the free market.

The scale of this strategy's early successes can be seen by the results of the sixth Five Year Plan (1981-1985). The plan called for average annual increases of 4 percent in both industrial and agricultural output—the actual growth was 12.6 percent in industry, and 8 percent in agriculture.[3] This growth led to probably the largest changes in everyday life in China's history. Living standards soared in the early 1980s—average incomes doubled in both the cities and the countryside, while there was a boom in both food consumption and the availability of consumer goods.

The new leaders also admitted that the Cultural Revolution had been a disaster and dismantled many of the state controls which had characterised life under Mao. In part this was a necessary part of the market reforms, but it was also done to win back a measure of popular support for the ruling class. The political liberalisation was substantial, and quickly created political problems for the ruling class that have plagued them ever since, as intellectuals in particular have tried to push back the new boundaries of what was permissable.

The first challenge to the new rules began as soon as Deng Xiaoping had won the leadership of the ruling class. Oppositionists began to put up posters on a wall in Beijing (quickly labelled 'Democracy Wall') and produce magazines to sell to the crowds who flocked there. The activists were mostly ex-Red Guards, who found a mass base among the youth who had been sent to the countryside during the Cultural Revolution.[4]

The movement's dynamic eventually led it into open opposition to Deng Xiaoping, and it was finally destroyed in a law and order crackdown in 1983. The movement was important both because it showed very early the limitations of Deng's reforms, and because it has remained the reference point for opposition since then. The best history of the movement, with substantial extracts from its writings, is David S G Goodman's *Beijing Street Voices*. But *Wild Lilies, Poisonous Weeds*, edited by Gregor Benton, remains the best anthology of the movement's writings. Andrew Nathan's *Chinese Democracy* places the movement in the context of earlier protest movements, and gives an excellent account of its subsequent influence.[5]

Important as Democracy Wall was, it was undoubtedly a minority voice. The early success of the economic reforms made Deng Xiaoping's government probably the most popular in China since Mao took power in 1949. But by 1985 the new economic strategy was running into substantial problems, as it became clearer that the market was failing to deliver what had been promised. By 1988 raging inflation, growing rural unemployment and rampant corruption among state officials and managers had created a powder keg which was to explode in the Tiananmen Square revolt of 1989.

Since 1989 the economy has recovered from the (state induced) recession of the late 1980s, but is once again wracked with inflation, unemployment and overheating. The last two years have seen a series of riots and attacks on local officials spread across the countryside, while strikes are becoming more and more common in the cities. With Deng Xiaoping due to take his place in the deepest circle of hell any time now, the Chinese ruling class has never faced a more uncertain future.

The evolution of China's reforms since 1978 has been covered in depth in previous issues of *International Socialism*, and in my *The Road to Tiananmen Square*,[6] but they have also been covered in a wealth of other works. These break down into three broad categories: Western journalism, Western academic studies and writings from within China. I intend to look at each of these categories in turn, before discussing the revolt of 1989 and the literature it has produced.

Journalistic works

This is the shortest section, but the best place to start if you don't know much about China. In the early years of the reforms much the best coverage of the changes in China came from journalistic works. Two early works that capture the scale of the changes and the expectations they aroused are Orville Schell's *To Get Rich is Glorious* and Roger Garside's *Coming Alive: China After Mao*.[7]

The two most important works, however, are Lynn Pan's *The New Chinese Revolution* and John Gittings's *China Changes Face*.[8] Both books are comprehensive surveys of the changes in China's economy and society during the 1980s, informed by a far deeper knowledge of China than most other writers, and both were written after the first bloom of naive enthusiasm for Deng Xiaoping had worn off, giving them critical insights into the contradictions that the economic reforms were beginning to produce.

Orville Schell's *Discos and Democracy*[9] focused on the growth of political opposition and the fragmentation of official ideology, in the student protest of 1985-86. In many ways that year was a turning point as inflation began to wipe out increased wages, official corruption became more and more blatant, and the logic of the market led the economy into the beginnings of crisis.

Academic works

The two best general surveys of the reforms of the 1980s and their initial results are collections of essays—*Reforming the Revolution: China in Transition* and a two volume work *Transforming China's Economy in the Eighties*.[10] The second volume of this is especially useful as it focuses on industry and the cities, a major gap in most of the literature.

The more detailed surveys of the results of the reforms have tended to concentrate overwhelmingly on the countryside. The land reforms of the late 1970s were followed by an upsurge in industrialisation in many villages. By 1985 village industries employed some 70 million people and produced 19 percent of China's total industrial output.[11]

Zhu Ling's *Rural Reform and Peasant Income in China* is an excellent, if dense, survey of the changes in peasant income and the growth of inequality, based on a survey of three very different villages in the central province of Henan. *China's Peasants* by Shulamith and Jack Potter, is a similar survey of a village in Guangdong, particularly useful for giving an account of change in the village since 1949. Both give a vivid picture of the hopes aroused by the economic reforms and the ways in which they have been frustrated.[12]

One of the few attempts to provide a national picture is *State and Peasant in Contemporary China* by Jean C Oi, though her reliance on interviews with refugees in Hong Kong means the study is skewed towards the southern coastal regions. The most critical account of the rural reforms is William Hinton's *The Great Reversal*. Hinton is an unrepentant Maoist, who sees the reforms as a betrayal of socialism, but his deep knowledge of the Chinese countryside gives him a sharp eye for the reforms' adverse effects.[13]

Margery Wolf's *Revolution Postponed*[14] is a sharply critical account of how women's lives have changed for the worse since the reforms were introduced. She is particularly sharp on the coercion used to enforce the one child policy which began in 1979, and her insistence on talking to women workers in the cities makes this one of the best books on the changes in workers' lives. There are good accounts of workers' lives in two collections of essays, *Chinese Society on the Eve of Tiananmen* and *State and Society in China*,[15] both of which document the rise in living standards in the early 1980s, and how that was wiped out by inflation after 1986. Significantly, both were written after 1989, when workers' prominence in the Tiananmen rising brought them to the forefront of researchers' interests.

One of the very few detailed studies of city life is *Sex, Death and Hierarchy in a Chinese City* by William Jankowiak,[16] though because it's set in the Inner Mongolian capital of Hohhot, hardly a typical Chinese city, it's difficult to know how far one can generalise from his findings. The book is also useful for being one of the few to document the oppression of national minorities inside China—although there is a substantial literature on Tibet,[17] little has so far been written on other minorities.

Lastly, the ability to do proper research inside China has produced some fascinating re-evaluations of Chinese history. Anne F Thurston's *Enemies of the People*,[18] for instance, is a comparative account of the Cultural Revolution drawn from interviews with some 200 intellectuals, which makes it one of the most interesting Western books on the period.

Most importantly, a number of important studies on workers' lives and working class organisation in pre-revolutionary China have appeared, full of valuable insights into both everyday life and the activities of revolutionaries in the 1920s.[19] These are contradictory works, whose perspective is a mixture of E P Thompson influenced 'history from below' and feminist theories which focus on divisions among the working classes. Despite a certain theoretical incoherence they contain a wealth of detail about workers' organisation and the clashes in workers' lives between tradition and the pressures of the modern world.

Chinese works

Throughout the 1960s and most of the 1970s Westerners knew about China only through Western writing. The Chinese writing that was translated was unbelievably dull and cliché ridden propaganda, which read as though it had been assembled by committee. From 1978 onwards that situation was transformed. Deng Xiaoping's reforms, and particularly the open denunciation of the Cultural Revolution, released a pent up stream of poems, short stories, memoirs and other writings. Even after the suppression of the Democracy Wall, there was a far greater freedom to publish than before. Furthermore, firstly people with families abroad and then students were allowed to leave the country—most of the works translated into English have come from people who have left China and no longer have to worry about official retribution.

The most widely read book about the Cultural Revolution is undoubtedly Jung Chang's *Wild Swans*. Although it's well worth reading, both for its harrowing picture of the Cultural Revolution and (perhaps more importantly) for its insights into the loyalties of her parents' generation to Mao, its runaway success is primarily a triumph of marketing, for there are many other equally compelling accounts of the Cultural Revolution in translation[20]—and even these represent only the tip of the iceberg in terms of the literature in Chinese.

Most contemporary translated Chinese fiction is simply personal memoirs written in novel form: useful for a sense of life during the Cultural Revolution, but with little literary merit. There are important exceptions to this. Lu Wenfu's *The Gourmet and Other Stories* is a gently satirical collection of stories about everday city life, while Wang Anyi's *Baotown* is a simply sketched slice of life in a remote village.[21]

Zhang Xianliang's *Half of Man is Woman*, based on his years in a labour camp, is by contrast a violent, surrealistic and (by Chinese standards) sexually explicit novel. His style can be both dense and rambling at the same time, but it's worth persevering. Mo Yan's *Red Sorghum* (on which the film of the same name was based), is an even more violent and earthy story of the war against Japan. His is an important perspective because he was born into a peasant family, and only began to write while he was in the army. Most writing on rural China comes from intellectuals whose resentment at being sent to the villages is mixed with a disdain for peasant labour. Mo Yan, by contrast, understands the villages from inside, and can thus depict the vitality as well as the degradation of peasant life.[22]

For all the vitality of contemporary Chinese writing, it is important to remember that the voices of the vast majority of Chinese—the peasantry and the working class—are almost entirely absent. Two books do something to remedy this. He Liyi's *Mr China's Son*[23] is a classic work about peasant life today. A teacher who was sent to a labour camp and returned to his village in 1962, he relearnt English from the radio and wrote his memoirs in English. Although he describes the labour camp, the bulk of the book is an inside view of everyday village life in the remote south west.

Chinese Lives[24] was produced by two Chinese journalists, inspired by Studs Terkel's 'oral histories', who simply talked to people on the streets about their everyday lives and wrote down what they said as they said it. This produced a fresh and lively mosaic of ordinary people's immediate concerns and ambitions capturing, as few other books have done, both enthusiasm for the reforms and frustration at the pace of change.

Finally, although this is a review of books it is important to mention the renaissance of Chinese cinema over the last 10 years, beginning with Chen Kauge's *Yellow Earth*, from Tian Zhuangzhuang's bleak and savage *Horse Thief* to Zhang Yinou's violent Red *Sorghum*. A reported new generation of film makers seems to have been stifled by post Tiananmen censorship.

Tiananmen and after

Tiananmen Square was the most important movement of opposition since 1949 for three linked reasons: it brought millions of people onto the streets in opposition to the ruling class as a whole, rather than in support of one faction against another; it produced independent working class organisations for the first time since 1927; and when Li Peng declared martial law, opposition became open rebellion as millions of workers manned barricades to keep the army out of Beijing. Although the explosion caught everyone by surprise, seeming to come out of nowhere, it was a product both of the economic reforms' successes, and of the agitation of a minority of intellectuals over several years.

It was the growing gap between rich and poor that above all pulled millions of workers into the streets behind the students. But that student movement had been stirring for several years under the influence of a number of 'unofficial' intellectuals. Though often labelled 'dissidents' by the Western media, the term was inappropriate. Most were Communist Party members, and all saw themselves as working for reform from above.

All of them equally saw that the government would not listen unless it was made to, and thus pressed for action from below to bring about reform from above. It was that side of their ideas that above all attracted a mass student audience. For good accounts both of their ideas and of their influence, see Andrew Nathan's *Chinese Democracy*, Orville Schell's *Discos and Democracy* and Perry Link's *Evening Chats in Beijing*. Fang Lizhi's *Breaking Down the Great Wall of China* is a good representative account of their ideas in their own words.[25]

The two best general histories of the Tiananmen Square rebellion (although they only discuss events in Beijing) are Orville Schell's *Mandate of Heaven* and *Black Hands of Beijing* by George Black and Robin Munro. The second of these is particularly interesting both for its account of the growing gap between the reformist intellectuals and the mood on the streets, and for one of the most detailed accounts of workers' organisations and their activities. *Cries for Democracy* is a valuable collection of translations of the movement's wall posters and leaflets.[26]

Li Lu's *Moving the Mountain* and Shen Tong's *Almost a Revolution*[27] are two valuable memoirs from leaders of the students in Tiananmen Square, though they should be read more for their insights into what the students believed they were fighting for than as definitive histories. My 'Tiananmen Square and After' in *International Socialism* 44 contained invaluable eyewitness accounts of the rebellion, and in particular of the organisation of the barricades on the outskirts of Beijing.

Although the movement began in Beijing, and its dynamic was always determined by events in Beijing, it was far more widespread than any previous opposition movement. In this sense, there is as yet no good history of the movement. *The Pro-Democracy Protests in China*[28] is, as far as I know, the only book to concentrate on what happened outside Beijing, though its account is limited by the accidents of where the various authors happened to be. It is, however, particularly sharp on the different aspirations of the intellectual leadership and the workers who were drawn into the struggle. It also illustrates something that went practically unreported in the West at the time—the sheer scale and anger of the protests across China after the 4 June massacre.

Although the movement had the potential to topple China's rulers, the lack of any coherent leadership meant it was never able to realise that potential. But the massacre of 4 June demonstrated that the ruling class was unable to regain control except through brute force, and had nothing else to offer the Chinese people. That remains true today.

Their political crisis is rooted above all in the success of the economic reforms since 1978. The Chinese economy has expanded out of all recognition, but in the process the ruling class has lost control of both the pace and the direction of the economy. For the last ten years they have zigzagged from austerity packages to expansion and back again, depending on whether they faced overheating or recession. Yet each zig-zag diminishes their power, as local officials and managers find new ways around the controls imposed from Beijing. What the experience of the reforms demonstrates is that, while the market can expand the economy, it cannot do so in a way that benefits the majority of the population.

While few academic works on China after Tiananmen will go so far, all reflect a sense of crisis for which there is no obvious solution. *China in the Nineties* is a useful collection of articles tracing the roots of the crisis, while a more recent collection, *China Deconstructs,* illustrates the growing inequalities between different regions of China, and the loss of control by Beijing over economic development in China's provinces. Although it concludes (probably correctly) that the chances of China breaking up as a state are small, the fact that the question can be asked at all shows the depth of the problem.[29]

One key component of the crisis is the growing unwillingness of China's population to passively accept its effects. The last few years have seen an enormous increase both in strikes among urban workers and in demonstrations, riots and attacks on state officials across the countryside. In 1989 the ruling class could at least take comfort from the fact that the countryside kept quiet—in any future upheaveal, they cannot take that for granted. Elizabeth Croll's *From Heaven to Earth,*[30] a detailed study of the gains and losses of the reforms in the countryside, shows how that growing peasant defiance is based on the antagonism between peasants and officials and the fragility of the gains that most peasants have made.

Academic and even journalistic publishing tends to lag two or three years behind events, which is why the listing of books since Tiananmen is so sparse. One exception to this is the excellent *China Briefing*[31] series published annually, useful more as a snapshot of recent events than as in depth analysis, but the most up to date information you can get in book form. Otherwise, for the latest developments the *Far Eastern Economic Review*, *Business Week* and the *Wall Street Journal* all carry good reports of current events in China today. Precisely because these publications reflect Western capitalists' fears for their investments and export prospects, they follow unrest among workers and peasants closely.

If the number of books I've listed seems daunting, it should be remembered that I've only skimmed the surface of a vast literature. Despite that a number of topics remain uncovered. There are as yet, for instance, no good books on corruption among officials and managers, or on the growth of the 'floating population' (illegal migrants and travelling traders) in China's cities. Out of everything I've listed, I'd recommend four books to start with: Jung Chang's *Wild Swans*, John Gittings's *China Changes Face*, Margery Wolf's *Revolution Postponed* and Li Lu's *Moving the Mountain*.

But the first book that any socialist should read about China was written 40 years before any of these. Harold Isaacs' *The Tragedy of the Chinese Revolution*[32] is one of the classics of socialist history, a passionate and inspiring account of how Chinese workers and peasants rose up against their oppressors between 1925 and 1927, and how that revolution was betrayed by Stalin. Mao's victory was built on their defeat, yet the re-emergence of independent workers' organisation in 1989 opened the way for the rediscovery of that revolutionary tradition and the rebirth of the power that can put an end forever to the poverty and inequality imposed by the market.

Notes

The best books on a subject aren't always the ones that remain in print. For some reason this seems to be especially true of contemporary China. Books that are still in print are marked by *.

1   N Harris, *The Mandate of Heaven* (Quartet, 1978).

2   See for instance *The Chairman's New Clothes* (Allison and Busby, 1977), one of the best histories of the Cultural Revolution, and *Chinese Shadows* (Penguin, 1978) and *Broken Images* (Allison and Busby, 1979). All are out of print, but they remain some of the most essential books on modern China.

3   C MacKerras and A Yorke (eds), *The Cambridge Handbook of Contemporary China* (Cambridge University Press, 1991), p156*. This is a very useful source of facts and figures up to the mid-1980s.

4   In the late 1980s and early 1970s between 12 and 18 million young people were sent to the countryside from China's towns and cities—that is up to 10 percent of the urban population. For powerful descriptions of the alienation and deprivation

this caused, see Jung Chang's *Wild Swans* (Flamingo, 1991)* or Chen Kaige's film *King of the Children*.

5   D S G Goodman (ed), *Beijing Street Voices* (Marion Boyars, 1981); G Benton (ed), *Wild Lilies, Poisonous Weeds* (Pluto, 1982); A Nathan, *Chinese Democracy* (I B Tauris, 1986).

6   See G Gorton, 'China since the Cultural Revolution', *International Socialism* 23; G Gorton, 'China's "Market Socialism"—Can it Work?', *International Socialism* 34; C Hore, 'China: Tiananmen Square and After', *International Socialism* 44*; C Harman, 'Where is Capitalism Going? (part 2)', *International Socialism* 60*; C Hore, *The Road to Tiananmen Square* (Bookmarks, 1991).

7   O Schell, *To Get Rich is Glorious: China in the 1980s* (Mentor, 1986); R Garside, *Coming Alive: China after Mao* (Mentor, 1982).

8   L Pan, *The New Chinese Revolution* (Sphere, 1988); J Gittings, *China Changes Face* (Oxford University Press, 1989).

9   O Schell, *Discos and Democracy* (Pantheon, 1988).

10   R Benewick and P Wingrove (eds), *Reforming the Revolution: China in Transition* (Macmillan, 1988)*; 20) S Feuchtwang, A Hussain and T Pairault, *Transforming China's Economy in the 1980s* (Zed, 1988).

11   J Gittings, op cit, p140.

12   Zhu Ling, *Rural Reform and Peasant Income in China* (Macmillan, 1991)*; S H and J M Potter, *China's Peasants* (Cambridge University Press, 1990)*.

13   J C Oi, *State and Peasant in Contemporary China* (University of California Press, 1989)*; W Hinton, *The Great Reversal*, (Monthly Review, New York 1990)*.

14   M Wolf, *Revolution Postponed* (Methuen, 1987).

15   D Davis and E Vogel (eds), *Chinese Society on the Eve of Tiananmen* (Harvard University Press, 1990)*; A L Rosenbaum (ed), *State and Society in China* (Westview Press, 1992)*.

16   W Jankowiak, *Sex, Death and Hierarchy in a Chinese City* (Columbia University Press, 1993)*.

17   See for instance, A T Grunfeld, *The Making of Modern Tibet* (Zed, 1987).

18   A F Thurston, *Enemies of the People* (Harvard University Press, 1988).

19   See for instance G Hershatter, *The Workers of Tianjin 1900-1949* (Stanford University Press, 1986)*; E Honig, *Sisters and Strangers* (Stanford University Press, 1986)* about women textile workers in Shanghai; E Perry, *Shanghai on Strike* (Stanford University Press, 1993)*; J Stockard, *Daughters of the Canton Delta* (Stanford University Press, 1989)* about marriage patterns among women silk workers in Guangdong; D Strand, *Rickshaw Beijing* (University of California Press, 1989)*.

20   See for instance Liang Heng and J Shapiro, *Son of the Revolution* (Fontana, 1983); Nien Cheng, *Life and Death in Shanghai* (Grafton, 1986; reissued by Harper Collins1995)*; Luo Ziping, *A Generation Lost* (Avon Books, 1990); Gao Yuan, *Born Red* (Stanford University Press, 1987)*; Yue Daiyun and C Wakeman, *To the Storm* (University of California Press, 1987)*.

21   Lu Wenfu, *The Gourmet and Other Stories* (Readers International, 1987); Wang Anyi, *Baotown*, (Viking, 1989)*.

22   Zhang Xianliang, *Half of Man is Woman* (Viking, 1988); Mo Yan, *Red Sorghum*, (Minerva, 1994)*. He has also published a collection of equally vivid and earthy short stories, *Explosions* (Renditions, 1991)

23   He Liyi, *Mr China's Son* (Westview Press, 1993)*.

24   Zhang Xinxin and Sang Ye (eds), *Chinese Lives* (Penguin, 1986).

25   P Link, *Evening Chats in Beijing* (W W Norton, 1993)*; Fang Lizhi, *Breaking Down the Great Wall of China* (W W Norton, 1992).*

26   O Schell, *Mandate of Heaven* (Little, Brown, 1995)*; G Black and R Munro, *Black Hands of Beijing* (John Wiley, 1993)*; Han Minzhu (ed), *Cries for Democracy* (Princeton University Press, 1990).*

27   Li Lu, *Moving the Mountain* (Pan, 1990); Shen Tong, *Almost a Revolution* (Harper Perennial, 1991).

28   J Unger (ed), *The Pro-Democracy Protests in China* (M E Sharpe, Armonk, 1991).*

29   D S G Goodman and G Segal (eds), *China in the Nineties* (Oxford University Press, 1991); D S G Goodman and G Segal (eds), *China Deconstructs* (Routledge, 1994).*

30   E Croll, *From Heaven to Earth* (Routledge, 1994).*

31   The most recent is *China Briefing 1994* (Westview Press).*

32   H Isaacs, *The Tragedy of the Chinese Revolution* (Stanford University Press, 1961).*

The Socialist Workers Party is one of an international grouping of socialist organisations:

AUSTRALIA: International Socialists, GPO Box 1473N, Melbourne 3001

BELGIUM: Socialisme International, Rue Lovinfosse 60, 4030 Grivengée, Belgium

BRITAIN: Socialist Workers Party, PO Box 82, London E3

CANADA: International Socialists, PO Box 339, Station E, Toronto, Ontario M6H 4E3

CYPRUS: Ergatiki Demokratia, PO Box 7280, Nicosia

DENMARK: Internationale Socialister, Postboks 642, 2200 København N, Denmark

FRANCE: Socialisme International, BP 189, 75926 Paris Cedex 19

GERMANY: Sozialistische Arbeitergruppe, Postfach 180367, 60084 Frankfurt 1

GREECE: Organosi Sosialisliki Epanastasi, c/o Workers Solidarity, PO Box 8161, Athens 100 10, Greece

HOLLAND: International Socialists, PO Box 9720, 3506 GR Utrecht

IRELAND: Socialist Workers Party, PO Box 1648, Dublin 8

NEW ZEALAND: International Socialist Organization, PO Box 6157, Dunedin, New Zealand

NORWAY: Internasjonale Socialisterr, Postboks 5370, Majorstua, 0304 Oslo 3

POLAND: Solidarność Socjalistyczna, PO Box 12, 01-900 Warszawa 118

SOUTH AFRICA: International Socialists of South Africa, PO Box 18530, Hillbrow 2038, Johannesburg

UNITED STATES: International Socialist Organisation, PO Box 16085, Chicago, Illinois 60616

ZIMBABWE: International Socialists, PO Box 6758, Harare

The following issues of *International Socialism* (second series) are available price £3.00 (including postage) from IS Journal, PO Box 82, London E3 3LH. *International Socialism* 2:58 and 2:65 are available on cassette from the Royal National Institute for the Blind (Peterborough Library Unit), Tel 01733 370777.

International Socialism 2:66 Spring 1995
Dave Crouch: The crisis in Russia and the rise of the right ★ Phil Gasper: Cruel and unusual punishment: the politics of crime in the United States ★ Alex Callinicos: Backwards to liberalism ★ John Newsinger: Matewan: film and working class struggle ★ John Rees: the light and the dark ★ Judy Cox: how to make the Tories disappear ★ Charlie Hore: Jazz: a reply to the critics ★ Pat Riordan: Bookwatch: Ireland ★

International Socialism 2:65 Special Issue
Lindsey German: Frederick Engels: life of a revolutionary ★ John Rees: Engels' Marxism ★ Chris Harman: Engels and the origins of human society ★ Paul McGarr: Engels and natural science ★

International Socialism 2:64 Autumn 1994
Chris Harman: The prophet and the proletariat ★ Kieran Allen: What is changing in Ireland ★ Mike Haynes: The wrong road on Russia ★ Rob Ferguson: Hero and villain ★ Jane Elderton: Suffragette style ★ Chris Nineham: Two faces of modernism ★ Mike Hobart, Dave Harker and Matt Kelly: Three replies to 'Jazz—a people's music?' ★ Charlie Kimber: Bookwatch: South Africa—the struggle continues ★

International Socialism 2:63 Summer 1994
Alex Callinicos: Crisis and class struggle in Europe today ★ Duncan Blackie: The United Nations and the politics of imperialism ★ Brian Manning: The English Revolution and the transition from feudalism to capitalism ★ Lee Sustar: The roots of multi-racial labour unity in the United States ★ Peter Linebaugh: Days of villainy: a reply to two critics ★ Dave Sherry: Trotsky's last, greatest struggle ★ Peter Morgan: Geronimo and the end of the Indian wars ★ Dave Beecham: Ignazio Silone and *Fontamara* ★ Chris Bambery: Bookwatch: understanding fascism ★

International Socialism 2:62 Spring 1994
Sharon Smith: Mistaken identity—or can identity politics liberate the oppressed? ★ Iain Ferguson: Containing the crisis—crime and the Tories ★ John Newsinger: Orwell and the Spanish Revolution ★ Chris Harman: Change at the first millenium ★ Adrian Budd: Nation and empire—Labour's foreign policy 1945-51 ★ Gareth Jenkins: Novel questions ★ Judy Cox: Blake's revolution ★ Derek Howl: Bookwatch: the Russian Revolution ★

International Socialism 2:61 Winter 1994
Lindsey German: Before the flood? ★ John Molyneux: The 'politically correct' controversy ★ David McNally: E P Thompson—class struggle and historical materialism ★ Charlie Hore: Jazz—a people's music ★ Donny Gluckstein: Revolution and the challenge of labour ★ Charlie Kimber: Bookwatch: the Labour Party in decline ★

International Socialism 2:60 Autumn 1993
Chris Bambery: Euro-fascism: the lessons of the past and present tasks ★ Chris Harman: Where is capitalism going? (part 2) ★ Mike Gonzalez: Chile and the struggle for workers' power ★ Phil Marshall: Bookwatch: Islamic activism in the Middle East ★

International Socialism 2:59 Summer 1993
Ann Rogers: Back to the workhouse ★ Kevin Corr and Andy Brown: The labour aristocracy and the roots of reformism ★ Brian Manning: God, Hill and Marx ★ Henry Maitles: Cutting the wire: a criticial appraisal of Primo Levi ★ Hazel Croft: Bookwatch: women and work ★

International Socialism 2:58 Spring 1993
Chris Harman: Where is capitalism going? (part one) ★ Ruth Brown and Peter Morgan: Politics and the class struggle today: a roundtable discussion ★ Richard Greeman: The return of Comrade Tulayev: Victor Serge and the tragic vision of Stalinism ★ Norah Carlin: A new English revolution ★ John Charlton: Building a new world ★ Colin Barker: A reply to Dave McNally ★

International Socialism 2:57 Winter 1992
Lindsey German: Can there be a revolution in Britain? ★ Mike Haynes: Columbus, the Americas and the rise of capitalism ★ Mike Gonzalez: The myths of Columbus: a history ★ Paul Foot: Poetry

and revolution ★ Alex Callinicos: Rhetoric which cannot conceal a bankrupt theory: a reply to Ernest Mandel ★ Charlie Kimber: Capitalism, cruelty and conquest ★ David McNulty: Comments on Colin Barker's review of Thompson's *Customs in Common* ★

International Socialism 2:56 Autumn 1992
Chris Harman: The Return of the National Question ★ Dave Treece: Why the Earth Summit failed ★ Mike Gonzalez: Can Castro survive? ★ Lee Humber and John Rees: The good old cause—an interview with Christopher Hill ★ Ernest Mandel: The Impasse of Schematic Dogmatism ★

International Socialism 2:55 Summer 1992
Alex Callinicos: Race and class ★ Lee Sustar: Racism and class struggle in the American Civil War era ★ Lindsey German and Peter Morgan: Prospects for socialists—an interview with Tony Cliff ★ Robert Service: Did Lenin lead to Stalin? ★ Samuel Farber: In defence of democratic revolutionary socialism ★ David Finkel: Defending 'October' or sectarian dogmatism? ★ Robin Blackburn: Reply to John Rees ★ John Rees: Dedicated followers of fashion ★ Colin Barker: In praise of custom ★ Sheila McGregor: Revolutionary witness ★

International Socialism 2:54 Spring 1992
Sharon Smith: Twilight of the American dream ★ Mike Haynes: Class and crisis—the transition in eastern Europe ★ Costas Kossis: A miracle without end? Japanese capitalism and the world economy ★ Alex Callinicos: Capitalism and the state system: A reply to Nigel Harris ★ Steven Rose: Do animals have rights? ★ John Charlton: Crime and class in the 18th century ★ John Rees: Revolution, reform and working class culture ★ Chris Harman: Blood simple ★

International Socialism 2:52 Autumn 1991
John Rees: In defence of October ★ Ian Taylor and Julie Waterson: The political crisis in Greece—an interview with Maria Styllou and Panos Garganas ★ Paul McGarr: Mozart, overture to revolution ★ Lee Humber: Class, class consciousness and the English Revolution ★ Derek Howl: The legacy of Hal Draper ★

International Socialism 2:51 Summer 1991
Chris Harman: The state and capitalism today ★ Alex Callinicos: The end of nationalism? ★ Sharon Smith: Feminists for a strong state? ★ Colin Sparks and Sue Cockerill: Goodbye to the Swedish miracle ★ Simon Phillips: The South African Communist Party and the South African working class ★ John Brown: Class conflict and the crisis of feudalism ★

International Socialism 2:49 Winter 1990
Chris Bambery: The decline of the Western Communist Parties ★ Ernest Mandel: A theory which has not withstood the test of time ★ Chris Harman: Criticism which does not withstand the test of logic ★ Derek Howl: The law of value In the USSR ★ Terry Eagleton: Shakespeare and the class struggle ★ Lionel Sims: Rape and pre-state societies ★ Sheila McGregor: A reply to Lionel Sims ★

International Socialism 2:48 Autumn 1990
Lindsey German: The last days of Thatcher ★ John Rees: The new imperialism ★ Neil Davidson and Donny Gluckstein: Nationalism and the class struggle in Scotland ★ Paul McGarr: Order out of chaos ★

International Socialism 2:46 Winter 1989
Chris Harman: The storm breaks ★ Alex Callinicos: Can South Africa be reformed? ★ John Saville: Britain, the Marshall Plan and the Cold War ★ Sue Clegg: Against the stream ★ John Rees: The rising bourgeoisie ★

International Socialism 2:44 Autumn 1989
Charlie Hore: China: Tiananmen Square and after ★ Sue Clegg: Thatcher and the welfare state ★ John Molyneux: *Animal Farm* revisited ★ David Finkel: After Arias, is the revolution over? ★ John Rose: Jews in Poland ★

International Socialism 2:43 Summer 1989 (Reprint—special price £4.50)
Marxism and the Great French Revolution by Paul McGarr and Alex Callinicos

International Socialism 2:42 Spring 1989
Chris Harman: The myth of market socialism ★ Norah Carlin: Roots of gay oppression ★ Duncan Blackie: Revolution in science ★ International Socialism Index ★

International Socialism 2:41 Winter 1988
Polish socialists speak out: Solidarity at the Crossroads ★ Mike Haynes: Nightmares of the market ★ Jack Robertson: Socialists and the unions ★ Andy Strouthous: Are the unions in decline? ★ Richard Bradbury: What is Post-Structuralism? ★ Colin Sparks: George Bernard Shaw ★

International Socialism 2:39 Summer 1988
Chris Harman and Andy Zebrowski: Glasnost, before the storm ★ Chanie Rosenberg: Labour and the fight against fascism ★ Mike Gonzalez: Central America after the Peace Plan ★ Ian Birchall: Raymond Williams ★ Alex Callinicos: Reply to John Rees ★

International Socialism 2:35 Summer 1987
Pete Green: Capitalism and the Thatcher years ★ Alex Callinicos: Imperialism, capitalism and the state today ★ Ian Birchall: Five years of *New Socialist* ★ Callinicos and Wood debate 'Looking for alternatives to reformism' ★ David Widgery replies on 'Beating Time' ★

International Socialism 2:31 Winter 1985
Alex Callinicos: Marxism and revolution In South Africa ★ Tony Cliff: The tragedy of A J Cook ★ Nigel Harris: What to do with London? The strategies of the GLC ★

International Socialism 2:30 Autumn 1985
Gareth Jenkins: Where is the Labour Party heading? ★ David McNally: Debt, inflation and the rate of profit ★ Ian Birchall: The terminal crisis in the British Communist Party ★ replies on Women's oppression and *Marxism Today* ★

International Socialism 2:29 Summer 1985
Special issue on the class struggle and the left in the aftermath of the miners' defeat ★ Tony Cliff: Patterns of mass strike ★ Chris Harman: 1984 and the shape of things to come ★ Alex Callinicos: The politics of *Marxism Today* ★

International Socialism 2:26 Spring 1985
Pete Green: Contradictions of the American boom ★ Colin Sparks: Labour and imperialism ★ Chris Bambery: Marx and Engels and the unions ★ Sue Cockerill: The municipal road to socialism ★ Norah Carlin: Is the family part of the superstructure? ★ Kieran Allen: James Connolly and the 1916 rebellion ★

International Socialism 2:25 Autumn 1984
John Newsinger: Jim Larkin, Syndicalism and the 1913 Dublin Lockout ★ Pete Binns: Revolution and state capitalism in the Third World ★ Colin Sparks: Towards a police state? ★ Dave Lyddon: Demystifying the downturn ★ John Molyneux: Do working class men benefit from women's oppression? ★

International Socialism 2:18 Winter 1983
Donny Gluckstein: Workers' councils in Western Europe ★ Jane Ure Smith: The early Communist press in Britain ★ John Newsinger: The Bolivian Revolution ★ Andy Durgan: Largo Caballero and Spanish socialism ★ M Barker and A Beezer: Scarman and the language of racism ★

International Socialism 2:14 Winter 1981
Chris Harman: The riots of 1981 ★ Dave Beecham: Class struggle under the Tories ★ Tony Cliff: Alexandra Kollontai ★ L James and A Paczuska: Socialism needs feminism ★ reply to Cliff on Zetkin ★ Feminists In the labour movement ★

International Socialism 2:13 Summer 1981
Chris Harman: The crisis last time ★ Tony Cliff: Clara Zetkin ★ Ian Birchall: Left Social Democracy In the French Popular Front ★ Pete Green: Alternative Economic Strategy ★ Tim Potter: The death of Eurocommunism ★

International Socialism 2:12 Spring 1981
Jonathan Neale: The Afghan tragedy ★ Lindsey German: Theories of patriarchy ★ Ray Challinor: McDouall and Physical Force Chartism ★ S Freeman & B Vandesteeg: Unproductive labour ★ Alex Callinicos: Wage labour and capitalism ★ Italian fascism ★ Marx's theory of history ★ Cabral ★

International Socialism 2:11 Winter 1980
Rip Bulkeley et al: CND In the 50s ★ Marx's theory of crisis and its critics ★ Andy Durgan: Revolutionary anarchism in Spain ★ Alex Callinicos: Politics or abstract thought ★ Fascism in Europe ★ Marilyn Monroe ★